WINDOWS
to the
WORLD

Tales and Tastes from Our Travels

Laszlo Adler and Vera Princz Adler

We would like to dedicate the book to honor our parents,
Miklós and Helena Adler and Armin and Janka Princz.

ACKNOWLEDGEMENTS

To our family, Michael, Susan, Richard, Rachel, Hannah and Talia for their enthusiastic support and many comments to us for writing this book.

To Viktoria Martin for her excellent artistic contribution.

To Frank Gerace for his professional editing and many suggestions.

To Joe and Ibi Koenig for providing some photos.

To our immediate and our extended family as well as to many of our friends who shared our wonderful travels with us and made it more memorable.

INTRODUCTION AND BACKGROUND

Even though I started my travels at an early age, as of 2020 I have only visited a little more than a third of all the countries in the world, 68 out of 195. So, there are a lot more to go!

Countries visited as of 2020:

1.Slovakia, 2. Austria, 3. Israel, 4. Turkey, 5. Italy, 6. Vatican, 7. Hungary, 8. Romania, 9. England, 10. Germany, 11. USA, 12. Canada, 13. Brazil, 14. Argentina, 15. Uruguay, 16. South Africa, 17. Spain, 18. France, 19. Belgium, 20. Poland, 21. The Czech Republic, 22. Norway, 23. Denmark, 24. Japan, 25. Hong Kong, 26. Taiwan, 27. Serbia, 28. Bosnia-Hercegovina, 29. Croatia, 30. Montenegro, 31. Slovenia, 32. Greece, 33. Thailand, 34. China, 35. Switzerland, 36. Lichtenstein. 37. Monaco, 38. Luxembourg, 39. Chile, 40. Puerto Rico, 41. St. Thomas, 42. Martinique, 43. Grenada, 44. Venezuela, 45. Curacao, 46. Panama, 47. Mexico, 48. Russia, 49. Finland, 50. Sweden, 51. Australia, 52. New Zeeland, 53. Egypt, 54. Portugal, 55. Holland, 56. Ireland, 57. Bermuda, 58. Corsica, 59. Peru, 60. Honduras, 61. Guatemala, 62. Lithuania, 63. Latvia, 64. Estonia, 65. The Bahamas, 66. Cuba, 67. Cayman Island, 68. Ukraine.

Vera and I signed up for a trip to Morocco, which was supposed to leave from Paris on March 19, 2020, but had to be canceled because of the COVID-19 pandemic. Not able to go anywhere because of the quarantine, we decided to write this book on our travels and our experiences in different places. We include brief accounts not only of the history and culture of the various countries illustrating them with our photos but also of their culinary arts represented by the signature dishes of some of the countries that we visited.

I don't think anyone needs to be convinced about the many rewards of visiting different countries; learning first hand their history, seeing their customs, observing their politics, tasting their food, absorbing their culture, etc., rather than learning from books, reading the National Geographic, or watching travel shows on TV. In addition to all the new information described, **TRAVELING is FUN** and we both feel it keeps us young.

By the time I met Vera in 1962, I was ahead of her having already visited 6 countries more than she did, but she caught up with me, and now we both have been in 68 countries, hundreds of cities, and almost in all the states of the USA.

Traveling affected our lives. Had I not stopped in Toronto, on my way driving from Montreal to Flint Michigan, Vera and I would have never met. If I didn't travel to London to a Conference in 1976, where I met Gerard Quentin, professor at Université Paris 7, who invited me to Paris for my Sabbatical from the University of Tennessee, Paris would not have played such a major role in our lives. In this book, many more stories will illuminate how our lives were influenced by many of our travels. To start I will describe my early childhood and early travels.

MY EARLY TRAVELS

I was born in **Debrecen, Hungary** where I lived with my parents on Arany Janos utca 37. As far as I can remember one of the greatest pleasures I have always had was traveling. When I was maybe four or five years old, I took a streetcar several times a week to visit my favorite aunt and uncle, Malvin neni and Hermus bacsi, at their home on Csonka utca 10 in Debrecen. They had no children and I was treated like royalty.

Downtown Debrecen, Hungary 1930 - 40

Probably around the time I was seven years old I was taken on my first trip in a car; I think it was a Renault. We went to the small village of **Matrafured** about 100 miles from Debrecen for a two-week vacation with my mother and some of her friends. Kekes, the highest mountain in Hungary at 1014 meters, is near this village.

Driving from Debrecen to Matrafured   *Highest point 1014*   *Matrafured*

Another childhood trip was when I was 8 years old, I was taken to **Ungvar** by our neighbor an older lady whose daughter lived there. We went about 100 miles by train from Debrecen to Ungvar, which was my first train ride. My father had a cousin who lived in Ungvar with her family, and I stayed with them for a couple of days in this beautiful city on the border with Slovakia. My father was born in **Upor**, a tiny village in Slovakia.

After the First Vienna Award of 1938 when Czechoslovakia was partitioned, Hungary regained some territory in the Carpathian region which had been taken away after WW 1 by the Trianon Treaty. One of the cities which was regained by Hungary was Ungvar, which was taken away from Hungary again and given to Ukraine after WW 2, and today is called **Uzhgorod.**

Downtown Ungvar (Uzhgorod)

Trianon is a Chateau outside of **Paris** next to Versailles. It was the site of the Trianon Treaty in 1920 at the end of WW 1, which among other territorial adjustments took away Transylvania from Hungary, and awarded it to Romania. At the Second Viennese Award in 1940, the northern part of Transylvania was returned to Hungary.

I had the pleasure of having my second train ride at the age of 9 when we all went to **Ermihalyfalva** in **Transylvania** where my mother was born. Ermihalyfalva or Valea lui Mihai in Romanian is a small town with a population of about 7,000. She was very happy to take her family to her birthplace where several of her cousins, uncles and aunts still lived, and I was happy to meet many of my relatives, among them several kids of my age.

The town of Ermihalyfalva   *The Synagogue in Ermihalyfalva*

For the next couple of years because of the war, I had no opportunity to travel anywhere. The German Army occupied Hungary on March 19, 1944, and followed the process that they had developed in the rest of Europe, the deportation of the Jews for the "final solution". Soon, a large part of the close to eight hundred thousand Jews in Hungary was sent to concentration camps.

Jews are forced into cattle cars to be deported

Our extended family of 13, including my grandparents, aunts and cousins, in addition to my parents and me, were locked into a cattle car with 80 or 90 other people. After 5 days in subhuman conditions, we arrived at a concentration camp in a place called Strasshof, about 25 km from Vienna.

Strasshof Concentration Camp

From Strasshof we were taken to a Lager in the 15th district of Vienna, a former school that was altered to house Jewish laborers. At 11 years old, I had to work 10 hours a day loading bricks onto trucks. Somehow our family survived this hard labor for almost a year.

As the Russian Army was approaching the city, in April 1945 the Germans wanted to finish their goal of the "final solution". All thirteen of our extended family with several hundred others were sent back from the labor camp to Strasshoff from where the Germans planned to send us to an extermination camp. We were again jammed into railroad freight cars, 80 or more in each, and waited for the train to move.

All of a sudden, we heard planes dropping bombs around us. They were Russian planes. Because the planes bombed the railway tracks the trains could not proceed. For the next few days, we just stayed there without any food but eventually, the Russian army took over the camp and we were liberated. We had miraculously survived the concentration camp. We started home, first walking to Bratislava and then by train to our hometown.

After we returned to Debrecen, we learned that more than six hundred thousand Hungarian Jews had been murdered by the Nazis and by their Hungarian collaborators, including all our families in Ungvar and Ermihalyfalva.

A few weeks after I returned to Debrecen, I joined a Zionist movement, Hashomer Hatzair. At that time in 1945, the Hashomer Hatzair counted with about 3500 members in Hungary, girls and boys from age 6 to 18, and about 55 in Debrecen. Several of my few surviving schoolmates also joined the movement. In addition to learning new things like Zionism, socialism, and the songs and dances of many countries, new travel opportunities opened up for us. We traveled by truck and by train to entertain the small surviving Jewish communities in the neighboring villages of Nyirbator, Mikepercs, and Hajdunanas, in addition to the Jewish community in Debrecen.

I went with our group by truck to Budapest to participate in a national meeting for the Hashomer Hatzair. Budapest was one of the most beautiful cities in the world but was now full of destroyed buildings and bridges. Fortunately for us, some of the theaters had reopened and we had the pleasure of seeing the best-known Hungarian opera "Bank Ban".

The Main Boulevard, Nagy Korut in Budapest

During the summer our group went for two weeks to summer camps called Moshava, to participate in all kinds of sports and cultural activities besides having to listen to lectures. The first time I would go to a Moshava was in 1945 in Szilvasvarad, a beautiful mountainous area near the city of Eger. This area was famous for the *Siege of Eger*, where in 1552, a handful of Hungarian patriots led by Captain Istvan Dobo stopped the advance of the Turkish Army toward northern Hungary.

Eger

Scenery in Szilvasvarad Moshava

*from left me, George Gross,
above Tibi Gross and Janos Balog*

For the next three years, we participated in Moshavas in Borzsony and Bukk, beautiful, mountainous areas of Hungary. We even had a winter Moshava at Dobogoko.

When the State of Israel was established in May 1948, the Soviet Union and the other Communist countries, including Hungary supported it by voting for membership in the UN. However, by the beginning of 1949, this attitude changed and the Hungarian position followed the Soviet lead. Official Hungarian policy became more and more anti-Israel and legal emigration to Israel was not allowed and all Zionist activities, such as the Moshavas were banned.

1. SLOVAKIA

A clandestine route was organized to smuggle people out across the Hungarian border to Czechoslovakia. This border was less guarded than the border between Hungary and Austria, which was surrounded by minefields. During this time, Czechoslovakia was the only communist country where Zionist activities were still allowed.

A few years later in 1952, the head of the Czechoslovakian Communist Party, Rudolph Slansky was charged with "Zionist Conspiracy" and hanged. After that, all Zionist activities were banned also in Czechoslovakia.

We decided that we couldn't stay in Hungary to be captured and jailed. We took a train to a border village, where a Hashomer Hatzair agent was waiting for us. We moved two by two across the border and eventually, we arrived at Kosice (Kassa in Hungarian) the second-largest city in the Slovakian part of the country. It was Passover and we celebrated the holiday at the home of a young Jewish couple who were members of the movement. Kosice (Kassa) is a beautiful old city with the majority of its 250,000 people still speaking Hungarian. The famous Hungarian nobleman, and leader of the revolt against the Hapsburgs in the 18th century, Ferenc Rakoczi is buried here in the Saint Elizabeth's Cathedral.

Downtown Kosice (Kassa) Slovakia

We continued our route by train toward Bratislava (Pozsony in Hungarian), the capital of Slovakia from where, in the years 1945-49 more than 150,000 Polish, Hungarian and Romanian Jews crossed to the transit camp, the Rothschild Hospital in Vienna. We were told to not speak Hungarian on the train because there we were in danger of being sent back to Hungary, so we learned to say *Ne rozumien Slovensky*, "We don't understand Slovakian"

Bratislava (Pozsony) Slovakia

Czechoslovakia, which was created in 1918 after the Trianon Treaty, consisted of two parts, Slovakia with a population of around 5 million and the Czech part with a population of 10 million. After 1993, the two parts separated and became independent countries. For hundreds of years, Bratislava was part of the Hungarian kingdom and was the place where Hungarian kings were crowned. Until 1930, the majority of the population, about 42%, were Hungarians. Around 40% were Germans and about 10% were Slovaks and 10% were Jews. In 1806, a Yeshiva was established by Rabbi Moses Sofer in Bratislava. It was one of the most important in Central Europe and was attended by hundreds of students and graduated many famous scholars. After WW 2 the Germans and many Hungarians were expelled from the city. Today the majority of Bratislava's population, almost 90%, are Slovaks and 7-8% are Hungarians. The Jewish population is less than 1%, around 3000 persons.

This was my second time in this city. In 1945 after being liberated by the Russian troops, we walked about 100 km from Strasshof to Bratislava where we spent a few days before returning to Debrecen by train.

In the spring of 1949, we stayed in a crowded center run by a local Jewish organization together with several hundred people who also had escaped from other communist countries and were on their way to Israel. After spending a few days at the gathering point, we were transported in trucks to the American sector in Vienna.

Some fifty years later in 1998, with six of my childhood friends, we toured pre-Trianon Hungary for two weeks. We visited the Tatra Mountains, the highest in Central Europe about 9000 feet as well as Kassa and other cities.

Tatra Lomnitz, Slovakia

We stopped to spend a couple of days in Bratislava where we all had been before. This city had recovered from 40 years of communist rule and quickly became a vibrant and exciting place with well-dressed people and sidewalk cafes and restaurants. It was different from 1949, and so was our situation. We had a great time in this beautiful historical city.

We stayed at the very nice Hotel Tatra and after visiting some of the historical sites, we searched for a restaurant to find *Sztrapacska*, the Slovakian signature dish. It is one of my favorite dishes, a dark flour pasta cooked with potatoes sprinkled with goat cheese and with crispy bacon.

Sztrapacska

Serves 6

Ingredients:

20 oz. potatoes

10 oz. flour

8 oz. smoked bacon

10 oz. goat or sheep cheese

1 medium onion

1 egg

4 tbsp. sour cream

Salt to taste

A spätzle/nokkedli/sztrapacska maker

Directions:

1. Peel the potatoes, grate them add some salt, and let it rest for 10 minutes. Squeeze out the water from the grated potato.

2. Mix the grated potatoes with the flour and egg add enough water to obtain a spätzle/nokkedli type of dough, which is the STRAPACSKA.

3. With a spoon form the dough into small spaetzle/nokkedli-like pieces and drop into salted boiling water. If you have one, you may use a spätzle/nokkedli maker. See figure above

4. As they rise to the top, take them out and drain them. Save a quarter cup of the water.

5. Cut the bacon into small cubes and cook them until it is crispy. Take out the bacon.

6. Leave the fat in the pan add the chopped onion to the fat and fry it until the onion is lightly browned.

7. Add the goat cheese and half of the sour cream to the grilled onion, mix it well, add the quarter cup of water and cook the mixture for few minutes.

8. Add the Sztrapacska to the pan and roll it around several times in the mixture. Sprinkle with the bacon and serve it. You may top the dish with a spoon of sour cream.

2. AUSTRIA

In early May 1949, after a trip of about 50 miles from Bratislava to **Vienna** where we had assembled to start our emigration to Israel, we ended the first stage of our Aliyah. Our group of close to 30 young people arrived by truck at the Rothschild Hospital in Vienna, a transit camp for people on their way to Israel. Vienna was divided then into four parts just like Berlin: American, British, French, and Soviet zones. The once vibrant Vienna was still sad and gloomy in 1949, just a few years after the end of WW 2, but many of the structures damaged by the bombs had been restored.

A few years earlier in 1945, we were overjoyed when the Soviet Army saved our lives by liberating us from the concentration camp in Strasshof near Vienna. This time in 1949 we stayed in the American controlled part of Vienna and kept ourselves far away from the Soviet-occupied zone of the city to avoid the chance of being shipped back to Hungary. Times change!

Vienna Central District 1949

Nevertheless, we had the opportunity to visit the most important attractions of this magnificent historical city, which was the capital of the Austro-Hungarian Monarchy until the end of World War 1. At that time the Monarchy had a multinational population of over fifty million people. It was the third-largest country in Europe after Russia and Greater Germany, and Vienna was also the third most populous city in Europe after London and Paris. In addition to the Hungarians and the German-speaking Austrians in the Monarchy, there were groups of Serbs, Romanians, Slovaks, Poles, Ruthenians, and a sizable Jewish population.

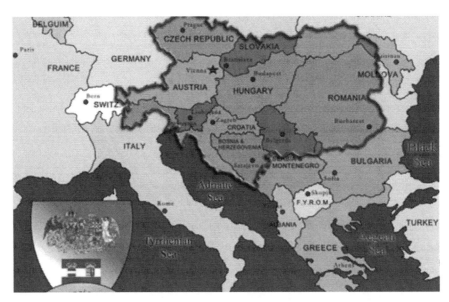

Map of the Austro-Hungarian Empire in 1914

Vienna was the world capital of music that hosted composers Johann Strauss, Richard Strauss, Mahler, Brahms, and others. It also was the home of the pioneers of psychoanalysis, Sigmund Freud, Josef Breuer, and Alfred Adler. Vienna was also the home of many wave physicists such as Mach, Doppler, and Schroedinger.

But Vienna was not only a scientific center; this exciting city was also a focus point for the arts.

The Vienna Secession was founded on 3 April 1897 by artists Gustav Klimt, Koloman Moser, Josef Hoffmann, Joseph Maria Olbrich, Max Kurzweil, Otto Wagner, and others. The Secession artists objected to the prevailing conservatism of the Vienna Kunstlerhaus with its traditional orientation toward Historicism.

Less positively, many worldwide known political figures resided here. Before the start of the First World War. Hitler, Stalin, Trotsky, and Tito lived within walking distance from each other and frequented the same pastry shops in Vienna.

After World War 1, the Austro-Hungarian Monarchy fell apart. Austria as well as Vienna lost their leading roles in Europe as countries like Yugoslavia and Czechoslovakia were established. The population of Austria dropped to 8 million at that time and has remained at this level.

In 1949, while I waited on my way to Israel, I had the pleasure of visiting Schonbrunn, the Royal Palace, one of the most significant tourist attractions in Vienna, which rivals Versailles in every way.

The Royal Palace in Vienna, Schonbrunn

I also had a chance to go to the Vienna Opera to enjoy Offenbach's *Tales of Hoffman*. Some 40 years later when Vera and I visited Vienna, the tickets were $200 apiece. I am not sure how much the organizers from the Hashomer Hatzair paid for the tickets in 1949, but surely it was not that much. Incidentally, in 1989 we saw an excellent performance of Mozart's *Marriage of Figaro*, one of our favorites.

Vienna Opera House

Among the many museums we visited, the most impressive was the *Technisches Museum*, the Museum of Science and Technology, founded in 1912 and one of the best I have ever seen.

Technisches Museum Vienna   *Museum Exhibit*

The first time I was in Vienna was in 1944 after I had been deported from Hungary and at age eleven was put at forced labor, loading bricks on trucks for the repair of bombed outbuildings. Almost fifty years later in 1993, I gave an invited lecture at an International Ultrasonic Conference at the TUW, the Technisches Universität Wien.

In addition to being in Vienna with the Hashomer Hatzair in 1949, I have visited Vienna many times since. I was there after the Hungarian Revolution was defeated in 1956, and again in 1965, 1983, and other times. A very special trip to Vienna was that of 1971with our two young children Michael and Suzika when we stopped to spend a few days there on our way to visit Hungary.

On several occasions especially in 1956, whenever I walked by the well-known and very expensive Hotel-Restaurant-Coffeehouse of the Hotel Sacher complex, located in the best part of Vienna, I promised myself that one day, I would come here and have their Sacher Torte with coffee.

Finally, on a beautiful warm sunny afternoon in July 1971, I arrived with Vera and the children at the Sacher Café and entered their coffeehouse to fulfill the promise. However, to our disappointment, we were not welcome because I wasn't wearing a jacket and necktie. The rejection was amusing and ironic, and it took me another 12 years before I finally made it back to the Sacher Hotel in 1983, not only to eat their Torte, but also to stay in their famous hotel. It is also interesting to note that during this stay at the great Sacher, a rather expensive gold bracelet was stolen from my suitcase, while I did my morning jogging in the streets of Vienna. The bracelet had been given to me for Vera, when I visited my aunt Manci in Budapest. Anything can happen even at the Sacher.

Hotel Sacher in Vienna

Other than that incident, all the times spent in Vienna were full of enjoyable experiences. When one thinks of Vienna, the first thing that comes to your senses is the aroma of coffee and chocolate in the air. You picture elegant, well-dressed people sitting in turn-of-the-century sweet shops eating pastries with mountains of *shlagsahne* (whipped cream) enjoying this typical Viennese past time. Most restaurants serve the signature dish of the city, the *Wiener Schnitzel.*

Wiener Schnitzel

The quality of the meat as well as a good crisp coating are decisive for the classic Wiener Schnitzel. The thickness of the individual cutlets is also important

Serves 4

Ingredients:

4 slices of veal or chicken breast, or pork chops

Salt to taste

1 pepper

5 oz. flour (for coating)

7 oz. breadcrumbs (for coating)

3 eggs (for coating)

2 tbsp. heavy cream or whole milk or water

Cooking oil, 1inch high in the frying pan

2 tbsp. butter

lemon wedges (for garnish)

Directions:

9. Carefully beat the meat pieces with a meat mallet until they are ¼ in. thick.

10. Season the meat on both sides with salt and pepper.

11. The classic Viennese breadcrumb coating: arrange two flat plates and one deep plate next to each other. Put the flour in one of the flat plates and the breadcrumbs in the other. Beat the eggs together with the cream in the deep plate.

12. Coat the meat in the flour and brush off any surplus. Then dip the meat in the eggs and coat generously with the breadcrumbs.

13. Heat oil and butter in the frying pan. Place the cutlets in the pan and fry with a cover until one side is golden-brown, turn the schnitzel over and fry them uncovered.

14. Remove the Wiener Schnitzel from the fat, place on a paper towel and dab off any excess fat. Serve with parsley on potatoes.

Hungarian Goulash

Most Viennese restaurants in addition to Wiener Schnitzel also serve Hungarian Goulash, one of the many influences of the Austro-Hungarian Monarchy. Both Vera and I felt that the Austrian version of this Hungarian dish was at least as good if not better than what you'd get in Hungary.

Serves 6

Ingredients:

4 tbsp. corn oil

2 Large yellow onion, finely chopped

2 Hungarian sweet bell pepper, seeded and finely chopped

4 cloves garlic, minced

2 large tomatoes, finely diced

3 pounds beef shank cut into 1-inch pieces

4 tbsp. Hungarian paprika

1½ teaspoons salt

¼ teaspoon freshly ground black pepper

Water

Directions:

1. In a medium saucepan, heat the oil and add the onions. Place a piece of wax paper on top of the onions and cook until the onions become transparent.

2. Add the peppers and garlic and cook for another two minutes.

3. Add the beef and cook for a couple of minutes. Stir in the paprika and remove from heat.

4. Add the remaining ingredients. Add one cup of water and return the pan to heat and bring it to a boil. Cover and reduce the heat to medium-low and simmer for 90 minutes. From time-to-time check whether more water is needed. If the stew is too watery, continue to simmer uncovered for a few more minutes so that some of the liquid evaporates. Add salt to taste.

5. Serve with boiled potatoes. Traditionally served with cucumber salad on the side. A spoonful of sour cream can be placed on top of each plate served. Sprinkle with hot paprika.

Before 1948 when the state of Israel was established, it took several months or sometimes even years to emigrate to Palestine, a British Mandate since World War 1. Boats with refugees who had survived the Nazi Camps were intercepted, and the passengers even under age children were forced to detention camps in Cyprus, another British Mandate. They lived there under harsh conditions for years until after May 15 1948 when they could legally enter the State of Israel.

In our case, when we left Hungary in 1949, we did not expect that it would take months to be able to get to the State of Israel. One of the reasons for the delay was that after the end of World War 2, there were around 250,000 Jewish DPs (displaced persons) in the so-called DP camps in Germany, Austria, and Italy. Most of them were Holocaust survivors who enjoyed priority processing of their exodus to Israel. Besides, there were also millions of non-Jewish refugees from eastern European countries who were looking to find a home in a new country.

After spending three weeks in Vienna, we went by train to one of the DP camps in **Salzburg**, about 200 miles from Vienna. There were thousands of people from many European countries in the camp waiting for Aliyah, emigration to Israel.

DP Camp in Salzburg 1949

The living conditions in the camp were rough and rudimentary. We slept on double bunks and the food was not very good, but most of us had gone through much worst before. We knew that it was only temporary and that sooner or later we would go on toward our destination. We were free to come and go from the camp and took advantage of the offerings of Salzburg, a beautiful city surrounded by mountains and castles. The *Berchtesgaden* part of the Alps was only 10 miles from the city center. Naturally, we took on the challenge of climbing to the 2000-meter (6500 feet) summit which was twice as high as the *Kekes*, the highest peak in Hungary.

Among the many castles, the most notable was the Hellbrunn Castle built in the 17th Century by an eccentric nobleman. A notable oddity of this castle is the stone dining room table with stone seats that sprayed water into the rears of the guests. When the mechanism was activated during a feast, hidden fountains sprayed the surprised guests' seats. Another surprise was a water-operated musical theater, built in 1750 that showed the actions of various professions doing their work. Outside in a rustic grotto, we saw jets of water move a crown up and down symbolizing the rise and fall of power.

Fountains in Hellbrunn Castle, Salzburg

This castle was a striking source of memories in 1949 and even more so in better times when Vera and I visited it again in 1993 with our friends Steve and Mary on our way from Switzerland to the International Ultrasonic meeting in Vienna. In 1993 we also visited the Hohensalzburg castle that is on the highest point in Salzburg. We all were fortunate enough to attend a concert with performances of Haydn's "Quinten", "Lark" and one of his Serenades performed by a Polish quartet.

Hohensalzburg Castle Salzburg

Street scene in Salzburg

Our conditions had improved significantly in the last 45 years and in 1993 we enjoyed walking, shopping, and dining in this lovely city. We always remember the *nockerl*, the light and fluffy dessert soufflé.

Salzburger Nockerl

Serves 8

Ingredients:

1 cup cream

¼ cup raspberry jam, you may use other jams

5 egg whites

3/4 teaspoon salt

3/4 teaspoon salt

½ cup granulated sugar

tablespoon all-purpose flour

2 egg yolks

1 teaspoon pure vanilla extract

Powdered sugar for dusting

Directions:

1. Preheat oven to 400°F.

2. Pour cream into a 9-inch pie plate and spoon raspberry sauce into the cream.

3. Put egg whites and salt in a bowl, then set the bowl in a larger bowl of hot water and stir whites to warm to room temperature, 1 to 2 minutes. Remove from hot water. Beat whites with an electric mixer at high speed until they just form soft peaks, then beat in granulated sugar, 1 tablespoon at a time, beating until whites just form stiff, glossy peaks. Sprinkle flour over beaten egg whites and fold in gently but thoroughly. Whisk together egg yolks and vanilla in a small bowl, then fold into whites gently but thoroughly.

4. Spoon large dollops of the above mixture onto the cream mixture and bake until golden brown and set, 15 minutes. Dust lightly with powdered sugar and cool 5 minutes before serving.

Our first stop in Austria driving to Vienna from Switzerland in 1993 was **Innsbruck** the beautiful Tyrolean city near the Brenner Pass. In 1949 from Salzburg to Trani Italy we passed through the Brenner by train.

The Brenner Pass

From Innsbruck together with Steve and Marika we drove to **Salzburg,** the beautiful historical city which I knew very well from my stays in 1949 and 1956. Our next stop was in the Wachau wine country, where we stayed in a lovely Inn near the city of Durstein. It was there that the English king Richard the "Lionhearted" was held in captivity in a castle by the Austrian Duke Leopold in the 12th century. Normally I drink only red wine but I enjoyed the white wine of the area.

By early June 1949, we were on our way by train to another DP camp in **Trani** in southern Italy, near the port of Bari. The first part of the trip was by train through the Brenner Pass that connects Austria and Italy at an elevation of close to 5000 feet in the Alps.

As we crossed the beautiful scenery of the **Brenner Pass**, we saw crowds of Italians lined up along the railroad tracks carrying large banners for an upcoming election.

Brenner Pass at the Austrian-Italian border

Most of the banners were promoting the Communist Party, the PC, the *Partito Communista*, and everyone was holding their red flags, and singing songs some of which we knew, like *Avanti Popolo.* During the war, the

Communist Parties in Europe, especially in France and Italy were the best organized resistance against the Nazis and Fascism. Because of their struggle and sacrifice, there was massive popular support for the Communists PC and the other leftist party the PSI, the *Partito Socialista Italiano*, the Italian Socialist Party. The PC and the PSI were the majority in the Italian parliament.

It was the same in France where the left had a majority in the parliament. Positive feelings toward the Soviet Union were the rule in many western countries after the war. Certainly, the siege at Stalingrad was a turning point in World War 2. The loss of more than 20 million people in the Soviet Union who died heroically fighting the Nazis attracted many sympathizers.

But by the early 1950s, the Communist parties in the West lost their leading roles as very disturbing news about the Soviet Union started to appear. The Gulags, the trials, and executions of many top Communist leaders and Jewish doctors and intellectuals disenchanted many. Khrushchev's famous speech accusing Stalin of atrocities, the uprisings in East Berlin, Poznan, and Budapest all caused hundreds of thousands to leave the Communist movements. Interestingly, there is still a Stalingrad metro station in Paris but that name no longer exists in Russia.

After a train ride of a couple of days across the most picturesque parts of Italy, we arrived at **Trani**, a seaport town on the Adriatic about 25 miles from Bari, where we spent the whole month of June of 1949.

Trani, Southern Italy

We stayed in a transit camp which was a military base under Mussolini. It was very much like the camp where we stayed in Salzburg. There were many such camps for displaced persons in Italy as well as in Austria and Germany.

Transit Camp in Trani

For most of us, this was the very first time in our lives to be near the sea. It was very exciting to be able to walk to the Adriatic to swim. We attracted quite a few local young boys of our ages when they spotted some of the pretty girls in our group. We could even communicate a little with them since most of us had learned some Latin in school so we could refer to the "Acqua" and use a few other words we knew. The main topic with the Italian boys, besides their eying our girls, was soccer, which we both called football, although more often the Italians called it *Calcio*. They insisted that Italian football was superior to the Hungarian. Tragically, just a month before our arrival in May 1949, all the players and coaches of Torino, the best Italian football team, died in an airplane crash. Such a tragedy!

The food in the camp was very bad. We only ate spaghetti with tasteless tomato sauce twice a day for three weeks. It took me several years to realize how great Italian food is. By the 2nd of July 1949, our group of close to 100 members of the Hashomer Hatzair was transported to **Bari** and onto an Israeli boat called Atzmaut, "Independence'", and we started our five-day journey toward Haifa, Israel.

Hashomer Hatzair Alia at Trani, Italy

3. ISRAEL

The ship was far from luxurious, and we slept on bunk beds four levels high. The food was something else; I recall eating only halva, a strange "oriental delicacy". Most of the people got seasick on this 5-day long trip to cover a distance of only a little over 1000 miles. On July 7, 1949, all of a sudden, we spotted the beautiful lights of the Port of **Haifa**. It was a very emotional experience. It was late when we arrived, so we stayed on the Atzmaut all night.

Haifa on the Mediterranean Sea 1949

Some 26 years later in 1975, I was invited to spend a two-month Sabbatical at the very prestigious Technion, the Israeli MIT in Haifa. I was involved with research and some lecturing in the Metals Institute associated with the Materials Science and Engineering Department. The Technion is on Mount Carmel from where you have a beautiful view of the Mediterranean Sea. Vera and our two children, Michael and Suzika came with me and we stayed in a very comfortable faculty apartment also on Mount Carmel.

The Technion in Haifa

24

Twenty years later in 1997, I toured Israel with my childhood friends and visited Haifa again. We went to see the Baha'i World Center and the Shrine of the Bab. It is the headquarters of this monotheistic religion that emphasizes the spiritual unity of humankind. The garden is one of the most spectacular we had ever seen and is the most visited attraction for tourists in Haifa.

Bahai World Center in Haifa

In July 1949, about twenty-five of us who had come from Trani went to Kibbutz Hatzor in the southern part of Israel. We joined the group which came with the earlier transport, including my close friends from Debrecen, Janos Balog, Steve Szasz, and George Bozoki. This kibbutz was founded around the mid-1930s mostly by Bulgarian people and included a furniture factory in Rishon Lezion, a city about a 45-minute drive from Hatzor. Because I had been a carpentry apprentice in Debrecen, this is where I started to work.

In Kibbutz Hatzor (1949)

The idea of the kibbutzim was a necessity for the early pioneers who came to Palestine before the establishment of the State of Israel in 1948. To conquer the bare, undeveloped desert and to make it into livable conditions could not be achieved by only a few individuals but required a collective effort. As a result, a large percentage of the immigrants in the first half of the 20th century went to some form of collective farm, like the Kibbutzim, the Moshavim, and so on.

With industrialization and the development of machinery for agriculture, fewer and fewer people were needed to do the farming and more and more people got involved with the new industries. Even the kibbutzim started various types of manufacturing like the furniture factory of Kibbutz Hatzor in Rishon Lezion. The food in the Kibbutz was not gourmet by any means but the breakfast was especially satisfying, with the salads and the many dairy products, leben, lebenia, various kinds of yogurts with different fat content and ways of processing.

Israeli salad

At night we danced many Israeli and other national folk dances until midnight. Life was pleasant in the Kibbutz but the four of us, like many others, decided to try to build our lives elsewhere and in December 1949 we left Kibbutz Hatzor and moved to **Beer Sheva**.

Beer Sheva in 1949

Beer Sheva was a small Arab town in the Negev Desert with a population of a few thousand. After the war of Independence, most of the Arab population deserted the city, but around the time of our arrival, the population of the city started to grow and there were about a few hundred newcomers like us. The mayor of the city who was from Hungary told us that we could move into any empty house that we wanted. We found a house in Rechov 16th 80 beth (16th street). The house was an Arab's cottage with one little room with a hole in the ground for a toilet. There were two medium-sized rooms with no furniture, and the doors and windows had no frames. There was no electricity or running water and the roof was made of dry camel manure, which thankfully had no smell. This house became ours and within a few days, we built two beds, one for Steve and Janos, and one for George and me. We also fabricated wooden windows and a door for one of the rooms. We even built a brick fireplace for cooking.

Laszlo, Janos, Steve standing in Rechov 16, 80 beth in Beer Sheva 1949

Seventy years later in April 2019, when our granddaughter Hannah had her Bat Mitzvah in Jerusalem, our whole family came to Beer Sheva to celebrate Passover with our cousins Sanyi and Mari. We stayed in the Hotel Leonardo. We had a very festive dinner with our cousins and with their children and grandchildren in their home. Today Beer Sheva is a large metropolitan area with a population of over 300.000. It is the fourth largest city in Israel with a great symphony orchestra, theaters, many good restaurants and elegant stores, and the excellent Ben Gurion University, which has the best medical school in Israel, who could even dream in 1949 of such miraculous progress?

Beer Sheva 2019   *Hotel Leonardo*

The following day, we all had a wonderful Middle Eastern dinner together with our cousins in a restaurant called The Cave in the Bedouin village of **Djerat** near Beer Sheva.

From left to right: Mari, Irit, Boaz, Michaela, Rotem, Hagar, Hannah, Inbar, Dani, Sanyi, Me, Richard, Suzika, Talia, Vera, Eli, Ejnath, in front: Oded and the owner of the Cave Restaurant

Israeli salad, Humous, and pitta bread, home-made by Vera

One of our favorite holiday dishes is the Israeli orange/honey chicken.

Honey Orange Chicken

Serves 4

Ingredients:

cup orange juice

½ cup of cider vinegar

¼ cup honey

1 tbsp. chili powder (optional)

1 tbsp. ground cumin

2 lb. chicken legs, bone in and skin on.

1 orange peel cut into Julienne pieces

1 tbsp. olive oil

Salt and pepper

Directions:

1. In a large zip-lock bag mix orange juice, vinegar, honey, chili powder and cumin. Add all the chicken and refrigerate for 24 hours.

2. Take out the chicken pieces and the orange rinds from the marinade, wipe them very dry with a paper towel. Reserve the liquid

3. In a heavy bottom pan add olive oil and heat medium-high. Add the chicken and the orange rinds, sear them until well browned on all sides. Season with salt and pepper.

4. Add the marinade to the pot and cook on a slow simmer until the chicken is very tender and well coated with glaze. If it is needed add a small amount of water.

5. Serve on a platter decorated with fresh orange slices.

Vera's Challah with honey

In the spring of 1950, after several months living and working in Beer Sheva, we heard that the prestigious Weitzman Institute was hiring laborers for an excavation project near Eilat in the desert close to the Red Sea. We applied for the job and all four of us were hired. The pay was excellent, the equivalent of about $240 (around $2,650 today) a month, plus room and board. It sounded great. At that time there was no highway from Beer Sheva to Eilat. It took 14 hours on a huge commercial truck to make this adventurous trip through the hills and valleys of the vast Negev.

In Eilat, we were stationed in a large camp with about 300 other people. We slept on bunks in a large tent with 15 to 20 of us to a tent. The camp was about a couple of miles from the Red Sea. Every morning we were taken by a truck about 10-15 miles to an area where we worked in groups of two, digging in an area assigned to us by an army officer.

Eilat on the Red Sea

Years later, when I was on Sabbatical at the Technion, I drove my family from Beer Sheva to Eilat. But this time, the tents in the desert of the 1950s were replaced by a vibrant resort city, and the roads were so good that we made the trip in about 3 hours.

30

Eilat Israel

In 1975 on our way back from Eilat, we drove by the Dead Sea where the water is so dense because of the minerals in the water that you can float easily, as our son Michael showed us as floated comfortably while reading a book. The surface of the Dead Sea is 1300 feet below sea level, the lowest point on earth. The deepest point of the sea is 2300 feet below sea level! Michael liked the area so much that eight years later he spent one year in Kibbutz Ein Gedi where he worked as a volunteer in their resort spa at the Dead Sea.

Michael floating on the Dead Sea 1975   *in Kibbutz Ein Gedi 1983*

In 2013, our first granddaughter Rachel spent two weeks traveling through Israel with the *Birth Right* program and loved the area around the Dead Sea.

Rachel in the Negev near the Dead Sea   *with a group of Birth Righters in 2013*

Everybody in our family loved the Dead Sea.

Suzika floats with Talia while Hannah flies in the air at the Dead Sea 2019

In November 1949, a month before the four of us left Kibbutz Hatzor to move to Beer Sheva, we were thinking about maybe moving to **Tel Aviv-Yaffo,** a large twin city, where there could be lots of opportunities to start a new life outside the Kibbutz. I asked the kibbutz officials for a three-day vacation to visit my cousin Edi who lived with her family in the Kfar Lidice Moshav near Latrun. The moshav was named in honor of a Czechoslovakian town where all the inhabitants were murdered by the Germans in retaliation for the execution of one German officer.

It was true that I also wanted to visit Edi but in reality, I went to Jaffa to look for work. I applied for a job in a carpentry shop where I was hired but since I had no place to sleep, I was allowed to sleep in the shop. After a few days, both the owner and I both realized that my carpentry skills were pretty limited, even though I had been an apprentice carpenter in Debrecen for over a year. He offered to let me stay on with a very reduced salary until I learned the trade better. However, I concluded that I needed a different solution for my life and I didn't stay in the carpentry shop.

However, I was there long enough to learn some history of the region. Tel Aviv was established in 1909 by only 68 families as a small suburb of the ancient port of Yaffo which had a large Arab population. By 1949, the combined Arab-Jewish population of Metropolitan Tel Aviv-Yaffo was close to 400,000. By 2019 it grew to 4 million.

Old City of Yaffo

Dizengoff Street in Tel-Aviv in 1949

After working for several more months in Eilat, we saved plenty of money and could enjoy a vacation in Tel-Aviv. We even sent money back to our parents in Hungary.

George Bozoki and me in Tel Aviv café 1950

I have returned to Tel Aviv many times. In 1975 when we lived in Haifa and I was on Sabbatical at the Technion, we stayed in the Hilton Hotel facing the Mediterranean. In 1997, we toured Israel for two weeks with my childhood friends. In Tel Aviv, we met our schoolmate Jakov Barzilai after 47 years, who had become a world-famous Hebrew poet.

Me, Jakov Barzilai, George Burger, Janos and Steve at Tel Aviv Beach 1997

We also came with Vera many times over the last forty-five years to Tel Aviv and to other parts of Israel for weddings, Bar Mitzvahs and just to be with our extended family.

With family in the Dan Hotel, Tel Aviv 2001

Probably one of the most meaningful visits that we made to Tel Aviv was the time after our granddaughter Hannah had her Bat Mitzvah in Jerusalem in April of 2019.

By that time Tel Aviv-Yaffo was a world-class city offering everything with the nightlife and excellent restaurants of Paris and the endless beaches of Florida. Tel Aviv also is a cultural center with a very modern Opera House with excellent acoustics, as well as many museums and theaters. We visited the Museum of the Diaspora, a very unique institution featuring everything about past and present Jewish life, music, history, food, and more.

New Opera House in Tel Aviv

Having fun in the Museum of the Diaspora in Tel Aviv 2019

One evening, we had reservations in one of the best seafood restaurants in Tel Aviv, the Seal Club on Ben Yehuda Street which had an imaginative young chef. Next to our table in the restaurant, two gentlemen were talking in English about science. I walked over to their table assuming that I might know them. It turned out that one of the gentlemen was Morris Kahn, one of the richest men in Israel who financed the development of the rocket that Israel had recently sent to the moon. The other person was a cardiologist.

Morris Kahn with Suzika and me

We wanted to have some fun together on the last day of this wonderful family vacation. The flight to Boston was scheduled for midnight on April 22nd and all travelers had to be out at the airport three hours before departure. So, we had the whole day to enjoy.

We decided to walk to the Old City of Jaffa about 2-3 miles from the hotel. Everybody was in good shape and the changing scenery was very colorful, so it was easy going from the modern high-rise buildings of Tel Aviv to the ancient city of Jaffa.

Jaffa with the high-rise buildings in Tel Aviv in the background

We went by the large market called the *Shouk Ha Carmel*, where you can find anything you need or even what you don't need. A fun place!

Talia and Suzika in the Shouk Ha Carmel. Hannah is shopping alone somewhere

After a so-so lunch, we were ready to go meet a young artist who was going to introduce us to the art of Graffiti. To most of us, graffiti meant vandalizing walls and we never understood that most graffiti have some political or social message. We walked through several streets where she explained the meanings behind the various graffiti. We learned that although it is forbidden by the police to draw graffiti on the wall, the police have to catch the performing artist in the act to be able to arrest him or her. For that reason, most of the graffiti is produced at night way up high above the ground on the top floors of high buildings, sometimes endangering the life of the artists.

After a couple of hours of the "graffiti tour", we went into a place where we were supplied with everything needed to make our own graffiti, like paints, brushes, aprons, gloves, etc. The fun began and we produced graffiti with various degrees of success. Probably Vera was the best and I the worst with the rest falling somewhere between the two of us.

Vera the Champion with the message" Life is not by chance" hence the dice.

Happy family at the wall with graffiti symbolizing love, before the end of a great vacation.

My mother's oldest sister's two children, Edi and Ocsi Bishi lived in Moshav Kfar Lidice, on the old border facing Jordan with Latrun an Arab city on the other side. I visited them in 1949 before the name was changed to **Mishmar Ayalon**. Jerusalem was only 20 miles away but I could not cross the border.

It took me 25 years before I finally got to visit Jerusalem for the first time with Vera and Michael and Suzika in 1975. We stayed at the King David Hotel, well known for having been bombed in 1946 by the revisionist group Irgun to avenge the atrocities of the British. The hotel was the target because at the time it was the headquarters for the British authorities of the Palestine Mandate. This time in 1975, we were able to drive from Mishmar Ayalon through Latrun to Jerusalem because after the 1967 war, the whole area became part of Israel. Today, my cousin Ocsi's son Yitzhak and his family in Mishmar Ayalon are the owners of Bishiq one of the best barbecue restaurants in Israel where they even brew their own beer. It was truly a great experience to taste their barbecued ribs, grilled foie gras, homemade sausages, and their house beer.

Bishiq restaurant in Mishmar Ayalon

I can't think of any city which impacts a visitor more than **Jerusalem.** The different neighborhoods, the people, the thousands of years of history, the home of three major religions make it the most unique place in the world. It is the most important place for the Jews since it was built 3000 years ago as the capital city of their kingdom; for the Christians, it was where Jesus died 2000 years ago; and it is sacred for the Muslims along with Mecca and Medina. During the last 3000 years, the city has changed its rulers at least 12 times as shown below:

- **David** in 1100 BC made Jerusalem the Capital of the Jewish Kingdom.
- His son **Solomon** 40 years later built the First Temple.
- **Babylonians** occupied the city in 586 BC and destroyed the Temple.
- Fifty years later the Persian King **Cyrus** took over the city.
- **Alexander the Great** occupied Jerusalem around 300 BC
- **Herod** restored the Temple but the Romans destroyed the Second Temple in 70 BC.
- The **Early Islamists** ruled the city around 600 AD until the 1100 AD
- The European **Crusaders** occupied the land from 1099 to 1187 AD
- **The Ottomans** ruled the city from 1516 until the end of World War 1
- The **British** took over under the League of Nations Mandate for Palestine in 1922.
- When Israel became a State in **1948** the city was divided: West Jerusalem was under Israeli control and East Jerusalem under Jordanian control.
- In 1967, **Israel** united the two parts of Jerusalem and today it is the capital city of Israel.

Jerusalem

There are many important sights to visit: the Knesset, the Israeli Parliament, the Garden of Gethsemane, the Al Aqsa Mosque, Mea Shearim, the colorful markets, and more. We came to Jerusalem with Vera many times after 1975. During our tour in Israel in 1997 with my childhood friends, we went to the Garden of Gethsemane, where Jesus was preaching and praying with his followers when he was taken to be crucified by the Roman soldiers after the betrayal of Judas.

Garden of Gethsemane

The Al Aqsa compound on the Temple Mount in the Old City of Jerusalem has been cherished as a holy site for thousands of years by Jews, Christians, and Muslims. According to the Old Testament, this is the site where everything began, where God created Adam and Eve from a clump of earth, a place frequented by Jesus, and of course the location of Al Aqsa.

In 1997 when our group of friends wanted to visit Al Aqsa, they wouldn't let us in because we were wearing shorts. We all had to purchase "hijabs" from a vendor outside the Mosque to make skirts out of them. With our new outfits, they let us in.

In hijabs at the front of the Al Aqsa in Jerusalem 1997

Vera had a similar experience some years earlier in the Vatican where they wanted her to wear something over her sleeveless shirt. I took off my undershirt and gave it to her to cover her shoulders and this satisfied their norms. Mea Shearim also is restricted to women with short skirts or sleeveless blouses. Religious men are not allowed to look at any uncovered women other than their wives. I guess all religions (although I'm not sure about Hinduism and Buddhism.) try to protect people from temptation!

Vera in Mea Shearim in 1984

Mea Shearim is the most religious section of Jerusalem. Most of the people who live there are originally from Eastern Europe and they still live with the customs of 200 years ago. They don't use Hebrew in their conversations, only Yiddish or the language of their origins, and only use Hebrew for praying.

While we were walking on the street in Mea Shearim, we heard Hungarian being spoken by some religious men and we went up to talk with them. We found out that their families were originally from Debrecen. They were born in Jerusalem but spoke Hungarian with a clear but distinct dialect of the *Hajdusag*, the area which includes Debrecen. When the Hungarian Academy of Science wanted to make a study of ancient

Hungarian dialects, it sent a group of scholars to Mea Shearim, probably the only place in the world to hear pure unaffected Hungarian speech.

With my friends at the memorial (including Debrecen) in Yad Vashem 1997

To visit **Yad Vashem,** Israel's official memorial of the victims of the Holocaust is an emotional experience for anyone whether directly connected or not to the Holocaust. It is difficult to walk through its halls without crying. The names of the millions of victims including a million Jewish children are read out on speakers.

The names and heroic deeds of *Righteous Persons* who saved Jewish lives during the Holocaust are also displayed. We are in the process of submitting the name of Dora Hoffman, as a Righteous Person. She was a devoted Catholic lady of German origin, who hid Vera in O Buda in 1944/45, while her mother was taken to Auschwitz.

We visited **Abu-Gosh,** an Arab town near Jerusalem several times. They have many excellent restaurants in the area but we returned time after time to one of our favorites, also called Abu-Gosh. They have the world's best hummus and pitta bread as well as many other Middle Eastern delicacies.

Abu-Gosh restaurant in the town of Abu-Gosh

Our most memorable event in Jerusalem was Hannah's Bat Mitzvah in April 2019. We had about 100 guests at the ceremony, more than 75 were Vera's and my relatives who live in Israel. The rest of the invited were Israeli friends of ours. We probably could have had another 30 people. However, Vera's orthodox relatives would not attend because men and women were together at the ceremony, which they consider forbidden. We danced to traditional music right up to the Wailing Wall for the Bat Mitzvah ceremony.

Dancing up to the wall in Jerusalem 2019

Hannah read the Torah, chanting the difficult passages like a professional cantor. All the Israelis were impressed by her perfect pronunciation of the Hebrew.

Hannah is chanting from the Torah at her Bat Mitzvah ceremony in Jerusalem

Hannah (with the tallit) in the middle, after she concluded her Bat Mitzvah ceremony.

After the ceremony, the festivity continued with dinner and dancing at the Kedmah restaurant on the top of Mamilla Mall with a panoramic view of Jerusalem.

Kedmah restaurant with a view of the Wailing Wall

While some of the guests enjoyed their meals, others danced for hours to the traditional music provided by a three-piece band.

With friends at the Hannah's Bat Mitzvah dinner in the Kedmah

Everybody loves to dance even the little ones

Suzika, Hannah, and Talia with the IDF soldiers in Jerusalem

The day after the Bat Mitzvah celebration we all took a 10-day tour of Israel, starting in Jerusalem. The girls enjoyed connecting with the Israeli Defense Forces.

Nearly 70 years earlier, in late summer of 1950, while we were working in Eilat, I thought about my next move. I really wanted to continue my education, which was interrupted at the age of fourteen when I completed the 4th grade in the Gymnasium in Debrecen and became an apprentice in a carpentry shop. The opportunities to study in Israel at that time were rather limited so I decided to go back to Hungary.

After spending 15 months in Israel we sailed back from Haifa to Naples on an Italian boat but returned many times in the next seventy years. It was a wise decision because at last I could connect with my parents if only for a couple of years. Both my father and my mother passed away shortly after my return.

4. TURKEY

The Italian boat was rather comfortable and certainly much better than what we were accustomed to. In September 1950, we were only two in a cabin and the food was interesting but we were not familiar with shellfish so we ate mostly meat, cheese, and rolls. After a short stop in **Cyprus**, a few hundred kilometers from Haifa, we landed in **Izmir Turkey,** where we spent a good half a day just walking around.

Izmir is the third-largest city in Turkey after Istanbul and Ankara. It was part of Greece and was called Smyrna until the Ottoman empire made it part of Turkey. After World War 1, Greece defeated the Turkish army and recaptured the city for a short time, but by 1922 Izmir became part of Turkey again.

Izmir Turkey on the Agean Sea

Izmir is a picturesque city on the Agean Sea and in 1950 when we landed there, it had a population of close to 500,000 while today the population is close to 3 million. After the Inquisition in Spain and Portugal, a large number of Sephardic Jewish people settled in the city and by the early twentieth century, the Jewish population was over 50,000. The Kabbalist Zevi Shabbatai, who claimed to be the long-awaited Messiah of the Jews, was born here in the 17th century. He had many followers until he was arrested by the Turkish authorities and made to choose either to convert to Islam or to be executed. He converted.

As we walked along the busy streets of Izmir, several well-dressed gentlemen, who appeared to be wealthy and influential, came up to us and started to speak to us in Hebrew. They probably assumed we were from Israel by our clothing. We explained to them that we had just come by boat from Haifa and that in the evening we were going to sail to Naples and then back to Hungary. They tried to convince us not to go back. They said that life in Hungary is horrible and that we should stay in Izmir, where there were good jobs that they could get for us. They stressed that in Izmir many eligible young Jewish girls were looking for husbands but there was a shortage of local eligible candidates.

As we walked around, they introduced to us a Turkish specialty called **yumurtali pide**, an excellent dish, flatbread with eggs, cheese, peppers, onions, tomatoes, and various spices. For years, I would still dream about yumurtali pide, especially in Hungary when everything was rationed in the 1950s and it made me wonder if it was a wise decision not to stay in Izmir. I thought of it when I was on the wrestling team as a university student in Hungary and one of the team members who was in his last year of medical studies said, "the first thing I will do as a doctor, is eat as much scrambled eggs as I can".

Yumurtali Pide

Serves 2

Ingredients:

2 ½ cups all-purpose plain flour

2 oz. dried yeast

tsp. sugar

tsp. salt

½ cup warm water

⅓ cup warm milk

tbsp. olive oil

2 eggs

sliced Havarti cheese

4 oz. grated mozzarella

tomato thinly sliced

small bell pepper, thinly sliced

Red pepper flakes

Directions:

1. Preheat the oven to 350 F

2. Stir in the dried yeast and sugar in a small bowl and pour in ½ cup warm water. Dissolve and mix the yeast in water. Set aside the yeast mixture for 5 minutes.

3. Combine the flour and salt in a large bowl. Make a well in the middle and pour in 2 tbsp. olive oil and the yeast mixture. Also, stir in the warm milk to the flour mixture. On a marble or floured surface, knead for 3 -5 minutes, until you reach a soft, smooth dough. The dough may get sticky as you knead, so pour the remaining 1 tbsp. olive oil and add a little more flour if needed to help shape into a soft dough.

4. Grease a large bowl with a little olive oil, place the dough and cover with a cling film. Leave the dough in a warm place for 1 hour to rise.

5. Once the dough rises, place the dough on a lightly floured surface. Knead the dough for a minute then divide the dough into two pieces and roll into two balls. On a lightly floured surface, roll the dough balls into 2 oval shapes of 8"x16", and a ¼ inch thick.

6. Line a large baking tray with baking paper and place the 2 oval flatbread dough on the tray.

7. Spread the grated mozzarella cheese, havarti, sliced peppers, and tomatoes evenly over the 2 flatbreads, leaving 1 in at the edges as a border with no filling. Fold up the sides to act as a border to keep the filling intact. Squeeze the oval dough at each end to make it pointy.

8. Beat an egg in a small bowl and mix it with 1 tsp. olive oil. Brush the edges of the dough with this mixture. Bake for 20 minutes, until the pide is golden and crispy at the edges.

9. Take the pie tray out of the oven and carefully crack an egg in the middle of each pide. Return to the oven and bake for another 6 minutes.

10. Sprinkle red pepper flakes over egg, cut into slices, serve while warm.

Many years later I found out that the Georgian flatbread called Khachapuri is almost the same as the Turkish Yumurtali Pide, which came first?

Despite all the temptation of the girls and the job offers, at the age of 17 I had other ideas besides settling in Izmir with a Turkish wife to eat yumurtali pide for the rest of my life. We thanked them for everything and went back to the Italian boat which left for Athens.

Some 40 years later in 1989, while taking a cruise along the Greek Islands, we landed in **Kusadasi** and visited **Ephesus** which is about 50 miles from Izmir. Ephesus was built around 10 BC and with its population of over 200,000, it was one of the largest cities of the ancient Greek Empire. The theater in Ephesus was the largest in the ancient world with a capacity of 25,000 spectators. Under Roman rule in the second century, the Celsus Library was constructed honoring Tiberius Celsus, a Greek who was the governor in Roman Asia. Later, a large earthquake destroyed the city and excavations only began in the 19th century; now the Austrian Archeological Institute has been entrusted with the re-discovery of this ancient city.

Celsus Library   *Theater*

Street scene in Ephesus Turkey.

In nearby Kusadasi in 1989, we were ready to continue our cruise, when Vera and I were approached by some Turkish men who were selling beautiful hand made carpets. They showed us 12 or more of their wares and although we liked one, we had no intention of buying anything. When we told the salesman that we had no cash and no credit cards, we assumed that was the end of the process. Not so! He said, "I'll take your check!" So we have a large 9x12 hand made rug in our living room in Paris.

In May 2010, Vera and I toured **Turkey** with an American group, including our friends, Ibi and Joe. Our first stop from Paris was **Istanbul.** The original city founded in antiquity was first called Byzantium by the Greeks. Later, the Roman emperor Constantine enlarged the city, which he named **Constantinople** in his own honor and he decreed that it to be the capital of the Eastern Roman Empire, which lasted 1000 years as the Byzantine Empire.

The Ottoman Empire took over the city in 1453 and changed its name to Istanbul. It was the Ottoman capital until 1923 when Ankara became the capital of Turkey. The population of Istanbul rapidly grew from 500,000 in the 1920s to 15 million today. During our two-week tour in Turkey, we learned many interesting details of Turkish history from our excellent tour guide.

The view of Istanbul and the Bosporus from the Grand Halic Hotel

We spent three days in this exciting colorful city, where we stayed at the luxurious Grand Halic Hotel in a room with a view of the **Bosporus** strait which separates Europe and Asia. We visited the most important historical sites with our guide, as well as walking a lot on our own to absorb the atmosphere of the place.

Hagia Sophia was built in 537 AD as the main Cathedral of the Greek Orthodox Church. It was the world's largest cathedral until it was converted to a Muslim mosque after the Ottomans took over the city. It includes a museum today which when we visited it was unpleasant for several people of Greek ancestry in our group. It was a painful reminder of their historical tragedy, and was repeated many places throughout our tour of Turkey, where practically everything was Byzantine Greek before the 15th century. History can be very cruel.

Hagia Sophia Istambul

To balance our visits to mosques historically and culturally, after seeing the medieval Hagia Sofia built by the Byzantines, we visited the more recent Blue Mosque also called the Ahmed Mosque, built by the Ottoman Empire in the 17th century and known for the beautiful tiles on its interior walls. Some of the ladies from our group refused to enter this mosque. I don't know why.

Blue Mosque Istanbul

In front of the Mosque   *The ladies were happier with Joe than with me.*

After hearing enough of political and religious controversies, it was refreshing to experience the Grand Bazar of Istanbul, one of the most popular tourist attractions in the world with 92 million visitors yearly. The Grand Bazar extends over 7000 acres and employs 26,000 people. As we walked through this colorful market with many thousands of booths, some of the merchants were happy to speak Hungarian with us. I guess they had 150 years to learn this difficult language after the battle of Mohacs in 1526 when Suleiman's Army beat the army of King Lajos in 2 hours and Hungary ceased to exist. Anyway, our conversation was very amicable, and we got very good deals on purchases of many things that we really didn't need.

With Vera in the Grand Bazaar in Istanbul

After the market, Vera and I did more sightseeing and explored the city, especially Istaklal Avenue in the Taksim area which is said to have the most crowded streets (after Osaka Japan).

Istiklal Avenue Istanbul

One of the evenings we had a very good supper in a leading nightclub where one of the best belly dancers of Turkey performed. It was hard to follow her movements without a stroboscope to slow down her gyrations.

Belly dancer

Regional folk dancers in a nightclub in Istanbul 2010

After eying a few slower-moving belly dancers, we enjoyed a program of regional folk-dance styles performed by groups in traditional dress and I enthusiastically joined in.

Dancing on a night club stage in Istanbul 2010

Our next stop was the city of **Bursa**, a couple of hours from Istanbul. We started the trip in an air-conditioned luxury bus of the tourist office and finished on a ferry.

On the ferry from Istanbul to Bursa

Bursa was the capital city of Turkey before Istanbul. Today it is a large city with over two million inhabitants. It was one of the largest silk producing centers in the world thanks to the contribution of the Jewish population of the city who lived in Bursa for centuries after they were invited by Suleiman to improve commerce. He was very lenient with minorities and historically there has been religious tolerance in Turkey.

We visited the Tumbekli Mosque in Bursa, which is composed of two sections. The first part is a structure with a dome and a cross on the tips of two pillars by the entrance to the building. From this point, a gateway leads into another building which is an old synagogue. So this building which includes a synagogue and a cross is also an active mosque. We spent a few hours shopping for silk products in the old picturesque part of the city.

The old city in Bursa

Panoramic view of Bursa

From a distance, we heard cheering and music. As we approached, we found out that the local football (soccer) team Bursaspor, had just beat the Besikta team *2 goals to 1* and became the 2010 National Champion of Turkey. We were very happy to share their happiness. Football is the major pride of Bursa, and their huge stadium is always packed

Football stadium in Bursa

Traveling through Turkey we usually stopped for lunch in the countryside. Most often, we selected their specialty, *gozleme*, a pizza-like flatbread, covered with cheese or yogurt, and sometimes meat. It was interesting to watch the women make gozleme from scratch. Their products were so tasty that we never get tired of eating them. Interestingly, when we asked for Gozleme in New York city's many Turkish restaurants, they never heard of it. They are truly *authentic!*

Authentic Turkish Name for "Sandwich House"!

Handmade Gozleme, Turkish flatbread

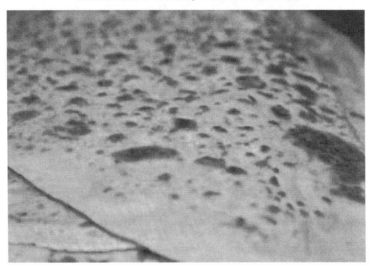

Gozleme, another Turkish flatbread

We stopped in **Ankara** the capital city of Turkey and with close to 5 million people, the country's second-largest city. It was established as the capital after World War 1 when Turkey was defeated by the Allies. Turkey was on the side of Germany and the Austro-Hungarian Monarchy, the losers in WW 1. Istanbul was occupied by the Allies and the Turkish National Movement headed by Ataturk named Ankara as the capital of the Turkish Republic.

Ataturk, whose real name was Mustafa Kamel was the heroic commander of a Turkish division, which stopped the advance of the Allies in WW 1 in the Battle of Gallipoli in the Dardanelles. Mustafa Kamel became the President of the First Republic of Turkey and took the name of Ataturk, father of Turks in Turkish. He was a true reformer who introduced many reforms that changed Turkey from a religious fundamentalist country into a modern secular nation. He introduced new laws that allowed women to remove their veils and achieve the right to vote and even changed the use of the Arabic alphabet to the Latin one. Anitkabir is a mausoleum In Ankara that honors him as the founder of modern Turkey.

Ataturk Mausoleum in Ankara

We continued our tour from Ankara toward **Cappadocia**, one of the most unusual parts of Anatolia, the Turkish homeland in Asia Minor. Only 5% of Turkey is in Europe and the rest or 95 % of the national territory is in Asia. This is one of the reasons why the European Union does not favor the admission of Turkey to the EU.

The rock formations of Cappadocia are amazing. They were used in the Middle Ages by the Christian population to build underground hiding places to escape from the advancing Muslim army and their cruel measures. There were even underground cities with four levels and as many as 20,000 inhabitants that had functioning schools for children that were able to survive for a year or longer. The area of Cappadocia is now a tourist attraction and elegant accommodations are provided for the visitors.

Rock formations in Cappadocia

Medieval Dwellings and Churches in Cappadocia

Cappadocia is also well known for its handicrafts and folk art, like ceramics, carpet making, and other skills. We visited one of their artisanal carpet manufacturing shops, where we purchased a beautiful blue carpet nicer than the one bought 20 years earlier in Kusadasi which we passed to Suzika and family.

Rug making in Cappadocia Turkey

Our next stop was **Konya,** a large city known for being one of the most religious centers in Turkey. The city is famous for the whirling dervish dancers, a group that practices a religious ritual which can go on for hours. We attended one of their ceremonies, and as much as I wanted to join the Dervish dancers, they would not permit a tourist like me to take part in their religious rites.

Dervish dancers in Konya

Next, our bus tour took us to **Pamukkale** a resort town with mineral water spas and baths. The name *Pamukkale* means "cotton" in Turkish because these very unusual springs look like puffs of white cotton. Russian tourists were all over the area which we discovered is one of their favorite spots.

Bathers at Pamukkale

We continued our bus tour to **Antalya** a large beautiful city on the Turkish Riviera with many expensive hotels.

In a hotel in Antalya Turkey 2010

61

At the beach in Antalya

From Antalya, we headed to what is thought to be the possible location of ancient Troy, a city that has been destroyed many times. We were told that there are nine levels of structures of the city built in different epochs of its long history.

In the Gymnazium in Debrecen, I had learned the story of Troy, the city described in the **Iliad** of **Homer,** the blind Anatolian Greek. His poem covers the end of the Greeks' 10-year war against Troy. The city was finally conquered by the famous tactic of the Greeks who pretended to abandon the siege but left behind a giant wooden horse with a group of their soldiers hidden inside. The Trojans were deceived and brought the wooden horse inside the walls of the city. At night the Greek soldiers climbed out of the horse and opened the gates for the rest of the Greek army that burned down the city and slaughtered all its population. Just recently during the COVID 19 period, by watching about 80 Operas from the Metropolitan Opera, we learned more about the Trojans via Berlioz's Les Troyens.

After we climbed up a wooden reproduction of the Trojan Horse in the area of **Troy** at the western part of Anatolia near the **Dardanelles,** we headed to **Gallipoli.**

Wooden horse in Troy

Our last stop of this two-week tour in Turkey was Gallipoli in the Dardanelles, a natural strait that connects the Aegean Sea to the Marmara Sea. In the map below, the Aegean Sea is on the left and the Marmara Sea is on the right. The Bosporus, the site of Istanbul, is another strait that connects the Marmara Sea to the Black sea.

Partial map of Turkey

The two straits, the Dardanelles and the Bosporus divide Europe from Asia. Gallipoli and the Dardanelles became well known as the place of one of the bloodiest battles of World War 1,

The war, which was called the Great War, took place from 1914 to 1918 with the Allied powers, England, France, Russia, and later on the United States on one side, and on the other side the Central powers, the Austro-Hungarian Monarchy, Germany, and Turkey. The minor players in the war counted Bulgaria on the side of the Central powers and Romania with the Allied Powers.

In 1915 the Allied forces wanted to capture the Dardanelles and Istanbul on the Bosporus, to be able to send supplies to Russia on the Black Sea. At the Battle of Gallipoli, the Turkish army stopped the Allies in a battle that lasted 8 months with casualties of close to 250 thousand on both sides. The total casualties of World War 1 were over 10 million. The successful defense by the Turks was led by Ataturk, who became the first president of the Turkish Republic. We visited both cemeteries, the Allied one and the Turkish one. There is a beautiful memorial by Ataturk honoring the casualties in the Allies cemetery.

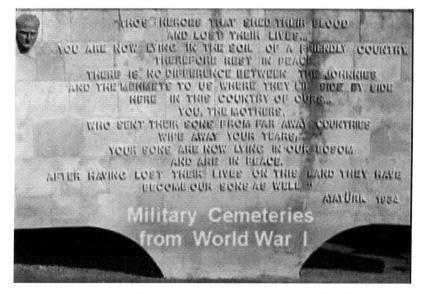

Memorial for the fallen soldiers at the Battle of Gallipoli in WW1

In the Turkish cemetery of Gallipoli there is a very evocative statue of an old man, clearly a veteran of World War 1, explaining to a little girl what took place in Gallipoli.

Statue in the Turkish cemetery in Gallipoli

Perhaps the memory of the battle at Gallipoli kept the Turkish government out of entering World War 2. By staying neutral, it saved many lives not only among the Turkish population but also provided a haven to many Jewish refugees fleeing Nazi-occupied Europe.

From Gallipoli, we drove back to Istanbul and departed from Turkey the next day with many wonderful memories of the country and its variegated history.

Sixty years earlier in September 1950, my friends and I sailed from Izmir to Naples on an Italian ship. The boat made another stop in Athens Greece. To our great disappointment, when we showed our papers to the Greek officials, they would not let us in even for a few hours visit, because we were going to Hungary, a Communist country. Greece had just ended a three-year civil war between the Royalists and the Greek Communist forces, led by Nikos Beloyannis. The war ended in 1949 after the Communist forces were defeated by the Royalists who got help from England and other Western countries. During the war, the Communists also received support over the Yugoslavian border from Russia and other Communist countries,

However, in 1949 the conflict between Stalin and the Yugoslavian dissident Tito brought about the separation of Yugoslavia from the Soviet-controlled eastern bloc, and Yugoslavia stopped helping the Greek Communists which led to their defeat. Many refugees, mostly women and children of the Greek Communists escaped and settled in other eastern bloc countries. Thousands went to Hungary which named a street after Beloyannis.

It took me another 39 years to visit Athens in 1989. By that time Hungary was not a Communist country, I was an American citizen, and the Greeks could not care less. In 1950, I only saw Athens from a distance from an Italian ship.

Athens, Greece

5. ITALY

It was a late September afternoon in 1950 when we got off the Italian ship in **Naples.** The Italian authorities were not as concerned about our Hungarian documents as the Greeks were, so we were free to roam this old Italian city.

Street scene in Naples

Just a few years after World War 2, Naples still had visible signs of the damage caused by the hundreds of bombings by the Allies as well as the destruction caused by the Nazis. Germany expected an Allied invasion at the seaport of Naples and destroyed many strategical points to place as many obstacles as possible to the invasion.

Our one-day visit to the city did not overly impress us and besides, we also had to make arrangements for the train to Rome, our next stop. We planned to take night trains to avoid paying for hotels since we had very little money. Nevertheless, we still were able to go back to Hungary including daytime excursions along the way to visit interesting sights on our stops at Rome, Venice, and Vienna.

Interestingly, the few hours of our stay in Naples in 1950, coincided with the turbulent period described by Elena Ferrante in her four very well-known novels. One of which," My Brilliant Friend" was made into a TV series. We did not have the pleasure of meeting the two main characters, Elena "Lenù" Greco, who portrayed Ferrante, and Lila Cerullo but we did see many other pretty Neapolitans, the best sights for us in the city.

I have not returned to Naples since 1950 but hopefully, I will have a chance to do so with Vera. Actually, some 50 years later in 2001, Vera and I were 20 miles from Naples while driving with our friends, on the Amalfi Coast. There was so much to see on that trip that we could not cover Naples. Maybe next time.

The Amalfi Coast is a 50 mile stretch of road from **Salerno** to **Sorrento** that goes through one of the most beautiful parts of Italy and is also one of the most challenging for the driver. Most of the route is a winding single-lane road through the mountains. On one side there is a steep hill and below there is the sea. It was a breath-taking view and sometimes we all had to hold our breath when a bus came from the opposite direction. I managed alright driving a rented Alfa Romeo, although Vera and our friends, Steve and Marika surely had to hold their breath more than once.

The Amalfi Coast Road

Our first stop, Ravello, which is not as well-known as Positano or Amalfi, is situated about 5 km off the main road on top of a cliff. It was highly recommended so fortunately, we decided to stop there for lunch. We found that the view from Ravello was probably the most beautiful on the Amalfi coast and we had a wonderful gourmet lunch in the garden of our restaurant.

Restaurant in Ravello on the Amalfi Coast

We stopped briefly in Amalfi before we drove to Positano our final destination, where we stayed for several days. Positano is a small town with charming restaurants and shops located on the side of a mountain facing the Mediterranean Sea. The beaches were not as nice as those of Florida but the area and its other attractions were our main reason to be there, not the beach. Vera and I even did our usual jogging which was not easy in the steep hills.

Positano, Amalfi Coast

With Positano as our base, we took several side trips, the first of which was to the ruins of Pompeii, about two hours' drive from Positano.

Pompeii was an ancient city near the present city of Naples with a population of about 20,000 persons. In 76 AD Mount Vesuvius, a volcano near Pompeii erupted violently and covered the city completely with hot metallic ash causing the death of all the inhabitants. After centuries, it was forgotten until about 1500 years later when a document was found which described the tragic destruction of Pompeii. It took another 150 years before a Spanish engineer discovered the existence of the city several meters below the surface of the surrounding fields, and excavation began. During the excavation, plaster was used to fill in the voids in the ash that once held human bodies which captures the exact position and even the facial expression of the victims at the moment of their death.

Vesuvius behind the ruins of Pompei

Several buildings and streets have been restored through the years which give us a picture of life in Pompeii before the destruction. They had theaters, sports arenas, very advanced water and sewage systems, and public and private buildings of all kinds. On the restored walls of the brothels, there are original graffiti showing the "various offerings" of the Pompeian madams. The "menu" has not changed much over the years.

Street scene in ancient Pompei

On our way back from Pompeii we stopped in Sorrento, where after a nice dinner of **gnocchi a la Sorrento,** (a tomato-**based** version; another way is with gorgonzola instead of tomatoes), and our singing "O sole mio", we returned to Positano.

Downtown Sorrento

Gnocchi a la Sorrento

Serves 4

Ingredients for gnocchi:

4 medium potatoes peeled

4 cups of all-purpose flour

2 eggs

Directions:

1. Bring a large pot of salted water to boil. Add the peeled potatoes to the pot and cook about 15 minutes, until they are tender but firm. Drain, cool, and mash with a potato masher.

2. Combine mashed potato, flour, and eggs in a large bowl. Knead until dough forms a ball. Shape a small portion of dough into a ½ inch diameter long cylinder. On a floured surface cut into ½ inch long gnocchi.

3. Bring a large pot of lightly salted water to boil. Drop in the gnocchi and cook for 3-5 minutes or until gnocchi rise to the top. Drain and serve with a spicy creamed tomato sauce and sprinkle with mozzarella cheese. Some serve it with gorgonzola sauce.

Ingredients for spicy creamed tomato sauce:

2 tbsp. olive oil

3 cloves garlic minced

Half tsp. red pepper flakes

Half tsp. dried oregano

28 oz. can whole peeled tomatoes, crushed

Salt to taste 1pinch of freshly ground pepper

¼ cup of cream

Two tbsp. vodka, optional

Directions:

1. Heat olive oil over moderate heat

2. Add garlic and red pepper and oregano stirring until garlic is golden yellow.

3. Add crushed tomatoes and salt. Bring to boil add black pepper. Reduce heat and simmer 15 minutes.

4. Add the cream and the vodka (optional) and bring to boil.

5. Reduce heat to low and a few minutes later add to gnocchi.

Cioppino

Serves 6

Ingredients:

3 tbs. olive oil

fennel bulb thinly sliced

1 onion chopped

shallots chopped

garlic cloves finely chopped

½ tsp. dried crushed red pepper flakes

¼ cup tomato paste

1 small can peeled tomatoes in juice

cups clam juice

1½ cups dry white wine

1 bay leaf

1½ lb. large scallops

1½ lb. large uncooked shrimps with tail on

1½ lb. assorted firm fish, mussels and clams.

Directions:

1. Heat olive oil in a very large pot

2. Add onion, shallots, fennel, + salt and pepper and cook on medium-low heat until the onion is transparent

3. Add garlic and pepper flake and sauté for two minutes

4. Stir in the tomato paste

5. Add tomatoes with their juice, wine. clam juice and bay leaf. Cover and bring to boil.

6. Reduce the heat to medium-low, cover and simmer for about 30 minutes.

7. If you are using mussels and clams add to the cooking pot. Cover and cook about 5 minutes until shell open.

8. Add shrimp, scallops and fish, and simmer until they are gently cooked and the shells are open. Discard any shells that do not open.

9. Remove bay leaf.

10. Divide into serving plates.

On another day, we went to Capri and took a boat to the spectacular **Blue Grotto** where sunlight passing through an underwater cavity shines through the seawater creating a blue reflection that illuminates the whole cavern.

Blue Grotto in Capri

In September of 1950, George, Janos, Steve, and I traveled on a late-night train from Naples to **Rome** a distance of around two hundred miles of stops in many small towns that took several hours. We arrived in Rome in the early morning and were happy to have the whole day to see some of the more important historical sites before having to take another night train to Venice. We realized that our time was limited so we selected the four most important sites (in our opinion): The Forum, the Colosseum, Vatican City, Castle Sant' Angelo. We all knew that we would have other chances to come back and see more of Rome.

The ancient Roman Forum was a central space surrounded by important government buildings during the days of the Roman empire. It was a place for political, social, and religious events. Already by the 7th and 8th century BC, many prestigious and wealthy people resided around the Forum.

Forum in Rome

The Colosseum was built in 70 AD by the emperor Vespasian, and at that time was Rome's largest amphitheater with a capacity for 80 thousand spectators at the performances of war games and gladiatorial combats. The various spectacles in the Colosseum were an efficient instrument of the emperor and the ruling classes to deliver *Panem Et Circences* (bread and circuses) to keep the masses in peace.

Colosseum in Rome

Also, in Rome, Vatican City is an independent state, the smallest state in the world in area .2 square miles. So while we were in Rome, we took the opportunity to visit the smallest country in the world.

6. VATICAN

Vatican City state, the smallest country in the world with 800 inhabitants, is not a member of the United Nations, is governed by the Pope and it is the center of the 1.2 billion Catholics worldwide. Saint Peter's Square is the home of the massive Saint Peter's Basilica and the Vatican museum, which has probably the world's most famous art collections. When we young travelers visited the Basilica, we conversed in Hebrew with a group of very friendly priests, whose Hebrew were considerably more refined than ours which we picked up during our digging in Eilat.

Vatican City State

The Castle Sant'Angelo was the tallest building in Rome when it was built to be the Mausoleum for emperor Publius Aelius Hadrianus, better known as Hadrian, who ruled the Roman Empire for twenty years in the 2nd century AD.

Hadrian's reign was very badly impacted by the revolt of Bar Kokhba in Judea which he considered a failure of his ambition to rule the world. Bar Kokhba was a Jewish military leader who successfully led a revolt against the Roman Empire and maintained an independent state for three years until Hadrian suppressed the Bar Kokhba revolt. The emperor even changed the name of Jerusalem to Aelia Capitolium, a form of his name that eventually was forgotten and the original name of Jerusalem prevailed.

In the 15th century, the Papal State converted the mausoleum into a castle which also served as a prison where several famous people were incarcerated because their ideas were not in line with Catholic doctrine. Giordano Bruno for example, a Dominican friar but also a mathematician, philosopher, and cosmologist, was imprisoned there for six years. He taught the Copernican concept that the Sun, not the Earth is the center of our world, and also proposed that the universe is infinite, which was contrary to the teaching of the church. Another prisoner was the sculptor and goldsmith Benvenuto Cellini, who eventually escaped from the Castle Sant'Angelo.

Executions were performed in the small inner courtyard of the prison, which was also the setting for the third act of Giacomo Puccini's 1900 opera *Tosca*. The heroine Floria Tosca leaps to her death from the Castel's ramparts after her lover Cavaradossi was executed. Maybe more because of Puccini than for Hadrian, by 1901 the castle became a very impressive museum.

Castle Saint'Angelo Rome

In 1950, after our very busy cultural exposure to the wonders of Rome, we walked to the railway station to continue our return to Hungary. On a busy street, we were approached by a man selling Parker fountain pens, the Cadillac of the fountain pen world at that time. When he asked the equivalent of $8, to the surprise of my friends, I started to bargain using my hands since I did not speak any Italian. To my surprise, he agreed to sell it to me for $2! So we bought four, one for each of us, one for George, Janos, Steve, and me. Today, the Parkers are selling for $225. I learned my lesson with the Parker pens and more than 32 years later when I landed at the Fiumicino Airport in Rome and asked a cab driver how much the fare was to my hotel and he replied, "eighty dollars", I asked, "how about twenty?", he said OK.

On my way to Erice Sicily in December 1982 I stopped in Rome for a day. The next day I took a flight to Palermo and from the airport, I was taken by car to **Erice.**

Erice Sicily

Erice is a small picturesque town, with a population of about 20 thousand located on top of the Erice mountain at three thousand feet above sea level.

I gave several lectures in the one-week workshop on Physical Acoustics at the School of Ettore Majorana in Erice Sicily in 1982. The "Ettore Majorana Foundation and International Centre for Scientific Culture" (see below) is named after an outstanding Italian physicist, Ettore Majorana, born in Sicily in 1906 who mysteriously passed away at the age of 36.

Every year the Erice Center hosts several workshops covering different scientific disciplines (e.g. physics, medicine, chemistry, life sciences, etc.) for hundreds of participating scientists It was founded 45 years ago and since then, this center has represented an important meeting place for scientists from all over the world. The School of Physical Acoustics was among the 118 schools that held workshops in Erice. I was invited to the first in December 1982 as well as to three more workshops on various subjects of physical acoustics in 1985, 1988, and 1991.

I participated in the Erice Center in Sicily (1982, 1985, 1988,1991)

All the attendees were guests of the city of Erice, and each of us had a name tag which was our passport to dine and wine in any of the local restaurants. The food was very good, starting with a *primo piato* of salad or pasta, followed by a *secondo piato* of fish or meat with a bottle of local wine. We finished with strong espresso coffee and a Sicilian dessert-like marzipan which the Sicilians know how to make very well. We had this treatment twice a day and by the end of the week, we knew the pros and cons of all the restaurants.

Erice, Sicily

My route back from Erice was almost always via Palermo and Rome to the USA. Only once in 1991, I decided to return via Milan instead of Rome so I could see an opera at *Il Teatro alla Scala* in Milan. But I was unlucky because the day I stayed in Milan for the opera, the Scala had no performance, so instead, I could only see the exterior of the theater, hum an aria from Rigoletto, and buy Vera a Missoni cardigan.

Teatro La Scala Milan

Vera and I visited Rome in 1983 and stayed in the elegant Eden Hotel for her first visit to the Eternal City. On the second day, we found out that the personnel at the hotel were on strike and for four days we didn't get any clean towels or sheets. Vera wanted to change the bed herself but because the laundry people were also on strike, no clean laundry was available. Nevertheless, we had a great time seeing all the historical sites of the city and eating Fettuccini Alfredo in a restaurant which claimed to be the first to serve the dish. Later, we found out that half a dozen other restaurants in Rome also claimed to be the first.

Hotel Eden, Rome

We discovered an excellent restaurant called Piperno located in the area of the Old Jewish Ghetto. It became one of our favorites and we returned to it many times.

Piperno Restaurant, Rome

Their signature dish is **Carciofi alla Giudia** (deep-fried artichoke) the way the Israelites used to prepare it 2000 years ago.

Carciofi alla Giudia

After that, Rome became one of our favorite destinations and we have returned at least half a dozen times. The one visit that we will never forget was in September 2001! After the 17th International Conference in Acoustics in Rome, we drove with Steve and Marika to the Amalfi coast where we spent a week. Our flight back to the US from Rome was scheduled for September 12, so we decided to stay on the Amalfi coast until September 11, when early in the morning, we left to drive to Monte Cassino which is about 170 km from Rome.

The Monastery of Monte Cassino, famous for its battle in 1944, is on the top of a 500-meter-high hill which was used by the Germans to stop the advancing American Army. Despite the continuous bombardment, the Germans held out for several months. Finally, the Allies decided to use ground forces, mostly the Polish Army, to capture the monastery. It was one of the bloodiest battles of WW2. When we drove up to the monastery, we visited the large Polish Cemetery where over a thousand Polish soldiers were buried. In a separate part of the cemetery, we found a large number of graves with the Jewish symbol of the Mogen David.

We had a nice lunch at the bottom of the hill in a cozy little restaurant. At around 3 in the afternoon, we took off to drive to Rome. As we were leaving the area, the young waitress made gestures trying to tell us something but we were already too far away to go back and assumed she was just saying goodbye.

Monte Cassino, Italy

When we arrived to Rome's Hilton Airport Hotel to check in, a woman told us that the **World Trade Center** had been destroyed by an airplane and that there were hundreds of casualties. First, we thought that she had lost her mind, but soon we found out the tragic truth. Most likely, this is what the young waitress of Monte Cassino was trying to tell us. The next day our flight was canceled because of 9/11 and we had to stay another week in Italy before we could fly out. The Italian people were wonderful and sympathized with stranded Americans. We could stay in the Hilton even though all the rooms were booked and the car rental company did not charge us for the extra week.

It was difficult to get a plane back to the US. There were thousands of people waiting at Rome's Airport, many of them sleeping on the floor for days. We finally got a flight out of Rome to end our very special experience of the memorable events of 2001.

Five decades earlier in September 1950, we four young travelers were in Rome on our way back to Hungary, we took a 50-mile night-train ride from Rome to our next destination **Venice**. It was a beautiful sunny morning when we arrived and we were mesmerized by the view of this unusual city on the Adriatic Sea. Venice contains over a hundred islands separated and connected by canals with no streets, so to get around you go by boat or by walking across the many bridges that connect the parts of the city.

In the center of Venice, the biggest tourist attraction is the Piazza San Marco which is always crowded with hundreds of pigeons and thousands of visitors so we started our one-day tour there. It was interesting to take the boat which crossed from one canal to the other. It was much cheaper than the gondola.

Piazza San Marco of Venice

Boat travel in Venice

In 1516, Venice was probably the first place to establish a Ghetto for the Venetian Jews who were confined to the defined area from 6 PM till 6 AM. They were also forced to wear identifying clothing to distinguish them from the rest of the population. William Shakespeare's famous *The Merchant of Venice* gives a graphic description of the conditions of the time. In the 18th century, Napoleon abolished the Ghettoes in Venice and in other cities, which was a welcome reform for the Jewish population.

Ghetto in Venice

Some 33 years later in 1983, Vera and I came to Venice. It was Vera's first time in the city and we stayed at the famous Danieli Hotel where the film "Death in Venice" was filmed. When we entered the hotel, we felt out of place among the well-dressed English ladies sipping their afternoon tea. It looked very elegant and proper, but it definitely was not our style.

Hotel Danieli Venice

Rather than sit around and drink tea we took a boat to the Lido Beach. On the boat, we were approached by a nice older lady from New York who was carrying a briefcase with the name tag of a New York Times correspondent. She was friendly and knowledgeable about all the attractions of the surroundings. We thanked her for the information and left her on the boat when we went to the Lido. Although the beach was very crowded with annoying beautiful people, we still had a very nice time and returned to the port to take the boat back to the Danieli. To our surprise, the same "New York Times Reporter Lady" was there happily greeting us like old friends.

After a few more anecdotes about Venice, she suggested we have dinner together in the evening at the Antico Martini, a well-known restaurant. We thought it was a nice idea and went to our room to change. When we came to the lobby of the hotel, she was waiting for us and we walked together to the restaurant which was across from the Fenice, the Venice Opera. The restaurant was very elegant and she had already made reservations for us and it appeared that she knew most of the restaurant personnel. I started to get a funny feeling that they were somewhat annoyed by her presence.

Antico Martini Restaurant Venice

We had a wonderful though very expensive dinner. I paid for hers of course. She walked us back to the hotel and we said goodbye to each other thinking that we would probably never see her again. Not so! The next morning when we were leaving the hotel, she was waiting for us again smiling and full of all kinds of ideas about what we could do together. By now, we realized that she was a con-lady taking advantage of visitors. We told her nicely that we were busy and wanted to do our own thing. Within a few minutes, we saw her cheerfully talking to another couple. There are many ways to survive even in Venice.

After another day at the Lido, we went in the evening to the Fenice Opera, a beautiful theater built in 1782, to see *A Midsummer Night's Dream* in ballet, which was excellent.

Teatro Fenice in Venice

In 2006, on our way to the Adriatic Sea coast in Croatia, Vera and I spent a few days in Venice with five couples who were friends of ours. On that occasion, I had a bad cold and stayed in the hotel while the rest of our group toured the city, so I missed Murano, the place where the famous glass products are made.

On other trips to Italy, we traveled across beautiful Tuscany on two occasions, in 1999 and again in 2005. Florence of course was the highlight of the trip. Florence is one of the most culturally rich cities in Europe that witnessed the birth of the Renaissance, the transition from the dark Middle Ages to modernity.

Florence Italy

Even after coming to the city two times, we could visit only a small portion of the many famous museums and important sites. We stayed in Florence in a small pensione owned by a very classy lady, who starred in the film, *"Tea with Mussolini"*.

We visited the Duomo, the unique cathedral, and the Uffizi Gallery museum in the Palazzo Vecchio and marveled at Michelangelo's sculpture of David in the Accademia Gallery. We even visited one of the oldest pharmacies, the 600-year-old Santa Maria Novella, where we discovered the Pot Pourri herbal mix which has become Vera's favorite fragrance for the home. The formula was developed by the monks during the time of the black plague to mask the odor of decomposing bodies.

Santa Maria Novella Pharmacy Florence.

Pot Pourri from Santa Maria Novella

After Florence, we visited Sienna and San Gimignano, a picturesque town built on the hills of Tuscany.

San Gimignano Tuscany

In San Gimignano, we visited the fascinating Leonardo da Vinci Museum which features many of this genius's inventions, clocks, weaponry, flying machines, and notes as well as his drawings.

I had already been in northern Italy in a region very different from Tuscany. A few years earlier in 1991, I lectured in Udine, the birthplace of Mussolini. Udine is located close to Slovenia in the north-east region of Italy, between the Alps and the Adriatic Sea. The Hungarians claim that Attila the Hun built a mountain in the area around 450 AD so he could watch his soldiers burn the neighboring villages. The modern city is very nice today since it was not totally burned down!

All in all, Italy is an amazing, beautiful country and one of our favorites in the world; the scenery, the culture, the people, and the food all make you want to return over and over again

At the end of September 1950, the four of us childhood friends took another night train from Venice to Vienna, the last stop before our return to Hungary.

7. HUNGARY

After almost two years, it was quite exciting to get back to my home in **Debrecen** and to be spoiled again by my parents. No matter how old you are and how many places you have seen, to your parents, you are still their child and your home is where they are.

The name of the 800-year-old and second-largest city in Hungary derives from the Turkish word *debrezin, "to live"*. When I was born the population was around 100 thousand. Debrecen used to be called the Calvinist Rome, because contrary to the rest of Hungary where the majority of the population are Roman Catholics, the majority of the people in Debrecen were Calvinist Protestants. Before World War 2, there was a sizable Jewish population in Debrecen, more than 10%.

Piac utca, the main street in Debrecen

Debrecen is located in the Great Plains (Nagy Alfold) of Hungary, and there are no mountains or rivers or not even a lake anywhere nearby. Certainly, it was not the scenery that attracted my grandfather Natan on my father's side to come from Upor in Slovakia, nor Jakab my other grandfather who came here from Ermihalyfalva in Romania.

But growing up in Debrecen with an extended family of more than 30, I never missed anything. Sunday afternoons the whole extended family, my parents, grandparents, aunts and cousins would go to the Great Forest of Debrecen, the nicest part of the city. While the adults discussed current events, we children just played. Every family brought their favorite dishes that were shared with everyone.

The Great Forest (Nagy Erdo) Debrecen

After I returned to Hungary from Israel on October 2nd, 1950, I lived in Debrecen for almost five years. For three of those five years, I worked full time as a grinder in Medicor, a Medical Instrument factory, and attended night-school in the Workers Gymnazium (High School).

Me on left George Burger on right, Medicor

I'm the second from the left at the Kossuth Lajos University Debrecen

In 1953 I started my university studies at the Kossuth Lajos University of Debrecen with a major in Physics and a minor in Math. I lived also a total of one year in Budapest, six months in 1951, and six months more before I escaped from Hungary again after the unsuccessful Revolution in December 1956.

Unfortunately, two years after my return my father passed away, and after one year my mother died also. But I had the support of my large extended family and my childhood friends.

My father is on my left and my mother in front of me Debrecen, 1947

George Burger, Steve Szasz, George Bozoki, Janos Balog, me, and Poncike 1952

Fifteen years later, in 1971, I came back to Debrecen with my little family, Vera my wife, and Michael and Suzika our two children. When I was a student at the university, I often walked by the famous historical hotel in Debrecen, the *Arany Bika* (Golden Bull), and looked at the menu of the hotel's elegant restaurant that was posted by the door. The **Arany Bika Tal** served on a wooden platter was the most expensive on the menu, at 500 forints it was more than my monthly stipend, so obviously I never ordered it, but promised myself to return one day to try it.

The Arany Bika Hotel in Debrecen

That day arrived in 1971 when our family went to the Arany Bika hotel's fancy restaurant and ordered the *Arany Bika Tal*, their signature dish that is served on a large wooden plate with an assortment of indispensable ingredients.

The Arany Bika Restaurant in Debrecen

Arany Bika Tal

The excellent traditional dish contains two kinds of Hungarian sausages both sweet and hot, fried pork wiener schnitzel style, fried pork only dipped in eggs Parisian style, plain pork and veal, grilled beef, stuffed cabbage, foie gras, thick-sliced bacon shaped into a crispy crown, roasted potatoes, rice, pickled peppers and tomatoes stuffed with sauerkraut. Our kids probably would have preferred a pizza.

When I was growing up, it was more common to eat starchy food every day after some soup. Hungarians start all meals with some kind of soup. One of my favorite meals was a Hungarian version of the Italian gnocchi, called **prezlis nudli,** gnocchi in sauteed breadcrumbs. Prune jam-filled ravioli called **derelye** in Hungarian can also be made from the same dough as the potato-based gnocchi.

Prezlis Nudli and Derelye

Serves 6

Ingredients:

4 medium potatoes peeled

4 cups of all-purpose flour

2 eggs

6 tbsp. of prune jam, or other jam of your choice

6 oz. breadcrumbs

½ cup cooking oil

Directions:

1. Bring a large pot of salted water to boil. Add the peeled potatoes to the pot and cook about 15 minutes, until they are tender but firm. Drain, cool, and mash with a potato masher.

2. Combine mashed potato, flour, and eggs in a large bowl. Knead until dough forms a ball. Shape 2/3 of the dough into ½ inch diameter long cylinders. On a floured surface cut into ½ inch long nudli/gnocchi.

3. The derelye/ravioli are made from the remaining 1/3 dough. Take half of the dough and flatten with a rolling pin to 1/8 in thick. Place 1/3 tbsp. of the jam on the flattened dough 2½ in. apart. Put the other half dough also flattened on the top and with your finger press around the jam to form the derelye/ravioli. With a ravioli cutter, cut into pieces of ravioli.

4. Bring a large pot of lightly salted water to boil. Drop in the gnocchi and the ravioli and cook from 3-5 minutes or until they rise to the top. Drain it.

5. Brown the breadcrumbs in heated oil in a pan, stirring it to make sure that it will not burn. Put the nudli/gnocchi and the derelye/ravioli in the browned breadcrumbs, cover the pan with a lid and shake it so that the gnocchi and the ravioli are covered with breadcrumbs and serve.

Fasirt

Another of our favorite dishes. fasirt, a kind of Hungarian Hamburger. Rachel could eat it every day.

Serves 6

Ingredients:

lb. ground meat of your choice, pork, beef, or chicken breast

1 medium-size onion chopped

slices of white bread

eggs

½ cup of breadcrumbs

1 tsp. Hungarian paprika

1 tsp. salt

½ tsp. black pepper

Mazola corn oil

Directions:

1. Sauté the chopped onion in a deep-frying pan until the onion is transparent. Take out the onion from the oil.

2. Place the ground meat in a large bowl

3. In a small bowl, add the paprika, salt and pepper to the eggs and mix well.

4. Soak the sliced bread in water and squeeze out the water

5. When the onion is cool add to the ground meat, the egg mixture, and the softened bread. Mix all ingredients well with your hand.

6. Form balls of about 3 in. in diameter and flatten to about 2 in thick.

7. Roll the hamburgers in the breadcrumbs.

8. Add additional oil 1 inch deep to the same pan where the onion was sautéd. Fry them on medium-low heat until brown on both sides and place them on a paper towel to absorb the excess oil.

9. The fasirt go well with some cold stewed fruits and compotes.

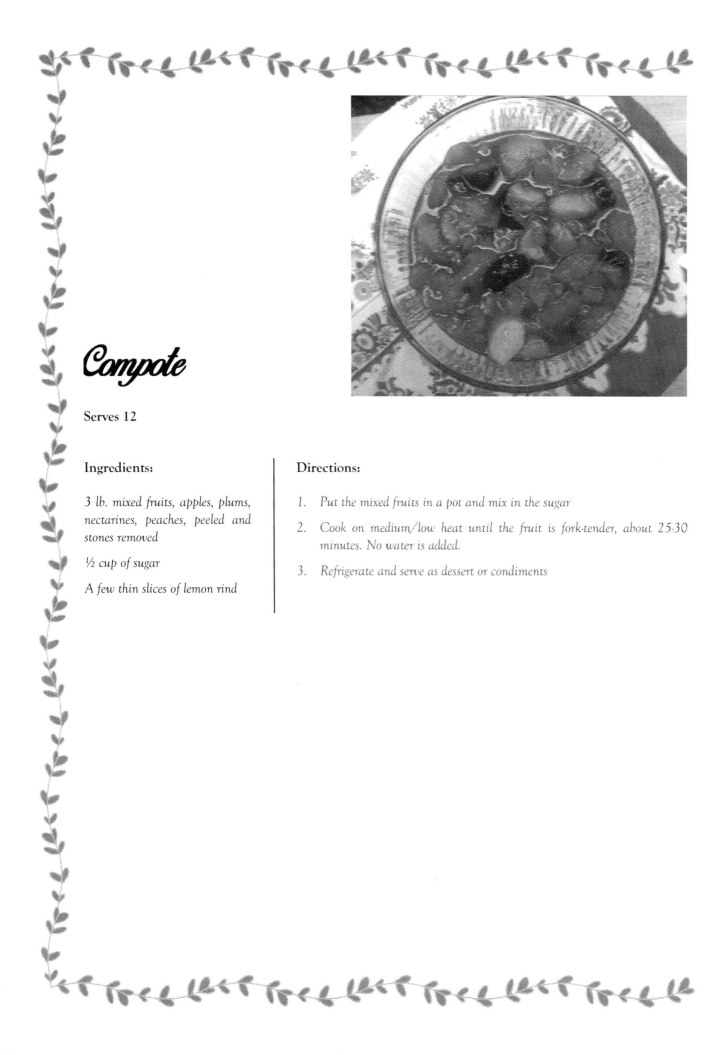

Compote

Serves 12

Ingredients:

3 lb. mixed fruits, apples, plums, nectarines, peaches, peeled and stones removed

½ cup of sugar

A few thin slices of lemon rind

Directions:

1. Put the mixed fruits in a pot and mix in the sugar

2. Cook on medium/low heat until the fruit is fork-tender, about 25-30 minutes. No water is added.

3. Refrigerate and serve as dessert or condiments

Töltött Paprika

Hungary has a greater variety of peppers than any other country, and one way to enjoy them is with meat stuffing.

Serves 6

Ingredients:

12– 15 mini peppers of various colors

1 lb. of pork or beef

½ cups of uncooked rice

1 onion

2 eggs

3 tbsp. corn oil

1 small can of tomato paste

2 tbsp. sugar

1 tsp. salt

½ tsp. black pepper

¼ tsp. red pepper flake

Directions:

1. In a frying pan pour the oil and saute the chopped onion in medium heat until it is transparent

2. Remove all the fat from the meat and grind it. Then put the ground meat in a large bowl.

3. Cook the rice in a bowl with 1 cup of water. When the water boils, lowered to simmer and cook for 20 minutes covered.

4. Remove the cooked onion and cool it.

5. In a small bowl beat the eggs, add the salt and pepper, and mix well.

6. Add the egg mixture, the cooked onion, and about a cup of cooked rice after it is cool to the ground meat. Mix it well with your hand.

7. Cut off the stem of the peppers. Slice cut down halfway leaving the tip intact.

8. Fill each pepper with the meat mixture and press the two sides of the pepper together. Set them aside. If you have extra meat mixture and not enough peppers you can make meatballs from it

9. In a large pot prepare the tomato sauce by mixing the tomato paste with 5 cups of water until it is thinned like a pancake mixture. Add the sugar and the red pepper flakes to the tomato sauce.

10. Put the stuffed pepper into the tomato sauce and cook at medium/low for 45 minutes to an hour, cover with a lid with a small opening to let the steam escape.

11. Serve for each person 1-2 stuffed peppers with the sauce.

We spent a couple of days in Debrecen visiting my family although by that time our large family was reduced to my uncle Lajos and his daughter Agi. Most of the older relatives were resting at the Jewish Cemetery of Debrecen and the younger ones were scattered around the world.

Our children enjoyed connecting with their father's past but appreciated even more spending time with their relatives at the outdoor spa, the Strand in the Great Forest.

In the strand of Debrecen 1971

Almost 40 years later we decided to bring our family to Hungary again. This time it was larger with the addition of Suzika's husband Richard and her two daughters, Hannah and Talia, and Michael's daughter Rachel, our first granddaughter.

In the Jewish Cemetery of Debrecen Susan on my left and Rachel on my right, 2009
The chain is not broken.

In early January of 1951, I was part of a group of about 70 people, young men and women who were sent to **Budapest** to be trained in the Medicor company's Budapest headquarters which was much larger and had more advanced technology than the branch in Debrecen. Ironically, although I was trained for 9 months to work in the manufacture of hypodermic needles, when I returned to Debrecen I was put to work at grinding dental equipment. Hungary's Socialist economic planning had strange outcomes!

Budapest was only out of the war for about 5 years and the city, as well as the whole country, was in bad economic shape. Everything was rationed even bread and we rarely saw meat or eggs. Historically, Hungary had always been a very productive agricultural country, so it was difficult to justify the food shortage and many felt that it was due to mismanagement.

Budapest in the 1950s

While in Budapest my schedule was like that of Debrecen, in that besides working in the Medicor plant from 6 AM to 3 PM, I continued my studies from 5 PM to 10 PM. I studied in the Workers' Gymnazium which was on the other side of the Danube River in Buda while Medicor was on the Pest side. Budapest which hosts roughly twenty percent of Hungary's total population, of 10 million is made up of two cities (Buda and Pest) divided by the Danube River.

Buda is on the left side of the Danube and Pest is on the right

The population of Hungary is practically unchanged in the last 80 years. Historically, the Hungarian Kingdom from 1000 AD to about 1600 AD had about one percent of the world's population, which if the same proportion were maintained today, it would mean that there should be seventy million Hungarians, not the current 10 million, given today's world population of seven billion.

One logical explanation for this population decrease, in my opinion, is that it is the sad result of the lack of clear vision and firm action by Hungarian leaders. For example in 1526, Hungary had a strong army but because of the incompetence of King Lajos at Mohacs, Hungary lost the battle against the Turkish army of Suleiman in just *two hours!* The result of this disaster was Hungary ceased to exist independently for 150 years. In contrast, Hungary's western neighbors, the Austrians, were able to withstand the attack of the Turkish army, thus saving western Europe.

Another tragic loss of two-thirds of its territory and close to half of its population due to poor political choices ensued around four hundred years later when Hungary joined the Central Nations, Austria, Germany, and Turkey against the Allies, England, France, Russia and the United States of America.

The territorial loss of Hungary after WW 1

Unfortunately for Hungary and especially for its Jewish population of close to eight hundred thousand people, the country's leadership made an even worse decision by joining Nazi Germany in World War 2. During the Holocaust, more than six hundred thousand Hungarian Jews were murdered by the Germans and by their Hungarian collaborators. For close to 1000 years of their existence in Hungary, the Jews had significantly better living conditions than their co-religionists in other European countries, especially during the so-called "Golden Years" from 1867 until the end of WW 1.

In 1918, Jews in Hungary had the same full rights as all other non-Jews. Because they could freely choose their occupation, Jews were disproportionately represented by more than 50 percent in many areas, like commerce, finance, medicine, and sports although their percentage of the population was only around 5 percent. All this changed drastically after the promulgation of the anti-Jewish laws of the 1920s which restricted the Jews' participation in most fields and which eventually lead to the brutal treatment and elimination of 75 percent of Hungarian Jewry.

In 1941, Hungary for no obvious reason declared war against the United States of America. An often-quoted humorous anecdote (which may or may not be true) describes the complexity and uniqueness of Hungary.

After Hungary declared war on the USA. President Franklin Roosevelt asked his aide if Hungary was a kingdom or a republic. The assistant answered, "It is a kingdom, Mr. President".

FDR: What's the King's name?

Aide: Hungary doesn't have a King.

FDR: Then who runs the kingdom?

Aide: A Regent by the name of Admiral Miklós Horthy.

FDR: Admiral? Then Hungary must have a powerful navy.

Aide: Hungary has no navy; it doesn't even have access to the sea.

FDR: Wars are often fought for religious reasons. What's the main religion there?

Aide: Catholicism, Mr. President. But Admiral Horthy is Protestant.

FDR: Did this admiral declare war on us because of territorial claims then?

Aide: Hungary's territorial claims are against Romania.

FDR: In that case, did Hungary declare war on Romania?

Aide: No, Hungary and Romania are allies.

FDR: Let me get this straight. Hungary is a kingdom run by a Regent who's an admiral without a navy, and it is allied with Romania against which it has territorial claims but it has declared war on the U.S. against which it has no claims.

Aide: That's right, Mr. President."

The anecdote is amusing but the history is very sad that such a small country with so many talented people, was misled by their leaders so many times in history.

In 1956, I returned to Budapest to start my senior year at the *Eotvos Lorand* University. In October of that year, the University students led an uprising against the Communist regime which was successful for two weeks and which briefly gave democratic government to Hungary. However, by November 4 the Soviet Army suppressed the Revolution and the Communist dictatorship regained power and many people were arrested and sent to Siberia.

On December 3rd, 1956, on my 24th birthday, I escaped from Hungary across the Austrian border with several of my childhood friends following the steps of more than two hundred thousand other people.

Fifteen years later in 1971, we came to Hungary with my family from Knoxville Tennessee. Hungary still had a Communist dictatorship, although under its system of so-called "Goulash Communism", it had better conditions than the other Communist countries. I now felt safe to bring my family here since I was an American citizen and invited to lecture at an International Scientific Conference. On the other hand, I was not naïve enough to think that the USA would attack Hungary to free me if for some reason I were arrested and jailed because I left Hungary illegally in 1956.

Both Vera and I still had some relatives in Hungary and our two children enjoyed getting to know them. Everybody had a great time during the six weeks we spent in Hungary. One of our favorite places was **Varosliget,** Budapest's City Park, which includes a Disney-like amusement park and a zoo. Besides these attractions for children, for the adults the area was host to *Gundel*, a famous restaurant established in 1896, and the Szechenyi Strand, a beautiful Spa.

Varosliget, City Park. Budapest

Another of our favorites was the Island called **Margit Sziget** (Margaret Island), with its beautiful park, swimming pools, restaurants and cafes.

100

The Palatinus Strand on Margit Sziget is one of the largest among the many spas of Budapest. It has at least seven or eight pools of various sizes and shapes from the very cold Olympic size pool for swimming to another at over 100 degrees temperature just to relax in. There is even one pool with artificial waves that our kids enjoyed the most.

Vera, with Suzika, Michael, and my aunt Magduska at the Palatinus Strand

We had a couple of weeks before my conference started, so we made another colorful out-of-town trip to **Balaton Foldvar**. Lake Balaton often called the "Hungarian Sea", is among the most enjoyable resort areas in Eastern Europe. During the summer of 1971, there were relatively few hotels available, and all private homes of any quality or price were fully occupied, mostly by East Germans, Poles, Czechs, and visitors from the other Communist countries. There were even some West Germans, who met here with their East German friends and relatives, meetings which were not possible in East Germany. Despite the crowding and scarcity of lodging for others, we had a fantastic situation. My aunt Manci, who was an accountant in Ferro-Globus, a large metal-manufacturing company, arranged a 10-day vacation for us in her company's hotel-resort.

Balaton Foldvar Lake in 1971. On the right, my Aunt Manci, On the left, my Aunt Magduska

The resort was near the lake with very nice facilities, excellent cuisine, and attractive clean rooms. We could not have wished for anything better. The resort personnel were very nice to us and loved our well-behaved children who were the only ones in the resort. We also were popular for being a lively Hungarian-American family among the mostly colorless East German functionaries, but mostly because of our generous tipping. The East Germans, who were selected by their government, loved to come to Hungary for the good food and the excellent resort in the lively and colorful Balaton Foldvar.

Lake Balaton

The Hungarians did not like them at all because of their rude manners and that they were so indoctrinated with Communist ideology that even in the late evening when everybody would sit around a campfire and sing, the East Germans insisted on singing songs hailing the glorious Soviet Union and Socialism. They gave you the feeling that these same people a few years earlier were singing the same way about glorious Nazi Germany and hailing National Socialism.

We came back to Hungary many times in the next 50 years and usually spent a week in Budapest and a few days at the Balaton. For the last ten years we stayed at **Balaton Fured,** the most attractive town on the lake where my childhood friend George Burger lived before, he passed away.

One of our best vacations in Hungary was in 2009 with our whole family (except Michael who couldn't make it) when we were invited to Vera's niece Cilike's wedding in Hungary. It was a good occasion to show our native country to Richard and to our three granddaughters. Certainly, Rachel was very excited by the experience, but I was not so sure about three-year-old Hannah and one and a half-year-old Talia.

First, we all gathered in Paris where we spent a few days. It was a little crowded for the seven of us in our two bedrooms but we managed. On the other hand, in Budapest we rented two suites in the Adina Hotel, each with two bedrooms and two baths which certainly was more comfortable. We hired a minivan from Arpad Kiss, whose son drove us during this two-week vacation. We also hired as a tour guide a bright pretty young Hungarian college student who spoke very good English so both Richard and Rachel got a good introduction to Budapest and to Hungarian history.

Hannah, Richard, Talia, Susan, Vera, Rachel, and me in Budapest (2009).

After our city tour, we went for dinner and entertainment to the *Rez kakas* (copper rooster) restaurant, where the girls enjoyed the musicians and the music. It was mutual as the musicians were charmed by the girls. I don't think that the food was well appreciated by my American family and even I have had better Hungarian food elsewhere. However, the idea was to enjoy the ambiance which we all did.

Talia is playing the cimbalom 2009

Hannah is improvising the Csardas dance 2009

Chicken paprikash is probably the best known Hungarian dish and in 1972, in Knoxville Tennessee, a newspaper reporter interviewed Vera and published her version. The detailed recipe can be found on the following pages.

Vera and her chicken paprikash recipe from a Knoxville Tennessee newspaper February 2, 1972

Chicken Paprikash

Chicken paprikash is probably the best known Hungarian dish, traditionally served alongside nokedli and cucumber salad.

Serves 8

Ingredients:

2 tbsp vegetable oil

2 tbsp butter

3 lbs chicken pieces, bone-in, skin-on

2 med. yellow onions finely chopped

2 medium tomatoes with seeds removed, finely chopped

1 bell pepper finely diced

3 or 4 tbsp of quality imported sweet Hungarian paprika

2 cups of low sodium chicken broth

1 ½ tsp salt

½ tsp freshly ground black pepper

3 tbsp all-purpose flour

¾ cup full fat sour cream

¼ cup heavy whipping cream

Directions:

1. Heat the oil and the butter in a heavy pot and add the chicken and brown on all sides. Transfer the chicken to a plate.

2. In the same oil/butter mixture sauté the onion until soft and transparent

3. Add the tomatoes and pepper and continue to sauté for 2-3 more minutes

4. Remove the pot from the heat and stir in the paprika, salt and pepper. (the paprika becomes bitter if scorched)

5. Return the chicken to the pot. Cover it and put it back on the flame.

6. Pour in the chicken broth to almost cover the chicken and bring to a boil. Then, reduce the heat to medium low and cook covered for 40 minutes. Remove the pieces of chicken to a plate.

7. In a bowl stir the flour into the sour cream/cream mixture to form a smooth paste.

8. Start adding the contents of the pot a little at a time stirring constantly to prevent lumps.

9. Place the mixture back in the pot and simmer it until the sauce is thickened, mixing it constantly.

10. Pour the mixture into a food processor and pulse until completely smooth.

11. Put the chicken pieces back in the pot and pour the mixture from the food processor over them. Simmer until all is heated thoroughly.

12. If you want it more spicy, you can add hot Hungarian paprika or cayenne pepper.

Nokedli

Ingredients:

2 cups all-purpose flour

2 whole eggs, beaten

1 tsp salt

¾ cup water

Directions:

1. Place a large pot of salted water on stove and bring to a boil.

2. Combine the flour and salt in a large bowl. Form a small well in the center.

3. Add the beaten eggs and a little water into the center of the well.

4. Blend the water, eggs, and flour using your hands.

5. Keep adding small amounts of water until the batter is thin enough to pass through the spätzle/nokedli/ strapacska maker or a colander (see photo)

6. Working in batches, press the batter through the holes of the colander or nokedli maker.

7. Allow the nokedli dumplings to boil until they begin to float (2-3 minutes)

8. Remove the nokedli from the water using a slotted spoon.

Put in a serving bowl, lightly salt, and coat with melted butter.

Hungarian Cucumber Salad

Ingredients:

2 large English cucumbers

1 cup water

3 tbsp sugar

2 tbsp white vinegar

2 tsp salt

Sweet paprika

Ground black pepper

Directions:

1. Peel the cucumbers and slice as thin as possible.

2. Place the cucumber slices in a bowl. Add the salt and let sit for 15 minutes. The salt draws out water from the cucumber.

3. The cucumber release some liquid. Take a handful of cucumber slices and squeeze out with your hand as much liquid as you can.

4. Place all the squeezed cucumber in a bowl.

5. Combine the sugar, the vinegar, and the water in a cup and stir with a fork until the sugar melts.

6. Add this mixture to the squeezed cucumber slices and mix well.

7. Sprinkle with the paprika and black pepper.

Strawberry Soup

Hungarians love to start their meal with a soup, sometimes hot like chicken soup or goulash soup but often especially during the summer they have a cold soup. Cherry soup is the most common but recently we found that they favor strawberry soup, topped with shredded goat cheese and a few pieces of pistachio and blueberries. It is delicious and you may have it as a dessert.

Serves 8

Ingredients:

1 and ½ lb. washed and cleaned strawberries

¼ cups of sugar

¼ cup of heavy cream

¼ cup of water

1 tbsp of sour cream

10 pieces of blueberries/serving

10 pieces of shelled pistachio/serving

A few pieces of crumbled goat cheese/serving

Directions:

8. Pour the strawberries, cream, water, and sour cream into a blender and make a smoothie turning on for 1 minute.

9. After cooling in the refrigerator, serve it as a soup or dessert. Top it with goat cheese, blueberries, and pistachios. Enjoy.

Stuffed Chicken Cooked in Soup

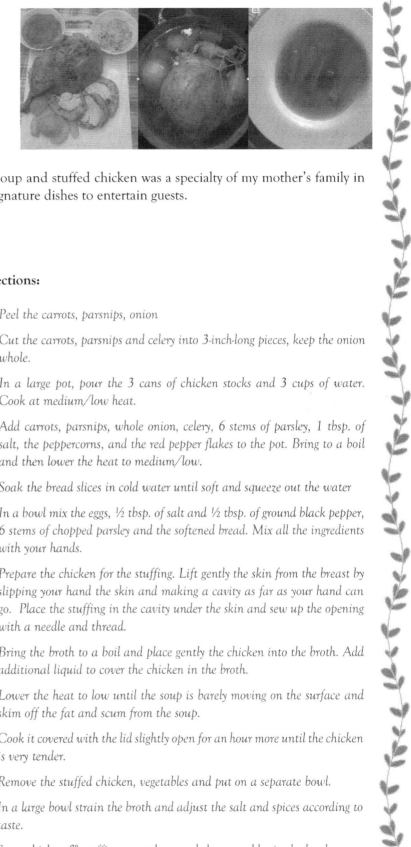

A rather unique combination of chicken soup and stuffed chicken was a specialty of my mother's family in Debrecen. Vera adapted it as one of our signature dishes to entertain guests.

Serves 6

Ingredients:

4 medium-size carrots

2 parsnips

3 celery stalks with leaves

yellow onion

12 stems Italian parsley

1 whole chicken

5 slices of stale white bread

cans of chicken stocks

eggs

10 black peppercorns

2 tbsp. salt

A pinch of red pepper flakes.

Directions:

1. Peel the carrots, parsnips, onion

2. Cut the carrots, parsnips and celery into 3-inch-long pieces, keep the onion whole.

3. In a large pot, pour the 3 cans of chicken stocks and 3 cups of water. Cook at medium/low heat.

4. Add carrots, parsnips, whole onion, celery, 6 stems of parsley, 1 tbsp. of salt, the peppercorns, and the red pepper flakes to the pot. Bring to a boil and then lower the heat to medium/low.

5. Soak the bread slices in cold water until soft and squeeze out the water

6. In a bowl mix the eggs, ½ tbsp. of salt and ½ tbsp. of ground black pepper, 6 stems of chopped parsley and the softened bread. Mix all the ingredients with your hands.

7. Prepare the chicken for the stuffing. Lift gently the skin from the breast by slipping your hand the skin and making a cavity as far as your hand can go. Place the stuffing in the cavity under the skin and sew up the opening with a needle and thread.

8. Bring the broth to a boil and place gently the chicken into the broth. Add additional liquid to cover the chicken in the broth.

9. Lower the heat to low until the soup is barely moving on the surface and skim off the fat and scum from the soup.

10. Cook it covered with the lid slightly open for an hour more until the chicken is very tender.

11. Remove the stuffed chicken, vegetables and put on a separate bowl.

12. In a large bowl strain the broth and adjust the salt and spices according to taste.

13. Serve chicken & stuffing on a plate, and the vegetables in the broth.

Restaurant Rosenstein in Budapest

On our recent visit to Budapest in September 2019, we connected with my only family still there, Peter my cousin, and his wife Ancsi. We went together to one of the best-known restaurants in Budapest, **Rosenstein**. We had a pleasant dinner and spent a few hours together with Peter and Ancsi chatting about family, past and present, and showing photos of the grandchildren. It was a beautiful start to our one week stay to eat at Rosenstein, which not only serves the best *halaszle* (a Hungarian fish soup) in Budapest but also provides many Jewish dishes, like ***cholent***, a traditional meal with beans and meat which is baked overnight on Friday, to eat on Shabbat.

Cholent

Serves 8

Ingredients:

2 lb. pinto beans

2 lb. beef shank

2 lb. smoked meat, duck, turkey, or pork shank (if you are not kosher)

large yellow onion

6 cloves of garlic

5 tbsp. of cooking oil or melted chicken fat

8 eggs

1 tbsp. of salt

2/3 tsp. of ground black pepper

1 lb. flour

1 tsp of paprika

Directions:

1. Soak the beans in cold water for 12 hours.

2. Drain beans and put in a large heavy pan, sprinkle with 2 tbsp. oil.

3. Cut the onion into 4 pieces and distribute them in the beans. Add the garlic cloves.

4. Cut the beef and the smoked meat into three pieces and distribute it in the beans.

5. Wash 6 whole uncooked eggs and place in the bean mixture

6. To prepare the **kugel**, mix the flour in a bowl with 3 tbsp. oil, and with 2 eggs mixed add 1/3 tsp. of the salt and ½ tsp. of the pepper and all the paprika. Make a dough out of the mixture and form an elongated shape out of it.

7. Add the kugel to the beans and pour enough water to cover all the ingredients in the pot.

8. Add the remaining salt and pepper. Cook the bean mixture until the water boils.

9. Preheat the oven to 200 F.

10. Put the pot in the oven and bake for 12-14 hours covered.

11. Take out the **Cholent** from the oven and let rest for 30 minutes.

12. Peel the eggs, slice the meats and the kugel and serve with the beans.

Falsch Hal Gefilte Fish

For holidays, not having any lake or sea near my home town Debrecen, an imitation gefilte fish made out of chicken was used as a substitute.

Serves 4

Ingredients:

1 quart of chicken broth

1 onion

1 white roll

3 carrots

3 potatoes peeled and cut in half

1 parsnip sliced

2 celery stalks

A handful of parsley chopped

2 eggs

1 lb. chicken breast

Salt and pepper

Directions:

1. Pour the chicken broth in a large pot, add 1 onion sliced, 2 carrots sliced, 1 parsnip sliced, 2 celery stocks chopped, 3 potatoes halved. Bring the mixture to a boil, then reduce the heat to simmer. Cover and cook broth while you prepare the chicken.

2. In a food processor place the chicken breast together with the remaining two carrots, with the parsley and the onion. Add salt and pepper and the two eggs and mix them well. Place the mixture in a bowl.

3. Place the roll in a bowl and soak it in lukewarm water. Squeeze out the water from the roll and add to the meat mixture and mix it well with the ingredients in the bowl with your hand.

4. Form oval shape patties out of the mixture about 2 in thick and 3 in long, place it on a plate.

5. When the vegetables are cooked, remove carefully from the broth and store it in a bowl.

6. Place the meat patties carefully in the boiling broth. Lower the heat to simmer and cook for about two hours covered.

7. Remove the meatballs from the liquid and place them in a serving dish with a rim.

8. Place the vegetables decoratively around the meatballs.

9. Reduce the broth to about half the volume and strain over the vegetables and the chicken patties.

10. Cool it in the refrigerator and serve cold with prepared horseradish.

Turos Beles

Shabbat morning we usually had a homemade cheese danish called *turos beles* in Hungarian. It is my all time favorite.

Serves 6

Ingredients:

Package frozen puff pastry sheet thawed, two sheets per package

2 Egg yolks

2 Cups cottage cheese grained in a strainer

8 oz. cream cheese

½ cup sugar or more for taste

tbsp. lemon juice

Directions:

1. Preheat oven to 400 degrees

2. Beat one egg yolk, cottage cheese, cream cheese, lemon juice, and sugar with an electric mixer.

3. Lay out the two sheets of puff pastry and cut each sheet into six 5x5 squares. You will and up with 12 squares.

4. Put 2 tbsp. of cheese mixture in the middle of each square of the pastry without spreading

5. Bring the opposite corners together and pinch the corners to seal.

6. Mix well one egg yolk with 1 tsp of water.

7. Brush the pastry with this egg wash.

8. Line the baking sheet with parchment paper.

9. Place the pastries on the paper and bake until they are puffed and golden brown.

10. Sprinkle with powdered sugar and serve.

Kremes

Vera prefers *kremes*, a Hungarian version of Napoleon. So she made both, to please everyone.

Serves 15

Ingredients:

Package of frozen puff pastry

¾ Quart of milk

¼ Quart of heavy cream

6 egg whites

Packages Dr. Oteker vanilla pudding or any other, but not instant.

8 oz. powdered sugar

Directions:

1. Heat oven to 400 degrees

2. Line baking sheet with parchment paper

3. Roll out one of the defrosted puff pastry on a largely floured surface. Transfer it to the baking sheet.

4. Place on the top of the puff pastry a sheet of parchment paper and on the top of that place another baking sheet.

5. Bake for 10 minutes. Remove baking sheet and parchment paper and put the pastry back in the oven for another 10-15 minutes until golden brown. Remove.

6. Repeat process for the second defrosted puff pastry. Let them cool. In the meantime, make the filling.

7. Mix the milk, cream, and pudding powder in a pot.

8. Put on the heat on medium-low, constantly whipping the mixture until the mixture reaches a thick consistency.

9. In a bowl beat the egg white with the powdered sugar until it is stiff.

10. Pour the stiff egg white into the pudding mixture and continue to cook for 2 minutes.

11. Spread the cream over one of the baked pastries.

12. With a serrated knife cut through the second baked puff pastry into a 3 in squares.

13. Place on the top of the cream and slightly press down with the palm of your hand.

14. Let it rest and before serving sprinkle the top with powdered sugar and cut through the cream to the bottom layer.

The following day, Vera was treated like royalty by her cousin Eva and by Eva's daughter Cilike. They took her to the Secret Garden a unique spa where all three were pampered with massages, facials, and all the possible beauty treatments imaginable. The Secret Garden is part of the 5 Star Mystery Hotel located near the Western Railway Station, *Nyugati*. The beautiful building was built in 1884 and for most of the time since then was the seat of the Hungarian Free Masons. During the Nazi and Communist eras, this elegant building was confiscated for political use. Under both the Nazi and the Communist regimes the Free Masons were not allowed to function because their liberal ideas threatened the dictatorships. The building was recently purchased and transferred to the Mystery Hotel, including the Secret Garden Spa. Vera had a great day spending time with her cousins Eva and Cilike.

Mystery Hotel Budapest

Vera with Cilike   *Vera with Eva at the Secret Garden Spa in Budapest*

116

As much as I liked to travel, the borders of Hungary were closed and the only opportunity for me to travel in the years from 1950-1956 was from Debrecen to Budapest and back again. I even joined the university wrestling team in order to travel to Budapest for tournaments which had the benefits of paid train tickets and generous portions of wiener schnitzel. By the middle of 1956, strict Communist policies in Hungary eased and more liberal programs were adopted, such as the possibility of travel to neighboring Communist countries. In September 1956, my childhood friend Janos Balog and I took a bus tour to Transylvania, a region of Romania,.

8. ROMANIA

I always felt a connection to Romania because my mother was born in Ermihalyfalva (Valea lui Mihai in Romanian). When I was a child, she taught me how to count in Romanian, I especially liked the sound of the word nouăzeci și cinci (95). My mother also used to cook mamaliga a Romanian dish like grits or polenta that even today is one of my favorites.

We visited Ermihalyfalva in 1942 when we had lots of relatives there. Unfortunately, all of my relatives together with the other 1400 Jews (about 20% of the population) were sent to Auschwitz and murdered in 1944. Jews had lived in Ermihalyfalva since 1780 when most of them moved there from Galicia but only three older Jewish men live there now. Interestingly, the grandparents of the 2020 Nobel Prize winner in literature, the American Louise Gluck came from Ermihalyfalva.

Synagogue in Ermihalyfalva, Valea lui Mihai

In 1956, the border between Hungary and Romania opened, although the borders toward the West were locked by mines. So, to be able to travel, I took a bus tour to Romania with my friend Janos Balog. Debrecen was only a 20-mile ride to the Romanian border and after a short ride, we arrived to **Nagyvarad** (Oradea in Romanian). Our bus just stopped on the outskirts of the town so we did not see anything but still were able to do business with the locals. Romania for some reason was loaded with lots of food products and some other items which were scarce in Hungary. On the other hand, even cheap watches were not available in Romania. So, knowing this in advance, we brought some very inexpensive Russian watches with us which we sold in the street in Oradea and bought cacao, black pepper and other items which were very valuable in Hungary and were easy to sell for a good price. Those days you had to be inventive to survive.

Nagyvarad (Oradea) Romania 1956

After a couple of hours, we continued our trip toward **Kolozsvar,** (Cluj in Romanian). Most of the cities in the Transylvanian part of Romania have names both in Romanian and in Hungarian because after World War 1, Transylvania bounced back and forth between these two countries.

Kolozsvar, Cluj Romania 1956

We enjoyed this beautiful city, the largest in Transylvania which had many cafes and good Hungarian restaurants with entertainment, music and dancing. We even danced with some pretty Romanian girls, with no language difficulty at all. The famous university in Kolozsvar is the *Babes-Bolyai* University. It is named after two scientists: the Romanian microbiologist Victor Babes, and Janos Bolyai, a Hungarian mathematician who developed Riemannian geometry before Riemann. In 1971 at the conference in Budapest I met some of their faculty.

University of Babes-Bolyai Kolozsvar, Cluj Romania

About 40 Years later in 1998, we traveled with my friends through pre-Trianon Hungary. After leaving Slovakia we drove across Hungary stopping on the way in the cities of Sopron, Pecs, and Szeged. Our next step was to drive from Szeged toward the Hungarian-Romanian border to start our venture in **Timisoara**, Romania. See map.

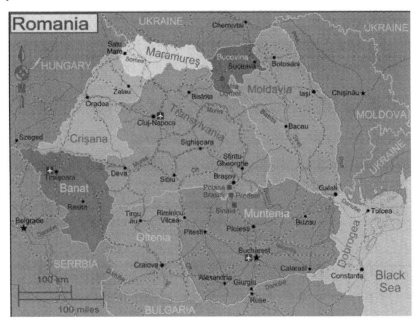

Map of Romania after WW 2

When we were ready to cross the Romanian border, a woman border guard informed us that people with American passports could enter freely, but the Canadians would have to pay $50. Steve who was Canadian at that time was ready to pay but Ponci who lived in Montreal refused, arguing that it was illegal and that he would call the Canadian Embassy in Bucharest and so on. The guard was not ready to change her mind and it looked like we would spend the rest of our vacation at the border arguing. Luckily, we could convince Poncike that he should pay and call the embassy later to get a refund. So, we continued our driving toward **Timisoara**, (*Temesvar* in Hungarian).

Temesvar, Timisoara Romania 1998

This city was famous for being the birthplace of Gyorgy Dozsa, a Hungarian peasant rebel leader of the 16th century. After the rebellion that he led against the landowners and aristocrats failed, Dozsa was put on a burning throne and burned to death. They taunted him with, "You wanted to become a king. Now you have it".

Gyorgy Dozsa

When we had our lunch at a local Hyatt Regency which was supposed to be the best hotel in the city, we were surprised to find chipped plates and cups and limited meal choices. The ideological and poorly-planned anti-Western policies of the last communist leader of Romania, Nicolae Ceausescu, destroyed the economy of the country. Otherwise, the city was very nice with a rich cultural heritage. The city has a sizable Hungarian and German population in addition to the Romanians. When we found Dozsa's statue we were surprised that his name was Georgiou Doja and not *Gyorgy Dozsa* the way we learned it in the Hungarian schools.

All in all, Romania gave us a much poorer impression than either Slovakia or Hungary. The roads were in very bad shape with lots of potholes which made it very challenging for our driver Sandor to reach our next stop in **Arad**, a famous city in Transylvania. In 1848 after the unsuccessful Hungarian uprising against the Hapsburgs, thirteen generals mostly Hungarians and a few Poles were executed by the Hapsburg rulers. They were all buried in Arad and they are referred to in Hungarian history as "The 13 Blood Witnesses in Arad". We looked for their graves or statues or any memorial without any luck. Finally, we found a dirty little corner in the city where geese were grazing and there was a little sign with the names of the thirteen generals. Hungarians are not the most favorite people in Romania!

Six friends at the Statue of the 13 Blood Witnesses of Arad, Romania (1998)

We also had a hard time finding the castle of King Matyas, the Hungarian king known as "Matyas the Trustworthy" in **Vajdahunyadvar** in one of the nicest mountainous area between Arad and **Kolozsvar** (Cluj in Romanian). Unfortunately, Ceausescu built a bunch of ugly factories in the area and there was so much pollution that when we finally found this once beautiful castle it was sad to see it all covered by smoke and soot. Nevertheless, the scenery in Transylvania is breathtaking which made this trip more than worthwhile.

When we arrived in Cluj and got settled in our hotel, some of the guys were ready to eat their dinner in the hotel right then. I convinced everyone that it would be better to go into the city first and then after sightseeing, go to one of their many restaurants for the dinner and entertainment choices that I remembered from 1956. So, we went first to see some of the highlights of the city like the theaters, the Babes-Bolyai University, and the statue of King Matyas.

After finishing our sightseeing, everybody was hungry and tired and ready to eat, but there was not a single restaurant anywhere. Another present from Ceausescu! I could not understand what happened to Cluj since 1956. All the guys were angry with me instead of with Ceausescu, and we went back to our hotel to eat the only thing they had, chicken liver with polenta. In fact, it was not bad. The Romanians eat that combination a lot. It is called *tocana de ficat de pui* and *mamaliga* in Romanian for stewed chicken liver and polenta.

Chicken Liver Polenta with Cheese

Serves 4

Ingredients:

½ lb. of fresh chicken liver

2 shallots

and 1 stick of butter

1½ tbsp. of sugar

tsp. of dried thyme

1½ cups of cornmeal

1 tsp. salt

4 cups water

¼ lb. soft cheese

½ tsp. salt

½ tsp. of freshly ground black pepper

Directions for the Liver:

1. Clean the liver of any fat, dry well with a paper towel.

2. In a small pot melt a quarter stick of butter.

3. Add the sugar and the roughly chopped shallots. Then add water and a pinch of salt just to cover the shallots. Cook uncovered slowly until the shallots are caramelized and all the water is gone.

4. Heat another quarter stick of butter and the thyme in a medium-sized frying pan and add the liver.

5. Cook the liver through until no visible blood is seen. Serve with polenta

Directions for Mamaliga (polenta):

1. Boil the water in a large pan.

2. Add the cornmeal gradually stirring with a wooden spoon.

3. Lower the heat to simmer and cook for 25 minutes covered.

4. Add the butter and after a few minutes when the butter melts remove the pot from the heat.

5. Pour the mixture into a Pyrex dish and cover with the cheese.

6. Put in the preheated oven.

7. Put a tsp. sour cream on each serving and sprinkle with dill.

Our last stop in Romania was **Oradea** (in Hungarian Nagyvarad), which was probably one of the most important cultural centers in the Austro-Hungarian Empire. It used to be called "Little Paris" because of its many elegant boulevards and outdoor cafes. It was also the center of many Jewish educational institutions before World War 2. At the time of our visit, we were disappointed to find a rundown city with lots of neglected buildings and poorly dressed people.

I always loved Romanian folk music and their colorful dances so Vera and I were both very happy when our friends Georges and Françoise connected us in Paris with Petrika Ionesco, a very flamboyant and interesting Romanian who is a world-famous opera stage director. Since then, we have spent a lot of time together in the last twenty years with Petrika who had a second home near us in Florida. He published a very imaginative and colorful science fiction book in French that recently has been translated into English.

"The song of the Mechanical Swan"

A few years ago, Petrika came from Paris to visit us with a Romanian friend of his, Ghighi (Georges Subovici). We immediately felt close to Ghighi, an architect and a very knowledgeable warm man. On our next visit to Paris, we connected not only with Ghighi but also with his wife Vera, a researcher and physician in pediatric oncology, and their very sweet and intelligent daughter Carla.

125

Carla and Vera   *Ghighi*

Ghighi introduced us to the museums and architecture etc. and many other faces of Paris, which were new to us, even after 40 years in this marvelous city. We jumped at the opportunity to take a tour of Romania with Ghighi and the Veras because my Vera had never been to Romania. Although it was the fourth time for me, I had only visited Transylvania and the Banath in the past. We also connected through Ghighi to another nice couple, Cristina and Andi, also from Romania originally but who live now in Paris in a most imaginative apartment of their own design and construction. Both of them are architects and we see them often when we are in Paris.

This time in September 2018, we took a flight from the Beauvais Airport, about 35 miles from Paris to the City of Jasi in the Romanian region of Moldovia, the second-largest city in Romania after Bucharest. The city was a center of Jewish culture before WW 2, with Jewish people making up 35% of the total population. The words for the Hatikvah, the national anthem of Israel were composed here by Naftali Herz Inbar. The original melody was composed by the Italian composer Giuseppe Cecci and adopted to many folksongs, such as "Carul cu Boi" in Romanian/Moldavian, "Pod Krakowem" in Polish, and so on. The same melody finally was chosen for the Hatikvah and recomposed by Samuel Cohen in the 19th century., The well-known song in Yiddish "Jasi mine shtetl Jasi" also knowns as "Rumania Rumania" also comes from Jasi. At one time there were 117 Synagogues in the city but today only two of them are functioning. In a few days during the war, 15,000 Jews were massacred in the city of Jasi, and later the rest of the Jewish population was also brutally killed.

The Grand Synagogue in Jasi, the oldest in Romania (1681)

Ghighi drove us in a nice rental minivan from Jasi all through Romania. First, we went to the picturesque region of Bucovina, to visit the famous monasteries where the walls and exteriors that are adorned with images of revered saints are masterpieces of Byzantine art. We also toured Gora Humor, Voronetz, Moldavici, Sevascici, and many more towns with monasteries that are listed by UNESCO as World Heritage sites. As we continued this trip to Romania we met some of Ghighi's very kind friends who invited us to their homes.

Monastery in Voronezh

Before 1960 the Hungarian population of Transylvania's largest city, Kolozsvar in Hungarian and Cluj in Romanian was the majority but this situation changed, mostly because of the forced relocations of the Ceausescu regime. In 1998, when we visited the city with my friends, it was a run-down city. Even though there were some beautiful historical sites, we could not find a single restaurant serving any food. However, by

2018 we found a vibrant world-class city with hundreds of great restaurants along with one Café which was on the level of Gerbaud in Budapest.

Kolozsvar-Cluj, the statue of Matyas Kiraly (King Mathias)

Toltott kaposzta, Hungarian stuffed cabbage is a perennial favorite of most Hungarians. The way it is made in Kolozsvar, Cluj, is very special, adding various kinds of meats and sausages in addition to the stuffed cabbages.

Kolozsvari Toltott Kaposzta

Serves 12

Ingredients:

2 lb. lean pork

2 lb. smoked ham

2 lb. beef shank

midsize cabbage

2 onions

2 packages of sauerkraut (about 2Lb)

3 eggs

1 cup uncooked rice

2 tsp Hungarian paprika

1 tsp black pepper

2 tsp. salt

1 can tomato paste

1 tbsp sugar

½ cup of corn oil

Directions:

1. In a large pot of water put the cabbages and cook until the water boils. This allows you to peel off the cabbage leaves.

2. In a frying pan sauté the chopped onions until lightly browned

3. In two cups of water cook the rice, when the water boils reduce the heat to simmer, and continue for 20 minutes covered with a lid.

4. Grind all the pork and half of the ham and place in a large bowl.

5. When the onion is transparent, take it out of the oil. When at room temperature add to the meat mixture.

6. Add the cooked rice to the mixture in the bowl.

7. Beat the 3 eggs and add all the spices, paprika, salt, and black pepper, mix it well and add to the bowl.

8. Mix all the ingredients in the bowl with your hand to have an evenly distributed stuffing.

9. Take out the cabbage from the water and start to peel off the leaves one at a time.

10. To make the cabbage roll, remove the middle hard stock from the center of the cabbage leaf place a handful of the meat mixture on one end of the cabbage leaf, and then fold over the top side.

11. Roll the cabbage leaf tightly and stick in the two ends. Continue until you used up all the stuffing.

12. Cut the remaining ham and the beef shank into 3 pieces each.

13. Rinse the sauerkraut with water its bitterness.

14. Slice the remaining cabbage into small pieces.

15. Take a large pot and put some sauerkraut and chopped cabbage pieces to cover the bottom of the pot. Start to put in the pot the stuffed cabbage rolls in a row, not too close together. Cover the rolls with the sauerkraut and cabbage mixture, repeat it until is all used up. Distribute the ham and beef pieces evenly. When all the stuffed cabbage rolls are in the pot fill the pot with water to cover the cabbages. If you don't have a large enough pot, you may divide into two or more pots.

16. Mix the tomato paste with a cup of water and mix in the sugar and pour over the cabbage, covering the whole surface.

17. On the top of the oven cook the stuffed cabbage on medium heat until the water starts to boil.

18. In a preheated 300-degree oven bake the stuffed cabbage for at least three hours.

19. You may serve the stuffed cabbage with a dollop of sour cream.

After visiting *Targu Muresh-Marosvasarhely*, a very old famous town, and the *Bran Castle*, also known as Dracula Castle (named after the legendary Count Dracula), we arrived at the home of a close friend of the Subovicis in Rasnov, a picturesque town in the Carpathian Mountains. The next morning Ghighi and I enjoyed a difficult run on the steep slopes of the Carpathians. The slopes at Rasnov are used for ski jumping competitions.

Picturesque Rasnov in the Carpathian Mountains

Bran (Dracula) Castle

We had heard lots of good things about the nearby city of Brasov from my cousin Vera and from her husband Moshe who was born there. My Vera and I considered it one of the nicest cities in Romania.

Brasov Romania

We continued our trip toward the capital city of Romania, Bucharest. We were told that it was a much more exciting and beautiful city before Ceausescu destroyed the precious historical buildings and avenues imposing his own "socialist realism" style of construction. But we still found the city to be very dynamic and more interesting than many other cities we had visited in Europe and elsewhere. After checking into the elegant Hilton Hotel, we had a nice dinner at the home of Iona, Ghighi's sister.

Hilton Hotel in Bucharest.

After dinner we met some friends of Ghighi and his family and all enjoyed the lively nightlife of this bustling city.

The old town of Bucharest

Dancing in Bucharest

In the next couple of days, we had several great tours, visited the universities, parks, and historical sites. One of the most unique museums was the *Muzeul Satulu, the* National Village Museum.

It is an open-air ethnographic museum showcasing traditional Romanian village life. The museum extends to over 100,000 m^2, (over a million square feet) and contains 272 authentic peasant farms and houses from all over Romania. It was created in 1936.

Exterior and interior of a southern Romanian house

As we finished this trip in 2018, I thought of when I visited this beautiful country, Romania in September 1956, I did not have the slightest clue that in just a few weeks the coming events would change my whole life.

134

9. ENGLAND

I arrived in Vienna after I escaped from Hungary in early December 1956. The October Revolution had been suppressed by the Russian Army and many people mostly students and intellectuals left to avoid reprisals and/or to look for a better life. Just like the other 200,000 Hungarian refugees, I was wondering what could my future be in the free world. If you lived in a Communist country, the government made all the decisions for you about what and where to study, and you did not have the freedom to make any choices.

But in Vienna, I was in control. The most important decision for me was how to continue my studies to get my diploma. I was in my 4th year at the Eotvos Lorand University in Budapest majoring in Physics before I left Hungary. In 1956 after the revolution, all Hungarian refugees were considered heroes who turned against their oppressors and were welcomed in Vienna and in most of the Western countries with offers of help. Many countries offered scholarships to the many University students among the 200,000 Hungarian refugees. Physics was a hot field in the 1950s, and I could easily go to Germany, Sweden, or Switzerland to continue my studies. I decided however to go to an English-speaking country, even though I did not speak the language because I felt that it would be the most important language for me in the future. I chose England because I was told that once I pass an exam given at the British Embassy in Vienna, in a few days I'd be in England. Going to the USA was much more complicated and Australia and New Zealand were too far away to consider.

British Embassy in Vienna

An official at the British Embassy scheduled me to take an exam and I assumed it would be on some advanced topics in Physics like Quantum Mechanics or General Relativity. To my surprise, the only question I was asked was, "How do you explain that most physicists in England are in the Communist party?" I was not prepared for such a question, but I figured I could probably answer better than most people could, being a physics major and having just escaped from a Communist country. I said, "Judging by the many physicists I've known, their thinking was so indoctrinated by abstract ideas that they probably had no judgment about the real world." Fortunately, there was a translator present and apparently, they liked my answer because a couple of days later on December 10, 1956, I flew to London.

I arrived in **London** on my first flight ever with 120 Hungarian students just a week after I crossed the Hungarian-Austrian border. We were placed in temporary housing in dormitories and were put in contact with some local students who were very helpful. One professor who spoke excellent Hungarian even though he was a native English speaker was in charge of our group and I was told right away that I'd be able to continue my studies in Cambridge, one of the best places in the world to study physics. Probably I was the only Physics major who left Hungary, many were too involved with their abstract ideas and may not have even realized what was going on, so I had no competition!

Still, I was not feeling happy with my decision to come to England. I hated the weather and the smell of their food. The mutton fat smell was hitting me from every direction, and the weather was gloomy. Everybody was kind but not very cheerful and every question was answered by" perhaps" or "maybe". I might have been misled by my limited knowledge of English but the cautious English mentality was foreign to me. I told my kids and grandkids much later, that "maybe" is not in our dictionary, but only either "yes" or "no"! I could tell right away that I would not become a good Englishman. Both the directness of the Hungarian mentality and my temperament were just too different from the English.

As an example: I was looking for a post office to mail a letter and asked a passerby for directions. He explained to me that I had to go until the first light, then turn left, and after three blocks it would be on the right side. I thanked him but as I walked away, I realized that it was 6 PM and that the post office might not be open. Since I was still near the man, I asked him, "Do you know what time the post office closes?" He said, "at 5 PM".

Nevertheless, the city of London was very impressive and even in the gloomy December weather, my childhood friend George Bozoki and I walked a lot and tried to see as much as we could. We were impressed by historic Hyde Park, the home of free speech for hundreds of years, by the bustling Piccadilly Circus, the most crowded center of London, and by the British Museum, probably one of the best in the world, as well as by many other sites in London.

Piccadilly Circus London 1956

I still was troubled by the thought that I should have waited for my turn in Vienna to make it to the USA. Hungarian refugees couldn't go to the USA from England. In the New World, you can carry the same identity from your home country. But once we left Hungary, we lost our citizenship and in Vienna, we all got the so-called *gray card* for identification which had to be given back to the authorities once we left Vienna for London. So we had no official documents. I figured that since all the planes that came to London from Vienna carrying refugees returned empty, there should be room on these empty planes for me and my friend. Eventually, with the help of the Hungarian speaking professor, we arranged our return from London to Vienna.

During my two week stay in London, I also connected with a distant relative who lived there. Back in Hungary, I was told by my uncle Zoli that my father had a cousin whose son Pista is a very wealthy man and the owner of a hotel in London. Zoli arranged for me to get some money from this man because I did not have a penny in my pockets. He gave the equivalent of 100 English pounds in Hungarian currency to Pista's father in Hungary and when I meet Pista in London he would give me the 100 pounds. I called Pista and when I visited "his hotel" he was waiting for me. He was the night manager and was busy working, so we met the next day in a newly opened Hungarian restaurant called *Budapest*.

Budapest Restaurant London

We had a nice conversation about old times in Hungary. I had never met Pista before because he had left Hungary before WW 2. We had a pretty good Hungarian supper, which was well appreciated after many days of English dishes. Pista paid the bill and before we left, he gave me 100 pounds minus my and my friend George's part of the restaurant bill. He did pay for his own, however.

The night before we left London for Vienna, we stayed in a hotel at the airport. This was also arranged by the Hungarian speaking professor who was also instrumental in our getting the return flight. He was a very caring person and helped us a great deal. Later on, we met several Hungarians who had to wait years to emigrate from England to the USA. We were very lucky.

In the hotel room in addition to George Bozoki, my childhood friend there was another Hungarian student who also wanted to go somewhere else rather than England. I don't remember exactly what we were talking about when he used a Hungarian expression to say, "I can smell a Jew even if there is no wind". My friend George got up from his bed and walked over to the guy, grabbing his shirt and snarled into his face, "Can you smell me?" George who died 11 years ago was a very husky guy with a hairy chest and even in the dark, you could sense the fear of this skinny little anti-semitic Hungarian. We did not want to hurt him, but I am sure he learned his lesson.

On the flight back to Vienna in the empty plane, he tried to sit as far away from George and me as possible. When we arrived at the airport, the pilot stopped the plane on the runway so we did not have to go through passport control. We jumped over the fence and the same day we went to get another gray card, reporting that we just came from Hungary and started the refugee process all over again. Those days security was not like it is now at the airports. I certainly would not try it today. So we were in Vienna at Christmas time and we enjoyed the fresh, cheerful, festive city of as we started our new venture.

In 1971, I came back to London with Vera and our two children when we flew back from Budapest where we had spent six wonderful weeks and where I attended and gave a lecture at the 7th International Conference in Acoustics.

In 1971, on our flight from Budapest back to London with British Airways, some of the passengers were Hungarians and some were English. At the airport exit, there was a long line for taxis. It was interesting to watch the Hungarians cut in front of the line to grab a taxi, while the British patiently waited in line. People in small countries had to learn how to survive.

Returning to London after 15 years, I tried to be more open-minded than in 1956. Nevertheless, coming from the sunny and cheerful city of Budapest to the gloomy and rainy London dampened our enthusiasm. Besides, our 4-year-old daughter Susan got sick. One of our reasons for stopping in London was to visit the University of Birmingham where I had some research interaction with one of their professors. My son Michael and I took a 2-hour train ride to Birmingham, the second-largest city in England. The University had a charming old campus, but the industrial city reminded me of some run-down midwestern towns in the US.

University of Birmingham

Birmingham England

In 1974, I came back to London for the 8th International Conference in Acoustics (ICA). The opening ceremony was held in a large reception hall connected to a wing of the Royal Palace. I remembered the reception at the previous ICA in 1971, where we were wined and dined in the Opera House in Budapest. So, I told my friends Mack and Joanne Breazeale to make sure not to eat anything before the ceremony because there would be more food than they could handle. I soon learned the difference between the English and the Hungarian approach to catering for a festive event like the reception at an international conference such as the 8th ICA. Where the Hungarians had provided caviar, foie gras, and the like at the Budapest meeting three years earlier, their British counterparts served open sandwiches of white bread topped by a piece of yellow cheese and a slice of cucumber. As they say in France, "a chacun son gout".

With Mack Breazeale (next to me) and Joanne Breazeale (front) in London (1974)

Feeling embarrassed in front of the Breazeales for my bad meal advice, I invited them to *Budapest*, the best Hungarian restaurant in London which I've known since 1956, to get something to eat after the "banquet". Not only did they experience delicious Hungarian dishes like chicken paprikash and *Gundel Palachinta* which they had never eaten before, but they were also exposed to a genuine Gypsy band playing Hungarian and Gypsy songs. I tried my best to sing along and give a simultaneous translation to the songs. They were especially thrilled by a well-known Gypsy song that tells of a boy who sings to his mother, "Dear mother I am going to die; I want to get married". The mother replies, "My dear son, don't die, get married in the dark". The Breazeales liked the humorous song and had a great time the whole evening which I think made up for the lack of food at the conference reception.

After the conference, I took a boat ride on the beautiful Thames River to Greenwich. The London area has a lot to offer and Vera and I have come back many times to enjoy the museums and the theaters. I also understand that there are very good restaurants to be found now.

The Thames River

In 1981, we flew to London and from there we took a train to **Brighton**, a picturesque town on the Atlantic about 60 miles from London in Southern England. Originally it was a little fishing village with only a few thousand people but by the twentieth century, it became a large resort town with many hotels and with a population of over 200,000. I attended a meeting there called "Ultrasonic International" which was rather small with about two hundred attendees, mostly Europeans.

I had heard about the famous English *fish and chips* and walking along the beach in Brighton I bought some from a vendor who wrapped some fried fish and French fries in a newspaper. It was awful! Greasy, smelly fish and soft fries. I dumped it into a nearby garbage can. Once again, I was reassured that moving away from England in 1956 was not such a bad idea! However, the truth is that we had a very nice banquet on the last night and the food was reasonably good.

140

Brighton England 1981

In 1988, we made another trip with Vera to the south of England across the Channel from Calais, France. We drove with our French friends Liliane and Alain to Calais from Paris and then took a ferry to England. Sidney and Jim, our friends and running partners in Columbus, had their wedding in a small spa resort, **Turnbridge Well** and we had the pleasure of participating. Two of our close friends for more than 32 years Mary and John also came to the wedding.

Mary, Sidney, Jim, Vera, I, Liliane and John at the wedding in Turnbridge Well 1988

The English deserts are exceptionally good. After a sumptuous dinner, the guests felt they could not eat another bite of food. The hostess however offered desert and said "this is just a trifle, my dears".

English Trifle

Serves 12

Ingredients for pastry cream:

Two cups whole milk

Half a teaspoon vanilla

Six egg yolks

2/3 cup of granulated sugar

¼ cup cornstarch

One tbsp. unsalted butter

Directions:

1. *Bring the milk to boil in a saucepan on medium heat*

2. *Add the vanilla and set the pan aside*

3. *Whisk the egg yolks and sugar until light and fluffy*

4. *Add the cornstarch and whisk vigorously until no lumps remain*

5. *Whisk ¼ cup of the hot milk mixture into the yolks until incorporated*

6. *Whisk the remaining hot milk mixture.*

7. *Pour the mixture through a strainer back into the saucepan*

8. *Cook over medium/high heat mixing constantly until thickened and slowly boiling.*

9. *Remove from the heat and stir in the butter. Let it cool slightly.*

10. *Additional note: If you don't have time to follow the above recipe, use a Dr. Oeteker original vanilla pudding.*

Ingredients for the cake:

Two lb of strawberries or any other berries.

For the cake use pound cake or ladyfingers.

¼ cup sherry or orange-flavored liquor

Two cups chilled heavy cream beaten with two tbsp. of brown sugar

Directions to assemble the trifle:

1. *Slice the pound cake (or ladyfingers) into ½ inch slices and moisten the slices with the liquor*

2. *In a glass bowl layer the ingredients: cake or ladyfinger, vanilla pastry cream, heavy cream, and strawberries.*

3. *Repeat until the glass bowl is full.*

4. *Ending with the whipped cream at the top layer.*

5. *Cover tightly with plastic wrap and let it rest overnight.*

6. *In the morning, decorate with more fruit.*

After the wedding, we drove around southeastern England and enjoyed the charming town of Canterbury and its magnificent Cathedral. Canterbury is probably our favorite place in England.

Canterbury England 1988.

10. GERMANY

While waiting in Salzburg for my entry visa to the United States from the later part of December 1956 through January 1957, I thought of visiting my uncle Jeno, my father's oldest brother, and his daughter's family in **Munich.** They escaped from Hungary in 1950 and settled in Munich. It was only 60-70 miles away, but not having any visa or money the idea was challenging. I thought I'd give it a try by staying in the toilet for the one-hour train ride from Salzburg until the train arrived in Munich. I was lucky and was not caught and after arriving, I walked over to the home of my uncle's family on Leopold Strasse, one of the biggest streets in the city. My cousin was reasonably affluent and had a nice apartment where I stayed for a couple of days before returning to Salzburg, by then knowing my way around Munich.

It was my first visit to Germany, although I spent a year in Vienna in 1944/45 as an 11-year-old forced laborer, after being deported from Hungary when Austria was considered to be part of Germany after the *Anschluss*, the annexation of Austria into Germany in 1938. The Austrians try to explain it as an imposition by the Germans. In reality, there was no resistance at all and the majority of the Austrians welcomed the arrival of the German Army.

Leopold Strasse Munich Germany 1957

Vera and I came back to Munich several times to visit the family until Uncle Jeno passed away in 1980. In 2002 however, I had a conference in Munich and we drove there from Paris with our friends Steve and Marika. The conference in Munich was held in the Convention Center and we stayed in a nice hotel connected to it. The first evening we listened to a concert in the Center by a Ukrainian group singing traditional folk songs. We also took an excursion to the castles built by the Bavarian King Ludwig 2 in the 19th century. Ludwig was a very troubled man and was even called "Mad Ludwig" who after visiting Versailles decided to build three marvelous castles in the Alps: Schloss Neuschwanstein, Schloss Linderhof, and Schloss Herrenchiemesee. We spent most of the day visiting these castles where we also learned that Ludwig was a huge fan of Wagner.

Schloss Neuschwanstein near Munich, built by "Mad Ludwig" the King of Bavaria

The conference banquet served *Eisbein*, the famous German roasted pig knuckle that was baked to a very crispy golden color, one of the best we ever had.

Eisbein (Pig Knuckle)

Serves 2

Ingredients:

One 3 lb. pig knuckle

Salt, pepper

Garlic

Bottle of beer

Directions:

1. Put the pork shank on a roasting pan

2. Rub with the garlic

3. Sprinkle with salt and pepper

4. Pour a little beer over it to keep it moist; some people prefer oil instead of beer.

5. After one-hour pour more beer over the roast and continue to pour beer over the knuckle every 45 minutes.

6. Roast for 4 hours.

7. When the internal temperature of the shank reaches 200F increase the oven temperature to 450F and bake for 15 minutes

8. Take out from the oven and let it rest for 20 minutes before serving

Almond Plum Kuchen

Another favorite German dish to go with the pig's knuckle.

Serves 8

Ingredients for the dough:

1 ½ cup flour

Pinch of salt

9 tbsp. unsalted butter cut into small pieces

1/3 cup of sugar

1 egg

Directions for the dough:

1. Preheat oven to 400 degrees

2. In a food processor combine the flour, sugar, and salt. Hit a brief pulse, add the butter and pulse, add the egg and pulse until all ingredients are evenly distributed and the dough forms into a ball. If the dough is not holding together add a tbsp. of ice-cold water.

3. Press the dough into a 10-inch removable bottom pan. Cover the bottom and sides with the dough evenly. Freeze the dough in the pan for 30 minutes.

4. Bake the dough in the preheated oven for 10 minutes, then lower the temperature to 350 degrees and bake until golden brown.

Ingredients for the filling:

1 cup almonds

1 tbsp. flour

½ cup granulated sugar

1 stick unsalted butter

2 eggs

6 pitted plums cut into wedges.

Directions for the filling:

1. In a food processor combine almonds, flour, and granulated sugar, pulse briefly until becomes a smooth batter.

2. Cut butter into pieces, add the 2 eggs and mix.

3. Pour the almond mixture into the prebaked pastry Flatten the paste evenly

4. Distribute the plum pieces decoratively on the top of the batter. Press the plum pieces gently down

5. Bake in a 350 degrees oven for 30-40 minutes until a test with a toothpick comes out clean

6. Cool and dust with confectioner sugar and serve.

In 1964 September, Vera and I with our 6 months old son Michael came to Germany , to *Göttingen*, a city of about 100,000 people. After teaching at the General Motors Institute for four years, I was fortunate enough to receive a National Science Faculty Fellowship and spend a year in Göttingen at one of the most prestigious institutes in the world, the *Drittes Physikalisches Institut*, also called the Institut von Schwingung Physik.

We took a nine-day long trip on the Franconia of the Cunard line which left Montreal and stopped on the way in **South Hampton** and Le Havre before arriving at **Rotterdam**, Holland from where we traveled by train to Göttingen, Germany.

The Franconia of the Cunard Line across to Rotterdam 1964

We could not find any milk to give to our 6-month-old boy on the train from Rotterdam to Göttingen, and when two men entered our cabin asking us, "Coffee or tea?", we thought they were vendors, so we answered, "milk for our baby", glad to find it for Michael. They started to laugh, explaining that they were custom officers, and were checking to see if any passengers were carrying coffee or tea from Holland to Germany which was illegal at that time. We understood our gaffe and joined in the laughter.

The University of Göttingen, the *Georg-August-Universität Göttingen*, was formed in the 18th century and was a Mecca for Physicists and Mathematicians for centuries. It was also famous in other disciplines such as the Medical and Biological Sciences, Chemistry, and the Humanities. No fewer than 45 Nobel Laureates were associated with the university either as graduates and/or as faculty, probably the largest number of Nobel Laureates of any university in the world before World War II, and it remained in the top ten even after WW2.

The list of very famous people associated with Göttingen is endless: Schopenhauer the philosopher, Heinrich Heine the poet, the Grimm Brothers the storytellers, Carl Friedrich Gauss, Bernhard Riemann, Felix Klein, Janos von Neumann the mathematicians and Max Born, Max Plank, Werner Heisenberg, Enrico Fermi the physicists. Many physicists were Hungarians like Jeno Wigner, Eduard Teller, and Leo Szilard just to name a few. Besides the scholars and scientists, many statesmen like Otto von Bismarck the "Iron Chancellor", Richard Weizsacker the former president of Germany, and many others were associated with the university.

Just for the record, airline fares have changed greatly in the last 50 years; the fare on the Franconia was less than a one-way airplane ticket! Upon arriving at Göttingen, we were surprised at the difficulty of finding suitable housing even though my stipend was extremely high by current German standards. My monthly stipend from NSF was over 3500 Marks, way above the average German academic salary. The reason for the housing shortage was that Göttingen as opposed to other German cities was saved from the Allies' bombings during World War 2, and consequently, there was very little new construction.

The United States had assigned a group of scientists headed by the Nobel Laureate Goudschmitt to identify the areas of large concentrations of famous scientists so as to not bomb those areas in order to save their lives and their facilities. Naturally, Göttingen was one of these locations with a large concentration of top scientists, even though many of the big names mentioned earlier were no longer there because in 1933 due to the anti-Jewish laws 250 professors and staff were forced to leave the University. Many who left, among them Wigner, Szilard, von Neumann, and Teller, landed in the USA and initiated the Manhattan project.

Eventually, we were able to get an apartment on Felix Klein Strasse, a street named after the famous mathematician known for his work in group theory and non- Euclidian Geometry. In Göttingen, many streets were named for famous scientists and mathematicians who were associated with the university.

Göttingen, Germany

We shared a five-bedroom apartment with a single bathroom and one kitchen with two other families. It was even more crowded when my childhood friend Steve Szasz joined us with his wife and their nine-month-old daughter after escaping from Hungary in 1965. We rented two rooms in the apartment for 300 German Marks from a German family the Lohls. When I found out from someone that Mr. Lohl was a teacher in a Trade School, I told Mrs. Lohl that I also was a teacher in the USA and I heard that Mr. Lohl also was a teacher. She responded in an angry tone, *"Er ist keine Lehrer, er ist Ober Lehrer,"* that he was not a simple teacher but a higher-level teacher. I guess he was teaching 3rd year plumbing students and not 1st year ones. Rank is very important in German society. At any rate, the Lohls were decent people and offered a room to Steve's mother to sleep.

The *Drittes Physicalisches Institut* (the Third Physics Institute) also called the *Schwingung Physik* Institute (Physics of Waves and Vibrations) was headed by Professor Erwin Meyer and was housed in a large building on Burger Strasse, about a mile from the center of Göttingen. All the buildings of the University were scattered all around the city of Göttingen. As in most European universities, there was no University Campus like there are in the USA. The institute had about 70 members, in addition to Professor Meyer, there were associate professors (Dozents), assistants, and doctoral candidates.

149

Ganseliesel fountain in Göttingen.

The landmark of the city of Göttingen is the charming *Ganseliesel* fountain. There is an almost three-hundred-year-old tradition here that when students receive their doctorate, they are carried by other students to kiss the Ganseliesel, the young girl with the geese.

Vera with Michael in Göttingen, 1964

Vera, Michael, and a friend in Felix Klein Strasse, 1964

We had a marvelous year in this old university town. People were genuinely kind, on several occasions when Vera was carrying packages and pushing the stroller, they came to help her. It was hard to imagine how such nice people could have committed such heinous crimes against humanity.

Werner Lauterborn was a student at the University of Göttingen when I spent a year there in 1964/65 as a National Science Foundation Fellow. Thirty-five years later he was the professor and chairman of the Drittes Physicalisches Institut, replacing Professor Erwin Meyer.

In 1999, Werner invited me to a conference held in the institute called "Nonlinear Acoustics at the turn of the Millennium". Vera and I were happy to go back to Göttingen.

The city had changed significantly in thirty-five years. In the sixties, the streets smelled of *bockwurst* the sausage sold by street vendors, while in 1999 the smell of shawarma and gyro was more prevalent as it now is all across Europe. Nevertheless, the city still kept the flavor of a small town with its world-famous university. We visited Felix Klein Strasse where we lived for one year sharing a five-bedroom, one-bathroom apartment with 9-10 people including Steve and his family who stayed with us when they came from Hungary in 1965.

Steve's mother hoped to get help from local Jewish organizations since she was an older Holocaust survivor and a refugee from Hungary, so I tried to locate such an organization and found one. We arrived with Steve's mother at a house owned by an old man with one leg. He explained to us that because he lost his leg in World War 1 in a heroic battle, he was awarded the Iron Cross, the highest recognition in the German Army which made him exempt from deportation by the Nazis. He was the only Jew to survive representing the Jewish Community in Göttingen.

Although we lived in Göttingen Germany for a year, we never had a chance to visit **Berlin** at that time because it would have required travel through East Germany which was not advisable. After 1990, when the famous Berlin wall separating East and West Berlin was knocked down, the city was united again. A few years later, we were able to attend a conference in 1995 in the eastern part of Berlin at the famous Humboldt University, which was established in 1810.

Humboldt University Berlin

In 1995 five years after the removal of the wall, one could see still the contrast between West Berlin with the elegant businesses and lively outdoor cafes on Kurfürstendamm Strasse and the huge grey buildings constructed by the Soviets in East Berlin.

Kurfürstendamm Strasse, former West Berlin

Unter den Linden, former East Berlin

Near the *Unten den Linden*, a famous large boulevard, there were still many empty buildings that had served the purposes of the Soviet secret police. Otherwise, Berlin is a very elegant city where Vera and I enjoyed visiting its many museums, the Pergamon museum being the most notable. We also loved the performance of The *Tales of Hoffmann* by Offenbach in the State Opera which in East Berlin. We never saw a more enthusiastic audience who could not stop clapping rhythmically which we call "iron clapping" *vastaps* in Hungarian. Most people who lived in the communist countries were indoctrinated to clap that way every time Stalin's name was mentioned. Perhaps that tradition has continued for performances of Opera?

We visited the Neue (New) Synagogue, the largest Synagogue in Berlin and the only Synagogue in Berlin which was not violated during Kristallnacht in November 1938 because the district police chief saved it.

Neue Synagogue in Berlin

Many newcomers to Berlin, mostly from the former Soviet bloc have increased the Jewish population to over 100,000. Vera and I were doing our daily run in Berlin when all of a sudden, we came across a street named after David Ben Gurion, the first prime minister of the State of Israel. I can't imagine a greater satisfaction than two Holocaust survivors jogging on Ben Gurion Strasse in Berlin.

Berlin 50 years after the fall of Nazi Germany

In 2002 on our way to Munich, we stopped in **Heidelberg** the famous university town. Seeing this calm beautiful city, one would not believe that seventy years earlier the professors and students in the University Platz were burning thousands of books written by Jewish authors. The university became infamous as the *Nazi University*. Ironically at the time of our visit, the windows of many book stores in Heidelberg were full of the works of the well-known Israeli writer Amos Oz.

Heidelberg

From Heidelberg we drove to another city made famous during the Nazi era; **Nuremberg**. It was here in the 1930s that Hitler dictated the so-called Nuremberg laws restricting Jews from civil service jobs and many other professions. The first law, *The Law for the Protection of German Blood and German Honor*, forbade the marriage of Jews and Christians, and was soon followed by many other infamous laws. Because these laws originated in Nuremberg, the trials to convict the Nazi leaders after the war were assigned to Nuremberg as a symbolic gesture.

153

Nuremberg historically was a center of culture where Johannes Guttenberg introduced printing to Europe in the early 15th century. Surely, he could not have imagined the barbarous acts of book burning that 500 years later would dishonor his name.

Models of the Guttenberg printing system

Vera and I drove to **Aachen** on September 9, 2019, where the 23rd International Conference on Acoustics, ICA was held for 5 days. Ever since the 7th ICA meeting in 1971 in Budapest, I have attended almost all the ICA meetings.

Given the fact that we had never been in Aachen, we did not want to miss this opportunity. Aachen, also known as Bad Aachen (Aachen Baths) because of its warm mineral springs, was one of the favorite places of the ancient Romans. In the 800s, Charlemagne the king of the Franks settled in Aachen and turned the small settlement into the capital of the empire which included western and central Europe. We spent a nice week in this ancient city whose old town like those of most European cities is a pleasure to visit. The Conference Hall was a modern complex near the best Spa in Aachen, the Carolus Thermal Spa, which we enjoyed several times during our stay.

Aachen has long been one of the financial centers of Europe ever since the Middle Ages, and to recognize this history, an imaginative statue describes how money goes around between the various participants in a transaction.

Vera is resting by the humorous representation of the Aachen "money mongers"

Another reason why we decided to come to Aachen so after the conference we could visit the part of Germany that was East Germany before 1990 when the East German government fell together with the Berlin wall. Even though we lived in Göttingen (Lower Saxony) for a year and traveled through most of West Germany, we were not able to go to East Germany because Vera was not yet a U.S. citizen and we were afraid to go into a Communist country.

The main place on our list to visit was **Leipzig**, called Lipcse in Hungarian, a commercial center for hundreds of years with a rich cultural history. The "*Lipcsei Vasar*", the Hungarian name for the Leipzig Market was a magic word for us. We hit the Autobahn and with a few hours of driving at 120 miles an hour, we arrived to the beautiful city of Leipzig. The city is located in the province of Saxony and it is the tenth-largest city of Germany with a population of 600,000. The next morning, on Sunday, September 15, we started a city tour at the center of the city, the *Augustusplatz* with a bright knowledgeable guide called Svetlana originally from Estonia who spoke at least six languages.

Augustusplatz, Leipzig 2019

The Augustusplatz was constructed in the 18th century and named after Augustus, the first king of Saxony. This main square contains most of the important institutions of the city, such as the Museum of Modern Arts, the Main Theater, the Opera House, and the 15th-century University of Leipzig, as well as the high rise building that was built in 1999.

In 1953 the name of the square was changed to Karl-Marx Platz but after 1990, it regained its original name. During WW 2, several buildings were damaged but by 1960 everything was restored to its original condition. Svetlana guided us around Leipzig telling us all about the history of the city and highlighting its most important points of interest. Leipzig is also known as the City of Music, where many famous composers like Bach, Mendelssohn, Schuman, and Wagner lived and are honored in several museums like the Bach Museum and the Mendelssohn Museum.

In 1937 the Nazis destroyed the Mendelssohn Museum to erase the memory of the composer, Felix Mendelssohn and his grandfather Moses Mendelssohn; the most famous Jewish philosopher of the 19th century. The mayor of Leipzig, Karl Goerdeler although a conservative politician, opposed the Nazi atrocities and resigned In 1944. Goerdeler later was executed because he was part of the group that attempted to assassinate Hitler.

Leipzig had many Synagogues and a Jewish population of more than 13,000 before the Kristallnacht in 1938 when 275 of Jewish Synagogues were burned down all over Germany. The most famous, the Moorish Revival Leipzig Synagogue which was built in 1855, and all the others except the Brody Synagogue were destroyed during the Kristallnacht.

Most of the Jewish population of Leipzig was murdered during the Holocaust and even after that, the East German communist regime also was not supportive of any Jewish activities of the few survivors. In 1990 when the reunification of Germany took place, there were only 86 Jews living in Leipzig. However, many Jews from the Soviet bloc countries have come to Leipzig like other German cities, and the Jewish population today is 1300 with a very active Jewish community. Svetlana, our tour guide, took us to the Brody Synagogue, the only surviving Synagogue after the Kristallnacht, The Synagogue is surrounded by buildings where non-Jews lived and although the Nazis destroyed the windows and the interior, they did not burn it down to avoid the destruction of Christian homes.

Svetlana introduced us to the Rabbi of the Brody Synagogue, Rabbi Zsolt Balla, a native of Budapest. We enjoyed our conversation in Hungarian with this bright young man, who became a Rabbi at the Berlin Orthodox Rabbi Seminary. Zsolt told us about the revival of Jewish life in Leipzig and all across Germany where the Jewish population has grown to close to two hundred thousand. We had the good fortune to participate in a concert held at the synagogue that same afternoon.

Rabbi Balla together with another Hungarian-speaking Rabbi, Rabbi Daniel Fabian from Temesvar (now part of Romania) played the guitar and sang traditional Jewish holiday and Israeli songs with the participation of the audience of more than 200 for a very memorable afternoon in a packed Synagogue. Happily, only a few days ago back in the U.S., we came across Rabbi Balla streaming on Facebook a Shabbat service to an empty Synagogue to maintain "social distancing" because of the COVID 19. I guess the Jewish spirit can never be destroyed neither by the Nazis nor by the Coronavirus!

The Brody Synagogue in Leipzig

After leaving the concert in the Synagogue we looked forward to have a nice evening with dinner in a typical local restaurant. Our experience with German food of the previous few days had been somewhat mixed. Even though we enjoyed their varied sausages, their cuisine was not on the level of the French, Italian or Hungarian dishes which are more to our taste.

The historic Madler Passage built in 1912 is one of the earliest commercial centers in Germany and the site of the famous Auerbach Keller, an underground pub that was established in 1438. The Keller (cellar) was favored in the late eighteenth century by Johann Wolfgang von Goethe, the famous German poet and is still highly recommended today.

It is said that when Johan Wolfgang was a law student at the University of Leipzig he often skipped his classes to enjoy spending time with his friends in the Auerbach Keller. As a matter of fact, he wrote **Faust** one of his most famous works below the Keller in the Mephisto Bar which was probably a favorite hangout of Goethe and his friends. Later, the French composer Charles Gounod made Faust into one of his best-known operas.

At the entrance to the Madler Passage, a Statue of Mephisto bewitching a student illustrates Goethe's main theme from Faust. We were not impressed by the food in the acclaimed restaurant; more than half of my roast boar and Vera's Wiener Schnitzel was left on our plates. Perhaps we did not drink as much as Goethe did before our dinner. But the beer was good so it was a memorable evening anyway.

The Statue of Mephisto bewitching a student at the entrance to Auerbach Keller

The next morning, full of many very meaningful memories of Leipzig, we drove to **Dresden**. Since Dresden was only a short drive away from Leipzig, we decided to swing by this city even though it was not on our way back to Paris. Dresden is the second-largest city in Saxony after Leipzig, and used to be a cultural center of Germany. In our times, It became sadly well known in WW 2 for the Allied air forces' repeated bombing the city more than any other in Germany, practically leveling it.

The Nazis used Dresden in their propaganda to blame the Americans and the British for their "inhuman atrocities against the German people, killing 200,000 women and children in Dresden", although the total casualties in Dresden were closer to 18,000. Whatever the number, it still saddens us. Those innocent children who died were not responsible for Hitler's bombing of Warsaw, London, nor for the creation of Auschwitz.

Another historical event occurred near Dresden at the Elba river, where the Americans coming from the west met the Soviets arriving from the east after defeating the German Army. The soldiers from both sides hugged and kissed each other celebrating their victories over the Nazi threat. A very good Russian film "Encounter at the Elba" makes the event unforgettable, Who would guess in May of 1945 that within a few years, a Cold War would develop to make enemies of these exultant soldiers celebrating together at the River Elba?

On our way back to Paris from Dresden we stopped in **Weimar** a small town in Thuringia, where after the loss of WW 1, the Weimar Republic was established in 1919 and was in existence until 1933 when Hitler came to power.

Because the victorious allies imposed severe sanctions on defeated Germany, the new Republic entered into severe economic ruin and hyperinflation. Hitler considered this period a shameful part of German history and in 1933 overthrew the Weimar Republik and established the Third Reich which lasted until the end of WW 2 in 1945. Near Weimar was the Buchenwald concentration camp, which we first considered visiting, but after having visited Auschwitz we did not feel like seeing another place where Jews were massacred. Too much emotion!

11. THE UNITED STATES OF AMERICA

S1. MICHIGAN

After returning to Vienna from London in December 1956, it took close to two months to approve my papers to be able to be an immigrant in America. I went to Salzburg which accelerated the process. Like about 40,000 other Hungarian refugees, I received a white card which gave me the approval of the American Congress to stay in the USA for two years until a final decision about my future would be made. I figured that two years is a long time so I had no problem taking the chance. We had no assurance that we could continue our studies and there were no promises. We also were told that America is a free country and the Government cannot dictate to the universities how to handle Hungarian students.

I arrived to New York on February 23, 1957, having come all the way from Vienna sitting on my suitcase on the plane. When I travel I never miss the opportunity to tell the stewardesses about how I crossed the Atlantic sitting on my suitcase whenever they warn me to stay in my seat until the plane stops.

My first residence in America was in New Jersey in an Army Camp where all the refugees stayed for redistribution. It was called **Camp Kilmer** after Joyce Kilmer a poet who was killed in World War 1. I enjoyed my stay there and found the army food fantastic because for the first time in my life I could eat as many eggs as I wanted. Some mornings I may have had as many as 8 eggs sunny side up with bacon.

Camp Kilmer, New Jersey 1957

When I was in Salzburg I had to have a medical examination in order to get an entrance visa to the United States. The X-ray showed a scar on my lung which needed further examination. From Camp Kilmer, I was sent to the Ingham County Chest Hospital, located in Lansing Michigan for the examination. When I was released, I went to **East Lansing, Michigan** to the Department of Physics at Michigan State University located in East Lansing to apply for admission to continue my studies.

I passed a test on various topics in physics and math, and although I had no transcript from Hungary, they accepted my Hungarian studies as the equivalent of a B.S. degree based on the results of my exam. I became a research assistant in the Ultrasonic Research Group and started my graduate studies in the MSU Physics Department where I received a 200 dollar a month stipend, which was more money than I had ever seen before.

Faculty and Assistants, Dept. of Physics at MSU, I am in the middle of the first row. 1958

The University was located in East Lansing. Lansing was the location of the Oldsmobile factory and the capital city of the state of Michigan.

Lansing the Capital city of Michigan   *Michigan State University Campus 1957*

I rode a bicycle the first couple of years but by 1959 I bought my very first car, a 1952 Oldsmobile. I was loyal to the city where they were built.

With my first car, a 1952 Oldsmobile, 1959

I was very content with my decision to come to America. My mentor, Professor Egon Hiedemann, was a German-born, world-famous physicist, and an expert in the field of Ultrasonics. He was one of the pioneers of Acousto-Optics, a discipline that studied and applied the interaction and effects of light and ultrasound. I was fortunate to start my studies with him which helped me pave the road to success in the field of Ultrasonics. In addition to taking many courses in Physics my major, and in Math my minor, I also took English and political science classes as well as other courses to better understand this great country because I wanted to become an American.

Professor Egon Hiedemann

Luckily after two years, Congress voted to give full immigrant status to all the 40,000 Hungarian refugees changing their white card to green and in 1962 I became an American citizen. At MSU I had the opportunity to learn many things about American life. Professor Hiedeman regularly invited his students to his home for dinner parties. Most memorable was my first Thanksgiving dinner which became my favorite holiday. I formed close friendships with the other assistants, especially with Bill Cook and Achutan Kotillil, and I learned how to play bridge, go bowling, and go out to eat pizza together although I was not too fond of hamburgers and so far have never yet been in a McDonald's but I do like Wendy's.

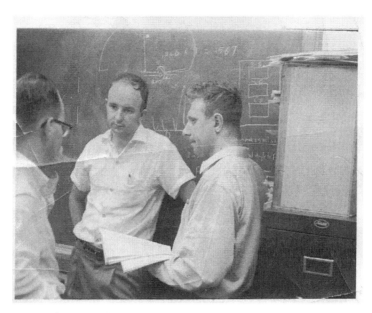

With research assistants Bill Cook and Bill Lester 1958

As I was finishing my studies and writing my dissertation, I got an offer for an Assistant Professorship in the Department of Physics and Environmental Engineering from GMI, the General Motors Institute, an Engineering College in **Flint, Michigan**. in July 1960, I started to teach physics courses and developed an ultrasonic laboratory in the college which was sponsored by the General Motors Corporation. A few weeks before starting to teach, I gave my very first presentation in Brown University in Providence Rhode Island at a meeting of the Acoustical Society of America. It went rather well and I also enjoyed my first lobster dinner paid for by Professor Hiedeman in a local seafood restaurant.

From the very beginning of my teaching at GMI, I knew that I wanted to have an academic career and I have stayed in academia through the next 60 years. Last year in September 2019, with the support of the Emeritus Academy of Ohio State University, I lectured at the 23rd ICA meeting in Aachen, Germany.

Teaching is fun and it is rewarding to be able to know immediately after a one hour class whether or not you have achieved your teaching objectives. This is something that is not so easily achieved in many other professions, and besides, as a teacher, you are constantly challenged by bright young university students who keep your mind active. But most importantly you have lots of freedom, which to me has always been very important.

I had a rather light teaching load of 7-9 hours a week and in addition, I was involved with several General Motors projects related to ultrasonics.

I had an excellent salary and many benefits of the General Motors Corporation, like a 35% discount on automobiles, and all expenses paid to attend scientific conferences, etc. In the 1960s, GM was in great shape and I learned that the city of Flint had the second-highest per capita income in the country. Unfortunately later on, like many other midwestern cities, it deteriorated quite a bit. I knew that I would not stay in Flint forever and that when other opportunities came up I would move on. I stayed in this position for four years until July of 1964. For a year and a half, Vera and I lived in Flint. We got married in January 1963.

Our town house in Flint 1963

I was proud of my position at a respectable Engineering College but still felt that I could do better. Professor Hiedemann suggested that I spend a year in a German university known for active ultrasonic research. Following this advice, I went to the Third Physics Institute at the University of Göttingen which at that time had one of the best research programs on both acoustic and electromagnetic waves.

In 1965 we returned from Göttingen to Michigan, where, I took a temporary teaching position at Wayne State University in Detroit and also an evening laboratory instructorship at Lawrence Institute of Technology (an engineering college) in a suburb of Detroit.

In 1965 the USA was troubled by the deterioration of many cities including Detroit. Once a thriving and dynamic industrial city with a very nice downtown, Detroit had started to be full of deserted and rundown houses and increased crime. The wealthy and middle-class white people moved to the suburbs, leaving the poorer mostly African American low-income or unemployed people in the area. Wayne State University was in the middle of downtown Detroit and the surrounding areas were neglected and unsafe.

With eighteen months old Michael in the front of where we lived in Detroit (1965)

We moved to an apartment in the "7 Mile Road" area, some 7 miles from the University but still bordering on some slums. We were very unhappy living in Detroit and even after almost 55 years, Vera and I consider the few months we spent there as the worst of our married life.

Vera, her parents, and Michael walking in our street in Detroit. (1965)

I understand that currently there is a revival in Detroit as in many other depressed cities in the USA. I hope that living conditions will improve there as well as in the rest of the State of Michigan, which was my "birthplace" in my chosen country.

12. CANADA

Once, while I was at Michigan State University in East Lansing, I tried to go to Montreal Canada, where I had relatives, the Vertes Family as well as my childhood friend George Karpati (Poncike). When I inquired at the Immigration and Naturalization office whether I could go to Canada with only the white card and a temporary permit to stay in the USA for two years, the official told me, "by all means, you can go". I had a funny feeling about his answer so I asked, "And will I be able to return?". "No", he said, "once you leave the USA you will not be able to return!" What a schmuck! I did not go. Never assume anything!

By the spring of 1959, after Congress approved the change of status of all Hungarian refugees and granted them the green card, I could come and go as a free man like everybody else. So when in August 1959, Professor Hiedeman made a generous offer to all his graduate students of an all-expenses-paid trip to **Ottawa** for an Acoustical Society meeting, I was able to join the group. Several of us graduate assistants drove to Ottawa, and stayed in rented rooms, while the conference and the professors' accommodations were in the beautiful Chateau Lauriel, near the Canadian Parliament.

Chateau Lauriel Ottawa Canada 1959

This was my very first scientific conference and it was exciting largely because it was an international event and I was able to meet and listen to the lectures of leading people in the field, not only from North America but from all across the world.

Professor Hiedemann was a very generous man and made sure that in addition to the scientific exposure we had some pleasurable social activities as well. In Ottawa, he took us out to *Madame Burger*, a well-known French restaurant which was my first experience with French food. He had been a professor at Strasbourg University while Alsace was under German rule and was very proud of the fact that his French was perfect. When the waiter in the restaurant took all the orders which Professor Hiedemann gave him in French, he clicked his heels together saying "Jawohl Herr General!" We all got a kick out of this.

I came back several times in 1976, 1981, and 1993 for scientific conferences to Ottawa, the capital of Canada. Ottawa is not only a pleasant city of nearly one million people on the Ottawa river, but there was also the additional or maybe main attraction that Montreal, one of my favorite cities was only a short drive away.

In 1959 August, after the end of the conference, I took a bus from Ottawa to **Montreal**, my first visit to this beautiful cosmopolitan city. I stayed with my only relatives on the North American continent, my aunt and uncle Lilike neni and Marci bacsi who came from Debrecen to Montreal in 1957. Lilike neni was a wonderful cook and a great hostess who always made me feel at home when I stayed with them many times in the coming years.

Montreal at that time was probably the most European city in North America, not only because it was the 2nd largest French-speaking city in the world after Paris, but also because it attracted many other nationalities from Europe who brought Old World flavors with them. After the 1956 Hungarian Revolution, tens of thousands of Hungarians came to Canada, probably more than to the USA because of Canada's more liberal immigration policies. Altogether, I found that the USA, with the possible exception of New York City, had the goal of being a melting pot for immigrants, where most newcomers would become "natives" immediately and raise their children without teaching them their parents' native language. On the other hand in Canada, the ethnicity of the new immigrants is much more preserved.

For example, in Montreal dozens of Hungarian restaurants, cafes and specialty shops opened on Stanley street, a small downtown street where I once counted 12 Hungarian establishments. They were all rather inexpensive and even with my low budget in 1959 I could afford everything I wanted.

Hungarian Delicatessen in Montreal

The city was very attractive and interesting. Friends told me that when you stand on St Lawrence Street, everything toward the East, all the eateries, nightclubs and other entertainment locals, are all French, and toward the West, everything is all English.

This changed significantly by the late 1970s and 80s when the Quebecois movement asserted more independence, and many of the English speaking people moved to Toronto and Vancouver which left Montreal with a very large majority of French speakers who got a law passed in Canada that in the Province of Quebec which includes Montreal, all street signs and commercial advertisements had to be only in French. In the other 10 mostly English-speaking provinces, like Ontario, British Columbia, and so on, all signs had to be displayed both in English and in French. Anyway, it didn't bother me if I wanted to eat a smoked meat sandwich the specialty of Montreal at Dunn's or Ben's, because I could read the כשר sign either as *casher* or as *kosher*. Everybody loves Montreal's smoked meat. Of my several friends living in Montreal, half of them favored Dunn's and the other half Ben's; to me, both tasted like pastrami.

The two competing smoked meat sources in Montreal, Dunn's and Ben's

After I started to teach at GMI in Flint Michigan, I preferred to spend my vacations and even some weekends in Montreal. Sometimes, when I finished my work on Friday evening I would drive 700 miles straight through to Montreal. By then, I had exchanged my 1952 Oldsmobile for a brand new one and I used to drive all night. If I got tired on the road, I would get out of the car and do a 7-8 minute headstand (I had become a devoted yogi). When I arrived in Montreal, I would go to my relatives' house, sleep a couple of hours, have some great Hungarian meals, and spend time with friends. I usually did not sleep Saturday night and would drive back to Flint on Sunday night to arrive at Flint on Monday morning. When you are in your twenties you can do a lot. One of my favorite sections of the city was Old Montreal with its colorful shops and eating places. In the evenings we always headed east toward the French part of the city to enjoy ourselves.

When I stayed longer than just the weekends, I would often go to the colorful Laurentian Mountains which are only a few hours' drive from Montreal.

Laurentian Mountains, Canada

My most important visit to Montreal, the one which most impacted my life was in the fall of 1962. I was asked by my family to drop off a lady in **Toronto** on my way back to Flint. She was from Debrecen visiting my family in Montreal but also had a sister in Toronto. Of course, I agreed although I never was too fond of Toronto. I had stopped there a few times but most of the time when I drove back and forth to Montreal I just passed by taking the direct highways. It was a rather colorless puritanical city, where cinemas, night clubs and so on were closed from Saturday evening till Monday morning so it didn't offer much to a bachelor visitor for the weekend. I heard that many people would go to nearby Buffalo to have some fun.

College Street Toronto 1959

It started to change once the large immigration of continental Europeans from Italy, Hungary, and the Slavic countries started to move in among the Anglo Saxon population. Numerous Hungarian and other ethnic restaurants opened across Toronto.

"Only an Ox Drinks Alone" Hungarian restaurant in Toronto

When I dropped the lady off at her sister's place, she fixed me up with a blind date. On November 24, 1962, I met Vera. We were married 6 weeks later and we have been married for almost 58 years.

With Vera's parents at our wedding in Toronto on January 6, 1963

Lately, Toronto has started to be much more attractive and today it is a world-class city with over 5 million inhabitants and is the largest city in Canada. Lots of people with big money moved to Toronto from Montreal which helped its economy.

Toronto Canada 2020

Every year the large ethnic population in Toronto puts on an "International Day" that we always enjoyed participating in. You get a small book, a "passport" when you register and it is stamped at the stand of each country that you visit. College Street shown in the 1959 photo above has changed significantly with the arrival of the new immigrants.

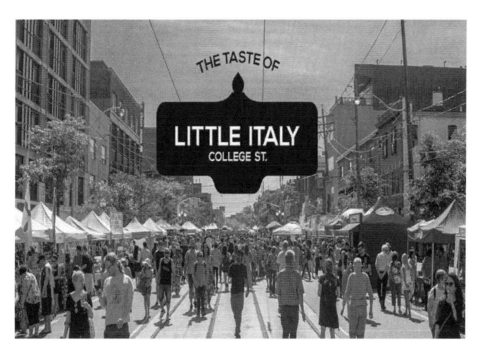
The changing face of College Street in Toronto

After our wedding, we came to Toronto often to spend time with Vera's parents, but we also went to Montreal very often to visit other family and friends.

We went to Montreal with our children for my cousin Agi's, (the daughter of Lilike neni and Marci bacsi) wedding on January 6th, 1973, ten years after our wedding. We all had a wonderful time even with the very cold subzero weather.

Wedding in Montreal 1973

Canada became our second home since we had family and friends both in Toronto and Montreal. For a short time, we even toyed with the idea of moving there since it is more European and there are many more social benefits such as health care and free tuition than in the USA. However, we dropped very quickly this idea of changing countries. We thought that for young, ambitious, hard-working capable people there was no place better than the USA where the opportunities were endless and hopefully would continue that way.

We visited the eastern part of Canada, many times, but by the Summer of 1993, we also had the opportunity to see part of the western area as well. My cousin Sanyi and his wife had come from Israel to tour the US and when we were with them in Seattle, we decided to take a ferry to *Victoria*, the capital of British Columbia, Canada.

When we got to the seaport around 6 PM we saw that there were already many cars lining up for the trip with people sitting in their cars or picnicking next to them. We found out that the next ferry, which was the last one that day, would leave at 9 PM. I hated the idea of sitting in a car for three hours but I realized that if we went somewhere, by the time we came back, there wouldn't be any place for us on the last ferry. So, I came up with the plan of leaving our car in the line and renting another car at the nearby rental place. This gave us time for a drive in our second rental car to the Olympic National Park across from the seaport. We even had a small meal before we returned car #2 to the agency and we came back to car #1. By that time all the spots were taken but we just took our place in line and within a short time our ferry took off to Victoria.

Prior to our departure, we had arranged for a B&B in Victoria. Once we arrived to the city it was quite late and I thought of driving downtown to ask for directions to the address for our B&B. On the main street we saw half a dozen young women lined up. When I approached one of them to ask for directions, her eyes lit up thinking I was a customer. Despite her disappointment, she was very polite and gave us the directions we needed. Victoria is probably the most English city in North America.

Victoria British Columbia Canada

From Victoria, we had a long drive to beautiful **Vancouver**. Even after our many returns to Vancouver, we still think that it is the most beautiful city in North America. It has everything one can hope for: a beautiful cosmopolitan city with a mixture of Asian and European immigrants, the sea, great mountains nearby for skiing and mountain climbing, excellent restaurants for any taste, lots of cultural activities and more. There are many great places in this world and it is wonderful to have the opportunity to see them.

Vancouver British Columbia Canada

We returned twice to Vancouver in 2007, once to go skiing in Whistler, about an hour drive from Vancouver, and the second time a few months later to sail to Alaska on the Ryndam of the Holland American line.

With Suzika and Richard skiing in Whistler British Columbia Canada 2007

S2. TENNESSEE

On New Year's Day of 1966, Vera and I (Michael stayed with Vera's parents) drove to **Knoxville** to take a look at the area and the University, where I had an offer for a faculty position. It is hard to say why we loved everything in Knoxville at first sight. Maybe it was the peace and quiet of a small hilly town of around 100,000, the beautiful surroundings, or that we just simply wanted to get out of Detroit. A few months after we moved to Knoxville a big riot erupted in Detroit; with looting and burning in a large part of the city. Unfortunately, there were lots of casualties. We felt very fortunate that we were out of the city and were safe.

Knoxville Tennessee, Market Square

Tennessee is a small southern state but as I was told it is like three different states joined together: East Tennessee where Knoxville is located, Central Tennessee with Nashville, and West Tennessee with Memphis. The locals insist that there are fundamental differences in scenery, politics, and even accents that I would not be able to differentiate. For example during the Civil War, East Tennessee was on the side of the Union while the other two parts seceded like the other southern states to become part of the Confederacy.

When we came to Knoxville in January 1966, we stayed at the home of the Breazeales and while I went for an interview with Dr. Nielsen, Joanne Breazeale drove Vera around the city to show her the different neighborhoods. Driving through an area called Sequoyah Hills, Joanne pointed out that this was the most desirable part of Knoxville where there were lots of very large beautiful mansions with very large gardens along Cherokee Boulevard parallel to the river. By sheer luck, we found a small 2-bedroom, 2-bathroom house in a small street off Cherokee Boulevard owned by a professor which he rented to us for $115 a month. So, we moved into 4206 Taliluna Avenue as our first residence in the best part of Knoxville.

Snow at 4206 Taliluna Avenue, Knoxville Tennessee, our first house

My teaching in the Physics Department started very smoothly. By now I had several years of teaching experience and I felt very confident teaching courses to sophomore engineering students, as well as to premed students, most of whom were juniors or seniors. I continued to enjoy teaching and even though they were mostly Southern students with their very special Tennessean drawl, I had no problem getting across to them not only the concepts of physics but also some old Hungarian jokes, all with positive responses.

In my first student evaluation (at the University of Tennessee each year a book of student evaluations of the teaching faculty was published) one of the comments was "he is a good teacher with a good sense of humor, but with a strong Eastern European accent". After reading the comments which were sent to me before publication, I walked into the class pretending that I was very angry and said, "This is not true; it is a lie; I don't have an Eastern European accent! Hungary is in Central Europe!" They enjoyed that comment.

My main problem was with the premed students who needed an A in their science classes including physics to get into medical school. I had about 45 students in my class and it was impossible to give A to every student. There was very fierce competition among them for the A. They tried to memorize everything I said, sometimes without thinking. Even when I quoted some laws of physics and accidentally left out a verb because the Hungarian language can have a sentence without verbs, they would memorize it that way.

In addition to my teaching, I was involved with research in Ultrasonics. After receiving my Ph.D. I stayed in the Physics Department at UT, the University of Tennessee, for thirteen years as an Associate Professor until 1980, when I was offered a full professorship at Ohio State University.

In the Ultrasonic Laboratory at UT

Living in the most exclusive part in Knoxville in Sequoyah Hills was very pleasant even though we had rented one of the least expensive houses in the area for $115. The house, built for an invalid lady and her nurse, had two bedrooms and two bathrooms, which was more than adequate for our little family of four. Besides, we had a screened patio where the children could play in rainy weather and where we ate most of our meals looking out at the dogwood tree in our backyard. Knoxville is known for its beautiful dogwood trees and its spring Dogwood Festival. We were all very content living in Knoxville.

Vera with Michael and Suzika under our dogwood tree in Knoxville (1968)

We even started to have visitors from the North or from Canada. Vera's parents came from Toronto mostly to escape the severe winter there. Knoxville rarely had snow and when it snowed all activity stops in the city. The schools are closed and no one dares to drive in the hilly parts of town.

We managed to have sometimes as many as 8-10 of us without any problem in our two-bedroom home. People loved to come to Knoxville. It was quite an attractive area, a short drive to the Smoky Mountains, where we picnicked almost every weekend during the nice weather. We either barbequed or took some cold fried chicken and potato salad followed by watermelon which we cooled in the running water of the creeks. It was always fun. On our way back from the Smokies we always stopped in Gatlinburg which we enjoyed although it was a rather touristic place.

Gatlinburg, Tennessee at the foot of the Great Smoky Mountains

A turning point in our life was when the landlord, the professor who rented us 4206 Taliluna, told us all of a sudden that he wanted to sell the house. I guess he was somewhat annoyed by the fact that the cost of repairs to the house was deducted from the rent, although this was his suggestion from the start. Since he didn't get much income from the rental he decided to sell and asked us if we had any interest in buying it. Not having any cash, it was difficult to imagine how we could even think of buying a house.

I often thought of how my parents, Vera's parents and so many others in Europe lost everything they owned, first to the Nazis in 1944 and later in the 1950s to the Communists, and I was sure that we never wanted to own any property. On the other hand, we did not feel like moving away from Sequoyah Hills, especially when our landlord offered us a super deal. We had already lived for a year in the house, so he said he would take the money paid for rent, approximately $1300, as the down payment on the house and sell us the house for $13,000. When we went to the bank and applied for a $13,000 mortgage, we were able to tell the bank that we could pay a 10% down payment. We got the mortgage approved and with taxes and insurance, our monthly payment was about the same as we used to pay for rent. So, we bought our first house without paying a penny. Only in America!

I also started to do some consulting in the nearby Oak Ridge National Laboratories, one of the most prestigious research laboratories established during the Manhattan Project when the first nuclear reactor was built in Oak Ridge. Vera enrolled in the University where she studied mathematics and computer science but eventually decided to open a retail store selling leather apparel, under the name of "Susane Suede and Leather Fashions". During the next several years she opened several more stores in Tennessee and in Ohio.

Susane Suede and Leather Fashions, Knoxville Tennessee

Life started to be easier and we did lots of traveling in the USA, to New York, California, and Maine. We also took the children to Hungary, to Israel, and other places. The children attended a private nursery school called Theakston Corner where we socialized with their friends' parents and they made lots of friends with the other kids. They were happy with our new Oldsmobile which they called Henry.

Michael and Suzika with our new Oldsmobile "Henry". (1970)

Barbecue Spare Ribs

Serves 6

Ingredients:

10 lb. of babyback spare ribs

Barbecue sauce of your choice

Directions:

1. Preheat oven to 350 degrees

2. In a heavy dutch oven place the spare ribs. Cover tightly with aluminum foil and place the lid on top of the foil.

3. Bake for two and half three hours until the meat is tender.

4. Carefully pour off all the liquids from the meat and generously cover the meat with barbecue sauce on both sides.

5. Cover with lid and bake another 46 minutes to an hour. Serve.

We had another addition to our family, a Collie, whom the kids called Rocky but we sometimes called him *Rakoczi bacsi* "Uncle Rakoczi" after Rakoczi, a famous Hungarian statesman. Rocky was a very gentle outdoor dog. The only time he came inside the house, was during a thunderstorm with lightning. Rocky was no hero! He was the favorite of my Aunt Manci who came to visit us often from Hungary.

Manci with "Rakoczi bacsi"

It was a great satisfaction coming back to the University of Tennessee in April 2017, to receive the Distinguished Alumni Award. Vera and I had three fun days in Knoxville, spending time with my cousin Agi and her family, and revisiting the city where we lived for more than 13 years.

Honors Day 2017

The physics department hosted the annual honors day ceremonies April 24, recognizing a distinguished alumnus, outstanding students, and the teacher of the year.

Dr. Laszlo Adler won this year's **Distinguished Alumni Award** "for his outstanding contributions to ultrasonics, nondestructive evaluation, and materials characterization." A 1969 PhD graduate, Adler was part of the physics faculty and also enjoyed a long and fruitful tenure as a consultant at Oak Ridge National Laboratory. He then joined the faculty at the Ohio State University, holding chaired professorships in in the departments of Welding Engineering and Engineering Mechanics. He developed OSU's interdisciplinary graduate program on nondestructive evaluation: the first such program in the United States. In 1993, he won Ohio State's Distinguished Scholar Award. Read more about Laszlo Adler and his life and career in the alumnus profile beginning on page five.

Physics Awards

Professor and Department Head Hanno Weitering (left) presents Laszlo Adler (PhD, 1969) with the 2017 Distinguished Alumni Award.

From the Newsletter of the University of Tennessee Physics Department

S3. NEW YORK

By the Fall of 1959, I was ready to take a trip to **New York City**. I had several friends from Debrecen who lived there, also my father's cousin, Uncle Moritz who left Slovakia after WW 1, had some furniture factories and stores in New York. One of the reasons I wanted to go to New York was to take a break in my research at Michigan State University and perhaps work for a couple of months in Uncle Moritz's shops since I knew some carpentry. Uncle Moritz was very nice but it was clear that he could not offer me any job.

Before coming to New York, I was told many times that life in New York is the basis of life in the USA, and it is where America gets its major influences. After living in the Midwest for more than two years, I concluded that in New York City you can experience the preservation of European customs and this is quite different from what main-stream America is all about.

Accordingly, as a "Midwesterner", I realized that my "New Yorker" friends did not know America like I did. When I talked about football and taught them the slogan which I learned to cheer the colors of the Spartans, the MSU football team at Michigan State football games, *"let's have a green, let's have a white, let's fight!"*, they thought of soccer, called "football" in Europe. In Michigan I enjoyed eating a good T-bone steak, medium rare (when I had the money) and singing with my buddies in East Lansing *"I've been working in the railroad"*, but in New York, we ate stuffed cabbage and listened to Gypsy music in a Hungarian restaurant, or listened to the Yiddish song "Rumania, Rumania" and ate *mamaliga* in a Romanian Jewish restaurant. Even today most Hungarians will not touch a bloody steak but eat it very well done when it is completely dried out like shoe leather.

I was very happy that I came and enjoyed all dishes that I had not eaten for some time which made me feel like I was back in Europe. I loved eating good crusty bread rather than the soft spongy sliced white bread, the only kind you could get in Michigan at that time. Things have changed significantly in the last few decades, and the rest of America has become more European, so now you can get very good crusty bread everywhere. I stayed in Brooklyn for a week in the home of an older couple, Sanyi bacsi and Ica neni, the parents of my friend from Debrecen. They were more like family to me and gave me the royal treatment.

When Vera and I got married on January 6, 1963, we decided to spend our honeymoon in New York City, and even though everybody suggested Florida. We stayed at a Holiday Inn on Amsterdam Avenue and had a great time for 10 days. We knew that we made the right choice. We saw Broadway shows like *"Little Me"* with Sid Cesar, one of the best comedians ever, and the musical *"The Land of Milk and Honey"* with Molly Picon, a great actress. We also enjoyed many good restaurants and even tried French food for the first time. We spent enjoyable evenings, ate great food, listened to good music, and danced in the Latin Quarter. No question about it! New York may not be typically American but one can find anything there.

Latin Quarter, New York City 1963

When Vera first started her leather goods business in 1971 in Knoxville, she was in partnership with Sanyi bacsi, who already had a similar store, *Alex Leather and Suede*, in the Village on Sixth Ave.

Sanyi bacsi's store, "Alex" on 6th Ave in New York City

We used to come to New York several times a year, to buy goods in the Javitz Center where wholesalers from all around the world showed their products. We combined these "necessities with pleasures", as the Hungarian saying goes *"ossze kottotuk a kellemest a hasznossal"*, and went to see several Broadway shows and discovered new restaurants. We normally would stay for 3-4 days in the Waldorf Astoria which at that time was the same price as the Hilton. We preferred the unique Waldorf which was the tallest hotel in the world when it was completed in 1931.

Waldorf Astoria on Park Avenue New York City

During the summer we used to go to Fire Island for a vacation with our children. We would drive from Knoxville to New York City to spend a few days before we took off to Fire Island. The children loved Radio City in the city. Once when we drove to Bayshore from where we had to take a ferry to a town called Seaview in Fire Island, and not knowing any better I left my car at a parking meter for ten days. By the time we returned to Bayshore, our car a 300 Mercedes Diesel, was not there anymore. When I called the Police, I was told that the car had been towed away because I parked illegally, and I had to pay a $180 fine (a lot of money in 1977!). On top of that, it cost another $55 for a taxi to a town 25 miles away to pick up our car. It was an expensive lesson but we still had a wonderful vacation and enjoyed the best seafood restaurants and beautiful beaches. Sanyi bacsi and Ica neni had a house there but we rented a house at Seaview together with my friend Poncike from Montreal who came with his wife and with his two boys to join us on vacation.

Sanyi bacsi, Vera, Ica neni and me

Probably the most exciting trip we ever made to New York was for our participation in the 1986 New York Marathon on October 31st,

1986 when six of us took a flight to New York City. Vera and I, my co-worker Peter Nagy, my students Wade Rose and Mike Mayes, and Mike's wife were all ready for the challenge. We all six had already registered for the New York Marathon months before so we avoided the elaborate registration process. The number of participants was limited to 21,000 in 1986, many less than the 53,627 finishers in the 2019 NYC Marathon.

Most of the registrants stayed at the Sheraton Hotel in Manhattan. The race was scheduled to start from Staten Island at the Verrazano Bridge on Sunday the 2nd of November at 11:00 am. On Friday evening, we went out with Sanyi bacsi and Ica neni to Gino's, their favorite Italian restaurant in Greenwich Village. The next day Saturday we just did an easy run of a few miles in nearby Central Park. We had loaded up early with a high carb dinner of gnocchi so we could have a good night's sleep.

Early in the morning on Sunday, we were taken out to Staten Island by the busses organized for the event. It was a rainy day so the runners stayed in a large tent to keep dry. Luckily, by 10 or so the rain stopped and the 20,000 plus people were ready to start their challenge. It is hard to explain the excitement we all felt. Even after running three Marathons in Columbus, it was quite different to participate in one of the largest events in the big metropolis. Hundreds and thousands of people were lined up along the route of the Marathon to observe and to cheer on the runners.

Map of the New York City Marathon Race on November 2, 1986

The race passes through all the boroughs where we were entertained by their different ethnic groups. Running through Williamsburg in Brooklyn, many of the Chasidic youngsters were singing and dancing to cheer on the runners. In Harlem, we were serenaded by alternating Latin and Soul musical groups, and it continued like this with many Jazz bands and western music in other areas. The 26-mile run was not easy (It is never easy!) but it certainly was a very colorful race.

Vera in the New York City Marathon drinking orange juice handed to her by a good friend

Benjamin Balshone (1986)

As we arrived at Central Park for the finish, we knew that lots of the star runners had already finished a couple of hours earlier than we did, but we still felt great because of our achievement. Vera finished in 3 hours 53 minutes and as always, I came in later at 4 hours 33 minutes. All six of us from Ohio State University finished. It was a wonderful day so Vera and I celebrated our event with dinner the next day at Le Bernardin, the well-known seafood restaurant in Manhattan. We knew the owners of Le Bernardin and had followed their success from Paris to New York.

While in Paris where I spent my Sabbatical at University Paris 7, I had read very good reviews about a small seafood restaurant across from the Notre Dame in Paris so we thought it would be a good place to try. We made reservations and Vera and I dined there with Mike Buckley the program manager of DARPA and his wife, who were visiting Paris in 1980. It turned out that we all had an excellent meal.

While dining at Le Bernardin, Mike assured me that it would be no problem to transfer my DARPA funding from UT to OSU, where I was going to work. After our meal, the owners, Gilbert and Maguy Le Coze, a very good-looking young couple joined us for a drink. We found out that they were siblings and were raised in a fishing village in Southern France. They opened their first restaurant in 1972 and 1982, they moved close to Etoile in the 17th Arrondissement where they opened a very fashionable restaurant which became one of the highly rated and much more expensive restaurants than the small one near Notre Dame.

Interestingly, in the early 1980s, we were invited for dinner at Bob and Ann Revesz's place in Ile Saint Louis. The Reveszes were our close friends from Columbus who for over 25 years every September for a month rented the same apartment in Ile Saint Louis where we again met Gilbert and Maguy who were also guests of the Reveszes. In 1986, the siblings moved to Manhattan and opened Le Bernardin on 51st Street and it became an instant success. Vera and I dined there that same year in November, the day after we finished the New York Marathon.

Unfortunately, Gilbert died of a heart attack in his early 40 s and Maguy has continued to run the restaurant alone. Today, Le Bernardin is listed among the 10-best restaurants in New York.

Le Bernardin in Manhattan

Our friends in Florida, Janie and Marty have a very nice two-bedroom apartment in Manhattan. For the last several years, they have spent their vacations in Paris staying in our place at 42 Rue Vaneau and in return, we stayed in their apartment in Manhattan. Their apartment is large enough so Susan and family can spend a week with us there also. Hannah and Talia love New York and it is always a happy time to share this exciting city with them. We love to go to the Metropolitan Opera and have seen at least 20 operas in the last 10 years. One can get cheap tickets a couple of hours before the performance starts.

After thirty years, I finally connected with two of my childhood friends from Debrecen, nagy Donci (Tibi Gross) and kis Donci (Gabor Gross). It was a happy reunion in Tibi's home where we even took Hannah with us. Unfortunately, Tibi was not in good health but still enjoyed reconnecting after so many years. From then on, we have kept our contact alive through telephone, e-mails, and with our visits. Gabor and his wife Judith always go out of their way to make our stay in New York pleasant. They always drive us around and fill up our refrigerator with Hungarian goodies. After my dear friend Tibi passed away, we continue to see his wife Agi together with Judith and Gabor who spent the 2020 New Year with us in Florida.

With Judith and Gabor in Florida, Jan 1, 2020

S4. CALIFORNIA

In the fall of 1972, I was invited to participate in a workshop at the Rockwell Science Center in **Thousand Oaks, California**. It was organized by the National Science Foundation, the Airforce, and Darpa. The aim of the workshop was to start a national program for an interdisciplinary field of **Nondestructive Evaluation**, which would include a dozen universities and few national laboratories. I flew to **Los Angeles** and drove to Thousand Oaks, a town in Ventura County about an hour's drive from the LA airport. This was my second trip to California, but my first to Los Angeles. In 1969 I attended an Acoustic Conference in San Diego. I knew quite a few people at the prestigious Rockwell Science center.

I had another mission while I was in California, that of visiting my childhood friend George Bozoki, who lived in the Bay Area. I had several childhood friends named George; this one and I went to kindergarten and all through elementary school and high school together. We came to the USA together and had many more ties over the years. George got his Ph.D. from Purdue in Operations Research, a specialized area in industrial engineering, and after spending a couple of years at Stanford, he got a faculty position at Sacramento State University. Eventually, he landed at the Lockheed Space Division as Chief Engineer. I had never been to the Bay Area before and was charmed by beautiful **San Francisco** so it was very nice to visit there and spend a few days together.

In the summer of 1974, I had a presentation at the QNDE meeting in Thousand Oaks and I took the opportunity to bring my family to California for a little vacation. In addition to Vera and the children, my aunt Manci, who visited us from Hungary in Knoxville, came along on the trip. We reserved a lovely hotel in nearby Malibu so I had to drive through the Canyons to Thousand Oaks to participate in the meeting. We took the cheapest flight, the "red-eye" special since we still had limited finances and five flight tickets were not so cheap. We arrived at 4 a.m. and had to drive around for several hours since we could not check into our motel in Malibu until noon. Despite this inconvenience, we all enjoyed our stay in Malibu and the surrounding area. My family even participated at the barbecue party organized by Don Thompson in his back yard for the participants of the meeting and their families. It was an informal atmosphere and continued that way through the years.

We extended our vacation by driving north from Thousand Oaks along the coast, stopping in Solvang, a picturesque Danish village, and at the Hearst Castle and Monterey before getting to San Francisco.

Solvang, a Danish Village in California

My friend Janos Balog, who was practicing medicine in San Francisco, had a pretty large apartment in the Embarcadero, which was available for us since Janos and his family were vacationing in Santa Barbara. Janos and his family were very close to us and stayed with us in Flint, Michigan for several weeks when Janos, his wife and their three little children arrived from Frankfurt in 1963.

We spent a few wonderful days in the city of San Francisco, sightseeing and enjoying the many wonderful restaurants. In one of the Greek restaurants where there was great music and dancing, we all participated in the Greek circle dances. By 11 PM when we were trying to go home, my daughter Suzika was upset and complained, "I'm having the best time of my life and you spoil it by not letting me stay". She was only seven years old and normally very shy but evidently, the music and dancing fired up her spirit. We stayed until midnight. Music and dancing have always played a big role in our family and still do.

I always took my family to the La Jolla meetings because everyone enjoyed them. In 1982, we decided to combine our trip to the meeting with a California vacation along with several of my childhood friends and their families. I registered my friends as attendees so this way they all got inexpensive housing on the University of California campus where the conference was held. Both adults and children enjoyed the week spent on the beautiful beaches of La Jolla. One of our most memorable dining took place in The Marine Room.

The Marine Room in La Jolla

We also went to the old city of San Diego to dine in the many Mexican restaurants and enjoy the Mariachi bands. After my co-workers and I presented our lectures at the meeting, all of us drove to San Francisco to spend a few more days with our friends who lived there. It was a memorable 10 days for all of us.

With friends in a San Francisco restaurant invited by Janos. (1982).

At the 1984 QNDE meeting in La Jolla the manager of the NDE group at Sandia National Laboratory, in Livermore California asked me if I could do some consulting for them. I agreed and a few weeks later I flew

192

to San Francisco and stayed with Janos Balog and family who lived in the Embarcadero close to the Oakland Bridge. I liked the idea of going regularly to San Francisco and spending some time with my friends Janos and George Bozoki.

Steve Szasz who had gotten tired of the ups and downs of our involvement in construction in Toronto talked about the possibility of moving to San Francisco to start a new construction business with our joint financial backing. Coincidentally, Steve was in San Francisco at the same time when I went to Sandia to consult and we looked around to see what might be the options. Livermore was a good 45 minutes to an hour drive from San Francisco where both Sandia National Laboratory and the Lawrence Livermore Laboratory were housed. On my first visit to Sandia, the manager of Lawrence Livermore came over to Sandia and asked me to do some consulting for them also. Lawrence Livermore did much more basic research than Sandia so it was more attractive to me but I figured I could kill two flies at the same time as the Hungarian proverb goes "*ket legyet egy csapasra*". It was quite exciting. Back in San Francisco, Janos told me that he was ready to buy a small apartment under construction across the Oakland Bridge in **Emeryville** and asked if I might be interested in doing so also. We went to visit the almost completed complex called Pacific Park Plaza. The agent showed me a one-bedroom one-and-a-half-bathroom apartment. It had a beautiful view of the whole city of San Francisco from the windows. The only catch was that it was on the 13th floor and the apartment number was also **13**. I have never been superstitious and always make quick decisions so I wrote a check right away for $3000, the down payment for the $168,000 purchase of apartment 13-13. I figured that with the two consulting jobs in Livermore and the potential for the construction business we had to put our foot into the Bay area. Besides, the real estate lady assured me that there was a big demand for rental in the area so I could not go wrong. Well, not quite so.

The first blow came after two weeks of me signing the contract when I discovered that they lowered the price of the condos by twenty thousand dollars, so if I had waited two weeks to buy, I could have bought the same apartment for twenty thousand dollars less than what I had committed to already, but of course, now my down payment would not apply to a new purchase. Next, Steve decided that with our limited resources there was no potential for our construction business in San Francisco. Still, I had the consulting jobs in Sandia and Livermore, and when the construction was finished, we closed the contract and ended up with monthly expenses of $1600 including mortgage, taxes, and condominium fees.

When I went to talk to the real estate lady and told her that we wanted to rent the place, she eventually got us a renter who paid $800 a month but the first month's rent went to the agent. So we had to pay the difference and after six months, the lady who lived in the condo died and the condo had to be rented again and the first month's rent once again went to the real estate lady. So, to make a long story short 13-13 was one of the worst investments we have ever made. After 10 years when we sold it for the same price that we paid for it, we ended up with a huge amount for a tax deduction. I still don't think that the number 13 was the problem.

Our apartment #13, on the 13th floor at Pacific Park Plaza, Emeryville California

A few months before our 15th QNDE meeting in La Jolla in 1988, I had the idea of injecting a little more fun into the meeting by introducing a 5K fun race. The people at Iowa State University who were working on the details of the yearly conference thought that it was a good idea. About 40 people signed up for the first 5K FUN Run held the day before the conference ended.

The organizers even arranged for nice T-shirts for all the runners at $15 each with drawings of all kinds of QNDE (quantitative non-destructive evaluation) techniques printed on the front. The colors and the designs of the shirts changed yearly. In addition to Vera and me, Michael and quite a few other people from our OSU group participated in the race. I was the director of the race but came in far behind the winners. Vera however got first prize among the women. Peter Nagy proved that he is not only an excellent scientist but also a good runner by taking first place in the race. Kent Lewis on the other hand, who by then he had received the first Ph.D. in the NDE Program from Ohio State University in 1986, came in last smoking a cigarette! The 5K Fun Run continued to be a tradition and has been held every year after 1988 at the QNDE meeting.

The first 5 K fun run in La Jolla (1988)

In 1993, Suzika was transferred to **Santa Barbara** by her company, E.F. (Education First) to be the regional manager of the company's western operation. During the next three years, we visited her many times in this colorful city before she was promoted to a higher position, that of Vice President of Sales and Marketing for Latin America.

Downtown Santa Barbara California

Vera and I went to the Lake Tahoe area a few times to ski with my friend George Bozoki who had a very spacious house at Tahoe Vista. Skiing was quite different there than in Colorado.

With George Bozoki at Lake Tahoe, California 2002

After our skiing trip, we also visited our friends Janos and Eva in San Francisco. We went to see a beautiful performance at the San Francisco Opera of *Fidelio*, the only opera composed by Beethoven. After the performance, we were served a super gourmet dinner in the Opera House.

Opera House in San Francisco

Unfortunately, in 2009, both George and Janos passed away in California, and Poncike another of my close friends also died in the same year in Montreal. The bad thing about getting older is that many of your friends are no longer around.

13. BRAZIL

In 1977, we extended our trip to Madrid by adding a couple of "stopovers". In addition to the 9th ICA meeting in Madrid, I also had another invitation to the Technion in Israel to participate in a research project activity. We decided to make our trip via **Rio de Janeiro**, Brazil, Johannesburg, South Africa, and then Israel before going to Madrid. This somewhat elaborate travel plan was ingeniously handled by our lady travel agent in Knoxville.

We took our flight from Miami to Rio with Varig Air, a Brazilian airline company. This was our first visit to Latin America and as the taxi was taking us to our hotel, we were shocked by the favelas (shanty towns) where people lived in unbelievable poverty. On a future trip, we saw much worse in Honduras.

Favelas in Rio de Janeiro

Later we learned that most of those gorgeous samba dancers who participate in the week-long carnival in February come from these slums. These poor working girls save most of their income to be dressed in glamorous costumes, to maybe try to forget their misery by dancing the samba during the festivities. The contrast between the depressed suburbs and the resort communities was overwhelming. Anyway, a couple of years later we came back to participate in the Carnival.

Girls dressed for the Carnival in Rio de Janeiro Brazil

The beautiful luxurious Ouro Verde hotel, a small hotel owned by a Swiss Company on the beautiful Copacabana beach, was better than we expected. The restaurant in this small hotel was listed among the top ten restaurants in the world.

Ouro Verde Hotel on the Cobacabana Beach

We spent a wonderful week in Rio. The sunshine, the beach, the great restaurants, the music, the dancing; we liked everything. A typical day started by our getting up late and going down to the beautiful Copacabana or Ipanema Beach where we did our 5-6 miles of running before we jumped into the water. Then we stayed around the beach for most of the day.

Copacabana Beach Rio de Janeiro, Brazil

Every night we picked a restaurant out of the many available, and like most of the locals, we usually started our supper around 10 or 11 in the evening. The first night when we went out to eat around 9 pm, the restaurant was completely empty because no one eats that early in the Latin countries. We learned this quickly in Rio and the lesson was also useful later on in Madrid.

After supper, we hopped from one dance club to another. Music and dancing are a major part of life in Brazil and we lived it up for the whole time we were there. The Carnival in February is the main event in Rio; we returned a couple of years later to participate in this Brazilian phenomenon. But the Brazilians don't wait for it, and whenever and everywhere you go, the nightclubs, the beaches, the streets, even the slums are full of music day and night. It was remarkable for us to see single women get up from their table in a night club or restaurant and dance alone just to enjoy it. In general, people are much more comfortable with themselves than in the US or Europe.

On the beaches, there are not only the many beautiful girls in bikinis, but there are also older women, skinny women, and fat women who all seemed to feel rather comfortable in bathing suits. By the time we got back to our hotel from the nightly entertainments, it was almost morning and we sat out on our balcony facing the beach and watched the sunrise as we had our breakfast which included many exotic fruits like papaya, mango, passion fruit, and others.

After breakfast, we closed our blinds and were ready to call it a day. We started over again in the afternoon. Although we had a wonderful time in Rio, we were disturbed by the scene of many young children hanging around at night, walking from table to table in the outdoor cafes trying to get a few pennies by shining people's shoes. We know that this problem of injustice exists all over the Latin American countries, just as everywhere else in the world. Nevertheless, we decided to return to the Carnival one day

That happened two years later. In February 1979 we flew from Miami to Rio again on Varig Airlines. At that time there was no restriction on smoking, not even cigar smoking on the Brazilian Airline. This affected me on the plane the day after a nice late evening dinner. When I tried to bend down to pick up something from the floor, I passed out. It was probably the combination of my low blood pressure and the heavy cigar smoke. First Vera thought that I was joking which would have been a stupid joke even though I had a history along that line. But when she realized that I was unconscious, she started to get worried and with the help of some other friends on the plane, she woke me up.

Besides this episode, everything was just perfect. We returned to the Ouro Verde, the same hotel on Copacabana Beach where we had stayed in 1977, and enjoyed the week's festivity with the Brazilians. The music, the dancing, the great food made it an unforgettable experience. One of the highlights of our stay was the celebration of the Grand Ball, held at the City Hall in Rio. It was quite expensive so we could compare how the "high society" differed from the masses in their celebration of the Carnival.

At the Grand Ball in the Rio de Janeiro Carnival (1979)

We were not only in the elegant Grand Ball but also in the popular street carnival, which lasted all night for several days and was much more colorful than the said ball. Hundreds of groups of performers in the most extravagant costumes danced the samba on the streets along with hundreds of thousands of spectators. It was an experience of a lifetime.

Carnival in Rio de Janeiro

14. ARGENTINA

While we were in Rio de Janeiro in 1979, we decided to take a three-day side trip from Rio to **Buenos Aires**, a very European city, which is much more like Madrid or Rome with its wide boulevards and fashionable stores. We were very impressed by the quality of the Argentinian steak and we are still dreaming about our meal in La Cabaña restaurant where the steak melted in your mouth like butter even though it was not even aged.

We looked up some old friends from Debrecen who had settled in the city after WW 2 and we also met Margarita's sister Fanny, who is a native of the city. We found it interesting that although about 400,000 Jews lived in Argentina in the early 20th century, no Jews could enter the country legally as immigrants but somehow, they managed! For entertainment, we went with our friends to some of the well-known tango places but we found the tango music, the elaborate dance steps, and the seriousness of the dancers to be a rather strange combination for us.

Vera and I were in Argentina for the 22nd ICA conference. It was our second time since our earlier visit to this beautiful city in 1979. We had lots of nice memories from that trip and we were happy to return in 2016. This time Conference was at Puerto Madero, a revamped dockside area. Its converted red brick buildings contain upscale steakhouses and many other entertainment venues popular with tourists, as well as the Catholic University of Argentina that was the location of the Conference. We stayed at the beautiful Madero Hotel across from the University.

Puerto Madero in Buenos Aires

202

The University is in the red building among the many buildings along Puerto Madero

The area has been restored in the last few years and is now very fashionable with expensive condominiums in high-rise buildings. We revisited some of the restaurants like La Cabaña, which we knew before it moved from the center of Buenos Aires to Puerto Madero. It was a disappointment this time. The steak did not melt in your mouth like thirty years earlier. Maybe it is the fault of the mouth! On the other hand, we discovered many new faces of the city this time around. The Sunday antique show with hundreds and hundreds of displays, and La Boca, the colorful neighborhood once almost exclusively populated with Italian immigrants.

La Boca in Buenos Aires

A sad sight in Buenos Aires are the demonstrations of the mothers carrying placards with photos of their children with the legend "Where are they?" After many years, they are still hoping to get information on their children who disappeared during the military dictatorship of the 60s and 70s.

15. URUGUAY

We took a one-day boat trip to **Colonia** in Uruguay across from Buenos Aires, a historic 17th-century town from the time of Portuguese rule. It was well worth it to see the preserved colonial scene and to have a very good lunch there.

Colonia a historic town in Uruguay

16. SOUTH AFRICA

My cousin Agi and her husband Avishai were waiting for us at the airport when we arrived to **Johannesburg** from Rio in 1977. They had lived there for a couple of years and to visit them was one of the reasons we went there in the first place. South Africa was still under the apartheid system and one could sense it from the moment of arrival. Apartheid means a state of separation or "apart-hood" in Dutch or Afrikaner. It was instituted by the South African Congress in 1948. It divides the country into four segregated groups: Black, White, Colored, and Indian. Housing and neighborhoods were completely segregated as well as the educational and medical systems. It was rather strange to see that black people were treated like they were invisible. When a black maid entered a room, people would not even turn their heads toward her.

Otherwise, we had a very pleasant few days in the city. Our host and hostess made sure that we had the best exposure to the city's highlights, both cultural and culinary. Since we both were long-distance runners, we were warned that Johannesburg was 7000 ft. above sea level. We must have been in good condition because the altitude did not affect our 5-6 miles daily runs. One of the most memorable events was the musical performance of the black residents with their beautiful costumes and dancing, called Ipi Tombi (roughly translated as "where is the girl?" in Zulu). We enjoyed it very much and the children all learned many songs from the recordings that we brought back for them.

Ipi Tombi Dancers and Singers in Johannesburg

17. SPAIN

In 1977 after spending a week in Rio de Janeiro and a few days in Johannesburg, Vera and I stopped in Israel on our way to Madrid. Our flight to Madrid from Tel Aviv was scheduled to leave on Sunday in the early afternoon. My presentation at the 9th ICA meeting in Madrid was set for Monday at 10 AM. On Sunday morning Mari, my cousin Sanyi's wife, woke me up to inform us that our Lufthansa flight from Tel Aviv to Madrid was canceled. We were rescheduled to an Air Italia flight to Rome in the evening and had to stay overnight there because our flight from Rome to Madrid was not until Monday morning. The news hit me right away that I would not be at the Conference in time to give my presentation which was the main reason for our elaborate trip. I called the airline and tried to explain my situation, but there was nothing that could be done.

Our plane landed in Madrid Monday at 10 AM exactly the time scheduled for my presentation at the 9th International Conference in Acoustics. It was clear that I could not be in two places at the same time, so I accepted the fact that I had missed my talk. By the time we got to our hotel, the 5-star Euro Building, it was close to noon.

However, when we got out of our taxi, I saw some people coming to the hotel from the conference site. I tried to explain to one of them who greeted me why I missed my presentation in the morning. To my surprise, he said, "No problem, the morning sessions were rescheduled for the afternoon, because King Juan who was supposed to speak at the opening ceremony of the Conference was late." I am still grateful to Juan.

During my presentation in the Physical Acoustics session, the slide projector broke down but this was certainly not Juan's fault. Spain in the 70s was more like a third world country and lacked many modern developments like workable slide projectors. Luckily, I had only two slides left to summarize my work, which I could just explain without the slides. The next speaker, who happened to be Michel de Billy from Université Paris 7, was not so lucky. He had to give his presentation in French without his slides, not an easy task. For years since then, we have told and retold with Michel our experiences in the Madrid conference of the ICA.

In the 1970s, Spain was still feeling the influence of more than three decades of the Franco era. As a teenager, very few historical events interested and affected me more than the Spanish Civil War. I read numerous books, saw several films, and learned many songs like "the brigade of a thousand languages but one heart", all about the glorious fight of the Spanish Republic against the overwhelming and powerful Fascist Falangists, led by Generalissimo Franco and supported by both the Italians and the Germans.

The Second Spanish Republic (the 1st Spanish Republic was formed in the 19th century) came to power in 1931 by winning an absolute majority in a democratic election with a joint coalition of Republicans, Socialists, Communists, Catalans and other splinter factions. The Falangists, supported by the powerful Catholic Church, rebelled against the Republic and a bloody civil war started which lasted from 1936 to 1939.

Although the Fascist countries helped the Falangists both with manpower and ammunition, the Western powers like England and France "stayed neutral" and effectively abandoned the legal government. The most significant help to the Republic came only from the thousands of volunteers from many countries all around the world, the so-called International Brigade. But their brave support was not sufficient and the Republic was defeated allowing Franco to rule Spain for over 30 years. After World War 2, because of the Fascist dictatorship of Franco, Spain was isolated which resulted in a very poor economy, a very low standard of living, and widespread suppressed unrest.

By the time of our conference even though Franco was dead and King Juan had acceded to power, Spain still suffered the consequences of Franco's political and social ideology. Most women were wearing unfashionable black dresses and even the streets were dark and unappealing. The sidewalks were in terrible condition causing unfortunate accidents for several of the participants of the Conference. Our close friend Joanne Breazeale broke her shoulder by falling on the street in Madrid. Mack Breazeale believed that an excessive dosage of X-rays resulted in Joanne's cancer and her early death.

Banquet at the ICA meeting in Madrid (1977)

Our conference was very well organized. We had a beautiful banquet, great food and entertainment with Flamenco dancers. We enjoyed sharing the local restaurants and night clubs with several old and new friends.

At a Flamenco Dance Club in Madrid. (1977)

By now I knew quite a few colleagues from many different countries and received many invitations during the conference which we followed up later. Among the colleagues were Oswald Leroy from the University of Leuven, Kortrijk Belgium, whom I had met in Budapest six years earlier; Professor Holler from Saarbrucken Germany, the Director of the largest non-destructive testing institute in Europe (Zehrstorungsfreien Werkstoffprufung); Michel de Billy who invited me to Paris on behalf of Gerard Quentin and so on.

While in Spain, Vera and I participated in organized tours to Avila, to Segovia, and to Toledo. Toledo impressed us most, especially the sight of the old synagogues which were transformed into Churches after the Inquisition. We also enjoyed an exhibit of the paintings by El Greco.

Synagogue in Toledo which was converted to a Church

In Madrid we spent quite a bit of time in the Prado, one of the best museums in Europe, learning about the Spanish painters, Velazquez, Goya and the more recent Picasso and Dali, etc.

Although the people in Spain were poor at the time of this visit, we were impressed by their honesty and hospitality. Once, when we were walking in Madrid, we decided to visit "El Corte Inglés", a department store which was well known to Vera for their leather goods. We walked to a taxi and asked the driver to take us there. To our surprise, he told us in broken English that there was no need to take a cab since the department store was just around the corner. We were so impressed by his honesty that we have repeated the story over and over to our friends.

In 1979 we made a business trip to Barcelona for Vera's store. Having been in Madrid two years earlier, we thought we knew enough of Spain not to expect anything new. We could not have been more wrong. It was way beyond our expectations. Barcelona is one of the most beautiful cities we have ever been in. Although we liked Madrid, Barcelona is so different from Madrid in every way: the location on the Mediterranean Sea; the cuisine; the architecture and so on. Even the language is different as a result of the history of the region of Catalonia. The Catalan language, which is different from Castellano, the official language of Spain, is the mother tongue of the Catalan people and has flourished anew despite having been forbidden under the dictator Franco in order to further oppress Barcelona for being 100% Republican.

The weather was beautiful and our host José, the US representative of one of the largest leather garment manufacturers in Spain was waiting for us at the airport. He and his wife took us to a very nice hotel near their home. José was a very kind Catalan gentleman, with a great sense of humor. He had visited us already in Knoxville several times. We dined in their home and were given a tour of the city during our stay. We were so impressed by the many beautiful and colorful buildings, mostly those designed by Gaudí who also designed the famous *Sagrada Familia* basilica, which was started in 1882 and is still not finished!

Sagrada Familia Basilica in Barcelona

We loved the many museums, the Miró Museum on Montjuic, and the beautiful views from the top of this mountain called the Jewish Mountain because it was the area occupied by the Jewish population. We had a great time in Barcelona. The owner of the factory took us out for dinner after we had visited the factory and we were delighted by the various cold cuts as appetizers, the tapas, and the variety of fish and seafood. Barcelona became one of our favorite cities and we return whenever we have a chance.

Suzika moved to Madrid in September 1987 to start her junior year there. She found a place in the home of a Spanish family headed by a lady by the name of Carmen (among many other ladies in Spain). She had six children and Suzika shared a room with one of the girls. In December, I had to be in Paris so I decided to stop on my way to Madrid to see Suzika. I stayed at the Hotel Eurobuilding, a 5-star hotel where we stayed ten years earlier.

Eurobuilding Hotel Madrid

Suzika and I had a lovely time together for the few days I stayed in Madrid. Carmen, who did not at all resemble the dancer from the Bizet's opera, invited me for dinner and made a huge bowl of paella. It was basically rice with one large clam on top. When all the hungry children wanted to grab the single clam, she hollered at Suzika, "No no, it is for *tu padre*!" (that was me). I felt sorry for the kids.

Vera's Paella

Serves 6

Ingredients:

2 cups uncooked Arborio rice

4 cups of chicken broth

½ lb. chorizo cut into ½ inch pieces

green pepper sliced

1 cup tomatoes chopped

A handful of chopped parsley

1 red bell pepper sliced

6 cloves of garlic smashed

1 yellow onion chopped

2 tbsp. olive oil

1 pinch saffron

½ Tbsp. red paprika

Salt and black pepper

15 shelled clams, washed

15 shelled mussels, washed

15 large shrimp, cleaned, deveined

Directions:

1. Brown the chorizo in a wok or paella pan on medium heat, remove the browned chorizo and place on a plate

2. In the wok, sauté e the chopped onion for few minutes adding one tbsp. of olive oil to the wok, add the smashed garlic, add the peppers, and after few minutes add the chopped tomatoes. Sprinkle with paprika, saffron add salt and black pepper to taste. Cook until all the vegetables soften about 10 minutes. Remove all vegetables from the wok and add to the chorizo.

3. Add another tbsp. of olive oil to the wok and pour in the rice and cook until the rice is transparent.

4. Add the vegetables and the chorizo to the rice and continue cooking for few minutes, mixing them well and add the 4 cups of chicken broth and the parsley and bring it to boil and then lower the heat to simmer, covered by a foil and let it cook for 10 minutes.

5. Place the clams on the top of the rice near the rim of the wok, cover it and cook for two minutes.

6. Uncover and add the mussels, and the shrimp and cook two more minutes covered.

7. After a few minutes check if all the shells are open. Serve

Suzika stayed with me in the hotel and one morning we went for a morning run (everyone runs in our family). When we returned, we found that my leather jacket, Suzika's portable radio, and a large sum of cash which we had left on the table was stolen. In fact, this was not the first 5-star hotel where things were stolen from me. It also happened in the Sacher Hotel in Vienna where they stole from my suitcase a gold bracelet which was sent to Vera by my aunt Manci. Later we had another situation in Vienna in the Intercontinental Hotel. We went with Suzika to the police station where she told them in excellent Spanish what had happened in the hotel. They were not too sympathetic, as it probably happened all the time. Despite the unpleasant experience we decided to move on and enjoy a great few day together.

We went to see some Flamenco dancers and walked a lot. But more than anything I was happy to see that my little girl was enjoying herself in Madrid even though she lived in Spartan conditions at Carmen's place.

Sobrino de Botin Restaurant Madrid   *Roasted piglet*

We went to one of Hemingway's favorite restaurants, the Sobrino de Botin, to eat suckling pig. On our return to the US, we arranged for a long overdue family portrait.

Our Family (1987)

In September 2002 we had a European Acoustical Society meeting in Seville, Spain. We decided to rent a car and drive from Paris to Seville. With the recommendations of some friends, we made arrangements in advance in hotels and in *Paradores*, the state-run hospitality enterprises in Spain, which are often in castles, palaces, fortresses, convents, monasteries, and other historic buildings. Our first stop was in Avila about 100 km north of Madrid. The old city of Avila has some of the best-preserved city walls in Spain and inside the walls, there is the Piedras Albas Palace, a Parador where we stayed for a day. This was our first experience in a Parador and it exceeded all of our expectations. It was a combination of a luxurious hotel and a historic setting.

We had visited Avila before in 1977 so we were familiar with most of the history so we only concentrated on a leisurely walk and a fabulous dining experience. Avila has its unique cuisine and we had one of the best veal steaks ever with a unique potato dish in paprika, which resembled a popular Hungarian dish called *paprikash krumpli*. We also had a very good bean dish, a kind of cross between the French cassoulet and the Jewish cholent.

Piedras Albas Palace, a Parador in Avila, Spain

We headed south from Avila and to avoid the traffic in Madrid, we did not drive through the city on our way to Cordova in Andalusia, one of the most picturesque cities we have ever seen

Cordova

In the Middle Ages, Cordova was one of the largest cities in Europe with over three hundred thousand people. It had a very significant Jewish presence at the time of the Moorish rule which attracted many intellectuals to the court. Many famous scholars were Cordovans, like Maimonides also known as *Rambam* who together with Rashi in France were the two most famous Jewish philosophers. Maimonides, an astronomer and physician was born in 1138 in Cordova. He died in Egypt but was buried in the city of Tiberias in Galilea. Another famous Jewish scholar in medieval Cordova was Hasfai Ibn Shaprut, doctor, diplomat, and scholar who served under the Moorish rulers. His family's subsequent wealth and power were major factors in the vibrant Jewish community during the height of the eminence of Cordova. Maimonides has been honored by having medical centers, such as the one in Brooklyn, New York named after him.

The statue of Maimonides in Cordova

After the Inquisition under Isabella and Ferdinand, the Jews and the Moors were expelled in 1492 from Cordova like everywhere else in Spain in order to preserve Catholic Orthodoxy. At the time of our arrival more than 500 years later, there was a revival of Jewish cultural heritage in Cordova. New synagogues, Jewish restaurants and stores have opened in the last few decades in the old Jewish Quarter called *La Juderia*.

In the evening we wanted to go to a good restaurant. Rather than choosing one randomly from a guide, we decided to follow a well-dressed couple to the restaurant of their choice. It worked out very well. We learned for example that there is a big difference between the gazpacho made in Andalusia, called Salmorejo, and that made in other places in Spain. We prefer the smooth creamy taste of the Andalusian one. We also had some excellent shellfish.

Andalusian Salmorejo

Serves 6

Ingredients:

1 lb. ripe tomatoes

2 slices of toasted bread

2 cloves of garlic

1 tsp. sherry vinegar

¼ cup olive oil

Salt

1 Hard-boiled egg

½ cup chopped crispy bacon

Directions:

1. In a blender puree the chopped tomatoes, toast, garlic, vinegar, and 1/3 cup of water for 2 minutes. Add the olive oil and continue to mix another 15 sec. Add salt to taste. Refrigerate.

2. Serve in a bowl. Sprinkle with the egg and the bacon. Drizzle with olive oil and serve

Our next stop was Granada, probably the most visited place in Andalusia because of the *Alhambra*, a Moorish citadel and palace. It is truly spectacular even from the outside. We could not go inside because you need to reserve tickets way ahead of arrival. However, we went to see the Alcazar in Seville and to some people, it is equal to the Alhambra. Walking away from the Alhambra, there was an unusually large crowd walking toward the center of the city. All of a sudden, I overheard a woman asking her husband in Hungarian "*hova megy ez a sok ember*", "Where are all these people going?" I could not help replying, "elore" forward. When she looked at me surprised, I said in Hungarian, "it is clear, isn't? If they went backwards, they would go like this" and I walked backward. Vera thought it was funny.

Late that afternoon we took off to Malaga on the Mediterranean Sea, the southernmost city in Europe. It is among the oldest cities in the world, built by the Phoenicians in 770 BC. After spending the night in a small hotel, we drove around the city and the seaport, and then we decided to drive to Gibraltar along the coast before going to our next destination the highly recommended city of Ronda.

The "Rock of Gibraltar "proudly shows off its gigantic size of over 500 meters high. Gibraltar has been a British Territory since 1704 when it was captured by the British from Spain. The people of Gibraltar are overwhelmingly in favor of staying with the British. Leaving Gibraltar, we got off the road quickly when we saw the sign "to Algeria".

Rock of Gibraltar, a British territory in the middle of Spain

The steep road to Ronda climbs up to the top of a mountain 750 meters above sea level which was so isolated that it took another hundred years for the Spaniards to regain it from the Moors. The city is famous for its three bridges that are 120 meters above the Canyon. Although we walked around the local arena and heard the cheering of the crowd for the bullfighting, we resisted the temptation to go in. We had a nice supper in Ronda breaking the fast of Yom Kippur. The next morning, we started out to Seville, our final destination.

Ronda, Andalusia

The conference of the European Acoustical Society that is held every three years started the day after our arrival. I knew quite a few of the European acousticians by now. Galego, my friend and singing partner of the song "Granada" who was born in Andalusia, was one of the organizers. Beautiful Seville, the capital of Andalusia, is the fourth largest city in Spain, after Madrid, Barcelona, and Valencia.

Vera, Oswald, Guler, Sabih, me, Agnes, Tony in Seville (2002

The most beautiful attraction in Seville is the Royal Alcazar of Seville, originally a Moorish fort. It is one of the most beautiful palaces in Spain and the oldest royal palace still functioning in Europe. It is the best example of Mudejar architecture in Spain.

The Royal Alcazar in Seville

The Mudejars were Moors who remained in Spain after the Inquisition but did not convert to Christianity like the Moriscos (converted Muslims) or Marranos (converted Jews). We spent several hours in the Alcazar on a tour organized by the conference. The other major attraction in Seville is the Cathedral, where we were present at an organ concert. The Cathedral was built in 1240 and is the largest Gothic Cathedral and the third largest Cathedral in the world.

The conference organized the banquet in a restaurant on a horse farm. During the dinner, a group of Flamenco dancers entertained us. At the end of the evening, Galego and his wife also performed a Flamenco routine quite well. After the banquet, we went to see a spectacular show with the famous Andalusian horses. The conference even staged a bull fight for us without killing the bull. Unfortunately, swarms of huge flies attacked us to dampen our spirits.

Seville was probably the scene of more operas than any other city. Fidelio by Beethoven, The Marriage of Figaro, Don Giovanni by Mozart, Carmen by Bizet, and the Barber of Seville by Rossini, all take place in this city. Just for the record, years before Rossini, Giovanni Paisiello composed his Barber of Seville before Rossini. Some of the music is quite recognizable.

I wanted to have a haircut in Seville to honor the famous barber before we left the city. The last day we walked with Vera for several hours from one hair salon to the other and we could not find a male barber. Finally, we found a young man trainee in one shop and I got my haircut by a Barber of Seville. We love all parts of Spain but undoubtedly our favorite is Andalusia.

The 19th International Conference in Acoustics (ICA) was held in Madrid in the fall of 2007. Mack Breazeale arranged a special session on "Parametric Excitation of Ultrasonic Waves". He asked me to give an invited lecture at that meeting. Steve and Mary had never been to Spain before so they joined us at that meeting also. The Conference was kind of Déjà vu, thirty years earlier we already had the 9th ICA meeting here. There were a few dozen of us who were at the meeting in 1977, including Oswald, Mack and a few others. We rented a car and drove around Spain with Steve and Mary. We stopped in Avila and Segovia which Vera and I knew quite well. I always wanted to visit Salamanca, where one of the oldest universities was established in 1218.

800 years old University in Salamanca

We arranged to stay in a Parador in Salamanca which in the new part of the city and was a much more modern structure than we had seen in other cities. For the few days we spent in Salamanca we visited all the interesting parts of the old town. In addition to the two universities, we were fascinated by the only museum that I am aware of to display both Art Deco and Art Nouveau pieces. Finally, I learned that Art Deco is the more geometrical of the two styles. From Salamanca, we drove to Toledo, where we also stayed in a Parador, and here again, we revisited the historic Jewish part of the city. On our way to Barcelona, we stayed in one of the oldest Paradores, one built in the 13th century in the town of Sigüenza.

Sigüenza

The Parador in Sigüenza

The original old structure with a modern interior was quite a contrast to the Paradores in Salamanca and Toledo.

In Barcelona we stayed in a modern hotel near the center of this beautiful city. We visited several museums, the Gaudi garden and we even had dinner at a Gaudi building in the restaurant called Casa Calvet. It was Rosh Hashanah and we enjoyed a festive meal.

Gaudi Building Barcelona

The Casa Calvet restaurant in the Gaudi building Barcelona.

On our way toward Paris, we stopped in Girona about 60 km from Barcelona. Girona's Jewish community flourished during the 12th century when it was one of the centers for Kabbalah studies but it all ended by in the fifteenth century with the inquisition. There is a Jewish Museum in Girona as well as remains of a *mikveh*, the ritual bathhouse.

Old Jewish quarter in Girona Spain

Driving from France with the family of our daughter Suzika in the summer of 2017 on our way to San Sebastian we stopped at a lovely border town in Spain, Hondaribbia. The town has an ancient old quarter with medieval walls and castle, as well as a very nice Parador. We knew that the Paradores are old castles, many 900 years old which were converted into comfortable modern hotels. So, naturally, we wanted to stay in a Parador in San Sebastian, our first stop in Spain. As we were driving toward San Sebastian, where we had booked a Parador, Suzika tried to find the best route by putting the address into her GPS. To our dismay, we found that our reserved Parador was 900 km (560 miles) away in the Canary Islands. The confusion was because there are six cities in Spain called San Sebastian. Did they run out of names?

The next morning, we headed toward Bilbao to visit the famous Guggenheim Museum. On the way, halfway between San Sebastian and Bilbao lies the famous city of Guernica which became tragically well-known during the Spanish Civil War, when Nazi Germany carpet-bombed Guernica helping Franco against the Spanish Republic. This was the very first-time carpet-bombing was used, killing thousands of the local population. "Guernica", the famous painting of Picasso named after the city is displayed in the Prado Museum in Madrid.

Guernica, by Picasso

The city of Bilbao, the capital city of the Basque Country in Spain, is a large seaport and industrial city. It is best known for the famous Guggenheim Museum, designed by the world-famous architect, Frank Gehry who was born in Toronto as Frank Goldberg, the son of Jewish immigrants from Poland. The Guggenheim Foundation co-sponsored with the city of Bilbao the construction of the museum which was completed in 1999.

With Hannah and Talia in front of the Guggenheim Museum in Bilbao, Spain (2017)

We had a beautiful vacation with our beautiful family and many more followed.

18. FRANCE

My first time in France was in 1978. Vera had already spent a few days in **Paris** with her parents in 1957 when they came from Hungary to Canada via a boat from Le Havre in France. She did not see too much of the city at that time, so we both had a new adventure from the time we left the Charles de Gaulle Airport till our taxi arrived at our hotel, the Lutetia on Boulevard Raspail on the left bank.

Hotel Lutetia Paris

Paris is divided by the river Seine flowing from east to west and the sections of the city are named according to their relation to the flow of the river: the left bank, *La Rive Gauche,* and the right bank, *La Rive Droite.* We were mesmerized by the beauty of the city and we both fell in love with it instantly. The five-star hotel was one of the best in Paris and we felt very happy staying there until we found that it was the headquarters of the Gestapo during the war. Of course, coming from Germany, we already had many other hard memories to deal with. We stayed there, but that was the last time we stayed in the Lutetia.

It was late evening by the time we settled into the hotel but we were ready to explore the city. We started to walk toward the Opera Garnier, crossing Port Royal, passing by the Tuileries Garden, the Louvre, and the Comedie Française, admiring the beauty of this unique city. By 9:30 we were ready to sit down in a nice restaurant for dinner.

Tuileries Garden Paris

Back in Knoxville some of our friends advised us about the French style of dining, which we tried to follow rigorously. First, one orders a Kir Royale, a drink with cassis, a sweet strong currant liqueur mixed with champagne. You start your meal with an appetizer or salad, then order a seafood meal with a bottle of dry white wine. This is followed by a meat dish, like *magret de canard* or veal accompanied by a bottle of red wine. Then you have your cheese plate, usually three or four kinds of cheeses, starting with the lightest and finishing with the strongest cheese. Then comes the dessert and finally an espresso, but not until you finished your dessert. For the last 42 years and about a hundred visits to Paris and dining probably in several hundred restaurants, we have never been able to have our coffee together with our dessert. We are still trying but the French insist that they know what is good for you. As we finished our elaborate first dinner in Paris, which by the way was excellent, and rolled out of the restaurant, we decided that we would moderate our eating in the future.

Early in the morning, we were awakened in our expensive hotel by a very loud knocking on the pipes as workers repaired a plumbing problem. Paris is a very old city and it requires constant maintenance even in luxury hotels. It was a beautiful morning in May and Vera and I were happy to go outside to do our morning jogging which we always do and have continued to do for over forty-some years, no matter where we are. Running along the Boulevard Saint Germaine and continuing along the quays, the streets along the left bank, we spotted the breathtaking view of the Eiffel Tower.

After an hour or so of running, we went back to our hotel and were ready to visit the University. The University of Paris, known as the Sorbonne for hundreds of years, became too small to accommodate large numbers of students, so after the 1968 student uprising in Paris, new university campuses were built all across the city. They were named by numbers like Université Paris 1, 2, and so on. One of the largest complexes was built in an area where earlier for hundreds of years there was a large open market of wine and spirits. The main entrance to the university complex is from the street Jussieu, on which there are two universities; Université Paris 6 and Université Paris 7, where I was to meet Gerard Quentin. The complex had about forty concrete buildings, each four stories high and rather unattractive due to the rapid construction to satisfy the

227

needs of the growing number of university students. Besides the academic buildings, there was a large 15 story tower for the university administration.

Université Paris 7 at Jussieu Paris

The total area of the "Campus" is rather small, yet at the time of our visit in 1978, there were about 50,000 students in the two universities which were not clearly differentiated in any way. It was not uncommon for people to share offices and laboratory spaces from both Paris 6 and Paris 7. The buildings were connected in a rather strange way. I've heard that a mathematics professor suggested designating the buildings by double numbers like matrix subscripts. For example, in building 23 where Quentin and his group worked, each floor in the building was connected by a corridor to the four neighboring buildings: 22, 33, 12, and 13. I wondered for a long time and still am not sure of the difference between Paris 6 and Paris 7. Later on, someone told me that the difference is that "all the faculty at Paris 6 are communists and at Paris 7, they are *gauchistes*, even more leftist than the communists". It was just a joke but the French intellectuals do lean toward the left.

It was almost noon by the time Vera and I arrived to Jussieu. Gerard welcomed us together with his three assistants: Alain Jungman, Michel de Billy, and Fred Cohen Tenoudji in building 23 on the third floor. After a short tour of the laboratory, we were informed that we were going to have lunch across the street. Because a wine market was in the area before the campus was built, there still were a large number of excellent restaurants around the university. We went to a small but very crowded restaurant called *Le Buisson Ardent*. Gerard knew his way around and a friendly waitress showed us to our table of six.

After the elaborate dinner of the night before, we had eaten a small continental breakfast of coffee and croissants but we still were not too hungry and we thought we'd have a small sandwich or omelet.

That will not fly in a French restaurant so we followed the advice of our hosts. We had a Kir again to start with, followed by a very tasty salad, called salad lardon, a frisée salad with chunky pieces of bacon with a salad dressing of hot bacon fat and vinegar. For the main course, we had their famous magret de canard, sliced duck breast almost raw with a peppercorn sauce accompanied by pomme de terre saarlandaise, a roasted potato dish cooked in duck fat with lots of garlic. With the meal, we had a heavy red vine called Cahor, from the southwest region of France. For dessert, we had a big slice of tarte tatin, a pastry with very sweet caramelized apple, named after the Tatin sisters who accidentally turned over an apple tart made in a wood fire oven which caramelizes the apple. Everything was so delicious and so inexpensive that for many years I have returned and ordered the same meal.

Le Buisson Ardent with Gerard and Liliane (1978)

Needless to say, such an elaborate meal took a couple of hours and by the time we returned to the university, it was close to 3 o'clock. I was glad that I did not have to give my talk until the next day at 11 a.m. I also found out that the day after my talk the university would go on vacation for a week because of some holiday. There are lots of holidays in France and also lots of vacations. Almost everybody gets six weeks of vacation and quite a bit more for academics. As I was told in Saarbrucken the "French work to live" and do not live to work, i.e. the French work to support the enjoyment of life. After the dinner at Le Buisson Ardent, I was beginning to understand it better.

It was our first time in Paris so Vera and I had no problem keeping ourselves busy for the next few days. Mostly we went sightseeing, which is a never-ending process in Paris, but we also went to visit some of the many wonderful museums, first of all, the Louvre which took us almost a whole day.

We went to see a very spectacular musical called the Volga in the La Chatelet and we continued to explore the culinary offerings of the French. On the Montparnasse, we decided to stick to the basics and tried an Alsatian restaurant called "Chez Hansi" but discovered that their Choucrute is not as good as the Hungarian *Szekely Gulyas*. I even tried to make a reservation at the famous La Tour D'Argent, a three-star restaurant in the Michelin guide, but because of my limited French when I tried to make a reservation on the phone and I was told *"ne quittez pas"* (do not hang up), I thought that meant that there was no possibility of a reservation! La Tour D'Argent, which faces the Notre Dame Cathedral, is one of the oldest restaurants in Paris and is reportedly the first place where forks were used for dining.

We would have completed a wonderful week in Paris if not for my excruciating toothache which started the day before our departure to Belgium. It was some national holiday as I mentioned and we did not know anyone in Paris other than my university contacts who had already left the city, so we were puzzled about what to do. Luckily, because many doctors and dentists have their offices in their apartments, we found a sign "Dentiste" on one of the streets. The lady dentist who did not speak any English just started to press my gum until I screamed, "that's the one" and she drilled into that tooth relieving the pain instantly. I am still grateful to her because of that.

When I returned to Paris to assume my duties in the beginning of January 1980, the weather was mild in Paris and I enjoyed walking in the city which by now was much more familiar to me. Just around the corner from the University was the Boulevard Saint Germain, one of the most fashionable streets in Paris and a nice walk of a couple of miles to Saint Germain des Pres, a real landmark in Paris.

Saint Germain des Pres, Boulevard Saint Germain, Paris

By going in the other direction across the Pont de Sully, one of the many bridges across the River Seine, you get to Ile Saint Louis one of the two islands on the Seine, and the city's most expensive real estate.

Ile Saint Louis Paris

The other island is the Ile de la Cité. Paris is probably the most walking-friendly city in the world. You can also start out on Rue des Écoles and walk toward the Jardin de Luxembourg, one of the nicest parks in Paris. So, there are lots of choices if you like to walk.

French Senate in the Jardin de Luxembourg Paris

I settled into the University the first day I arrived in Paris. They assigned me an office and I started to plan my work which was mostly to interact with the people on existing projects and to interface with them and our research capabilities back in the USA. My appointment, entitled *Invited Professor*, started in 1980, continued for the next 17 years when due to French law that calls for mandatory retirement at age 65, it was terminated.

I stayed in a hotel near the University complex for a few days, but I needed to find a place before the family arrived from Knoxville. All the people in the ultrasonic group tried to help me find a suitable apartment. Eventually, Lilian Jungman, the wife of Alain, found a place in Rue du Bac, which she highly recommended that I consider, because of its desirable location in the 7th Ar. I did not know at that time that although the 16th Ar. had some of the largest and most expensive apartments in Paris, the 7th was considered the best address in Paris. Rue du Bac impressed me right away. It starts at Rue de Sevres, where the oldest department store and supermarket, the Bon Marché is located and then continues crossing several nice streets like Rue de Babylone, Rue de Varenne where many of the government buildings and embassies are located, and finally over the Blvd. Saint Germain going all the way to the river Seine. On the way, along the Rue du Bac, there were many little boutiques, cafés, bakeries and restaurants following one after the other.

73 Rue de Bac Paris. Our place was the entire 3rd floor viewing Rue de Grennele as well (1980).

The prospective apartment for rent that Liliane took me to was located in a five-story building on the corner of Rue de Bac and Rue de Grenelle. When we rang the bell, the owner of the building, Mme Lefebvre and her maid, a young Portuguese girl came out and took us up to the 3rd floor where Mme. Lefebvre lived in a very large apartment by herself. She was an old lady in her seventies but clearly sharp and capable who appeared to be rather wealthy. Since I had limited ability in French conversation, Liliane talked about the details, but I could understand enough to learn that on the whole fourth floor there was a three-bedroom, three-bathroom furnished apartment to be rented for the equivalent of $1200/month. It was lots of money for us since our monthly mortgage in Knoxville was $270. But Paris is Paris and Knoxville is Knoxville. She wanted a security damage deposit of $2000. It was clear that, these were the prices in Rue du Bac, take it or leave it. I took it, even though I was not impressed by the Louis the 15th or 16th old antique furniture. I knew that in a few days Vera would arrive to Paris with Michael and Susan and we needed a place.

I moved in the next day and tried to clean it up to American standards, using lots of sprays mostly to eliminate the odors. In the morning when I wanted to take a shower, only cold water came out. When I called Mme.

Lefebvre and told her that I needed a plumber, roughly "J'ai besoin de plombier", she explained that because of the calcium deposits in the pipes, we would have only cold water and would have to heat water on the gas stove until the warmer weather, probably around March. I knew that Suzie used to wash her beautiful hair three times a day, so I could sense some challenges ahead. Otherwise, the apartment was large, bright and had many windows to watch the busy life on Rue de Bac as well as on Rue de Grenelle. I loved the location regardless of all the negatives.

After a long flight from Knoxville, Vera arrived at Charles de Gaulle airport with the children on a nice sunny Sunday morning. They were too tired to get much of an impression of the city through the window of the cab, and as soon as we got to 73 Rue de Bac, they all went to sleep. By late afternoon, I woke them up explaining, especially to Michael, that they had to adjust to the time change. While Vera was unpacking, I took Suzie and Michael for a walk. It was still very sunny even though we were in the beginning of January. Starting out from our building toward the Seine, we arrived at the crossing of Blvd. Saint Germain and Blvd. Raspail. The kids saw the Rue de Bac Metro Station and got excited with the possibility of taking the Metro. Instead, we turned into Saint Germain and I could tell that in a few minutes they had forgotten their bad experience of their trip of the previous summer.

The next few days were busy for all of us. Michael and Suzika had to start school. We found an international school called École Saint-Marcel on Blvd. Saint-Marcel, where there were kids from all different countries. Half a day the instruction was in French and the other half-day the instruction was in English. Not having a car, we all learned quickly to use public transportation, metro lines and metro stations. We made a little rhyme, which we still enjoy recalling: *first comes Odeon, then comes Mabillon and then comes Sevres-Babylone*. The kids mostly used the #83 bus which took them directly to Saint-Marcel. By now Michael was 15 and Suzika 12, and they both quickly adjusted to life in the big city.

Vera and I decided to enroll in an accelerated French course at the Alliance Française, located at Blvd. Raspail, about a mile walk from our place. Every morning it started at 8 and it lasted until 12. There were about 20 or so students from all different countries in our class and we made friends quickly with a few of them. Typically, Vera and I got up at 6 AM and went for a 3-4-mile run, mostly along the Seine up to the Eiffel Tower. Coming home we had a continental breakfast with the kids of the best croissants from the boulangerie across the street, and then we were all on our way. After the classes, I went to the University and normally got home around 6:30-7 PM. About half of the week, we had dinner at home, but at least 3 or 4 times a week all four of us went to a restaurant. I made a promise that we would never go twice to the same restaurant. And we kept the promise. We enjoyed eating out and tried many different types of restaurants with varying ambiances and prices.

One of our experiences in a restaurant taught us a lesson about French customs and attitudes. It was the second Sunday in Paris for us and we had a rather casual dinner in one of the tourist places on Champs Elysees although we improved our choices as time went on. It was a nice evening so we decided to walk home. We walked by the Place de Concorde and crossed the Point Royal, the bridge leading to the Rue de Bac. On Rue de Bac we found a restaurant called Les Ministeres, which was open and struck us as inviting for a dessert and a drink. The waiter gave us the extended menu in which we all found some dessert to our liking. I tried to show off my French and ordered the desserts. The waiter responded somewhat unexpectedly, "Monsieur, c'est un restaurant" implying that in a restaurant you have to eat through all the courses. We all got up and walked out being rather upset with their rigidity. For over 34 years we have walked by Les Ministeres but have never put a foot inside. Maybe one of these days we will try their food. As of this writing, the restaurant no longer exists!

The kids made friends in school. Michael went regularly to the Jardin de Luxembourg where there was a tennis court and played with his friend from Brazil and others. Suzika made friends also with some of the girls, one from Mexico and one from Vietnam. We even invited some of their friends to our house for dinner. We tried to use the French dinner codes and usually served cheese after the main course and before dessert. At one dinner, the cheese plate was going around the table and when it got to Michael, he pointed to one and asked, "What kind is this?" I knew that he liked brie, so I said, "It's Brie." By the time it got to Suzika, she asked the same question by pointing to the same cheese. Knowing that she liked Camembert, I said "It's Camembert." By then, Michael confronted me, "Before, you told me it was Brie and now you say it is Camembert. What is it?" Without thinking much, I quickly replied, "It's both." We had lots of fun!

Another memorable and oft-repeated story is when after dinner, sometimes Michael and I would go for a long walk. We usually ended up at *Le Drugstore*, a well-known establishment on Blvd. Saint Germain where we bought some wafers from Holland called Napolyi in Hungarian. There were 18 pieces in a package. I told Michael that we would divide the contents evenly. I gave him eight pieces and I kept ten. After a short while he said, "Dad, you didn't divide the Napolyi evenly; you should have given me nine pieces". I replied, "Then it would have been divided oddly; nine is an odd number, no?" It was convincing.

We rented a piano for Suzika and found a French piano teacher for her. She was progressing quite well, playing pieces from Chopin, Mozart and others. We tried to expose the kids to the many cultural offerings of Paris. When I was in high school, I was impressed by the French writer Moliere and read several of his plays in Hungarian translation of course. I was especially thrilled by his work *Tartuffe*. So, when we found out that Tartuffe was playing in the theater Comedie Française, founded in 1680 and the oldest active theater in the world, I bought four tickets. I also bought several copies of the play in English translation.

Comedie Française Paris

We sat down in our seats at the theater and were very excited with our first French theater experience. A few minutes before the play started an older couple stood by next to our seats claiming that they had the tickets to our seats. To resolve the dispute an usher came by and to our dismay pointed out that we had the right seats but for a week later. We got up and walked out and we all laughed but came back the following week at the right time. It was not easy to follow the play in French and we decided to go for musicals in the future.

We went to see Mozart's Magic Flute performed in a puppet theater, as well as Don Giovanni and many concerts.

We also visited many parts of Paris, using a Michelin guide and found many historic sites and current events on our walks. We all enjoyed the many museums of Paris. In the Pompidou Center, there was the largest exhibit of Salvador Dali's works which we went to see many times over and over. We liked the ambiance around the Pompidou Center where many performers entertained the crowd outside. Many parts of Paris were full of musicians and other entertainers and we all enjoyed these street performances which was quite new to us since they certainly did not exist in Knoxville.

We had friends from the USA and also my aunt Manci from Hungary visited us in Paris, Manci had lived in Paris in the 1930s and this was her first visit back after almost fifty years. It appeared to be a very emotional return for her.

We decided to take a family vacation after the conference in the latter part of March. We got various suggestions from our colleagues and friends and finally decided to take a week's vacation in **Chamonix,** in the Alps at the French-Swiss border. Living in Knoxville, none of us had any real exposure to skiing. Vera and I had rented one pair of skis once at the Harz Mountain when we lived in nearby Göttingen in 1964/65 and took turns skiing down a rather simple slope.

We thought it was a good opportunity to take a skiing vacation. We signed up with Club Med, a company founded in the 1950s, which was the first company to provide quality vacations in many exotic places like Tahiti, Guadeloupe, and of course the French Alps. The worldwide company is owned by Baron Rothschild who purchased it in 1961 from its original owner, the former Belgian polo champion Gerard Blitz. Initially, it catered to singles, later on, it became very attractive for families with children, which was the reason we selected to use it for our vacation.

After a long overnight train ride which left from the Gare de Lyon railway station, we arrived early in the morning at Chamonix. All the passengers arriving at Chamonix who were registered for Club Med were welcomed by a band playing lively music.

It was clear to us right away that it would be an organized and well-structured vacation. We were taken for a short ride in a limousine to our hotel. The Hotel Faucigny was very nice although the rooms were rather simply furnished with single beds. We had two connecting rooms for the four of us. Shortly after our arrival, all the guests were gathered in a large room, where we were welcomed by the Club Med director who introduced us to his staff of nice-looking young women and men. The staff would instruct us about our skiing, the entertainment, the room service, and the culinary arts of the establishment, etc.

They must have assumed, I guess, that during our night-long trip in a sleeper train, we all had a good night's sleep and were ready to go out to the slopes of the Alps to ski. So, after getting our skis and boots we had to show the level of our knowledge of skiing. Michael and I were placed in a slightly higher class than Vera and Suzika. The instructors all spoke French and it was obvious from the beginning that it would be tough training and not for sissies. We had to learn how to move upward on the slopes of the mountain which was not easy and which we rarely did later when we skied in Colorado. Brevent Mountain where we skied was across from our hotel. During the week we learned some of the basics and it was a good start for us to continue skiing for the next 26 years.

The four of us on our first ski trip at Chamonix, French Alps (1980)

It was a wonderful 10 days at Chamonix and probably the best family vacation we have ever had. In addition to the beautiful scenery of the Alps and the skiing, the accommodations provided by Club Med were way above what we expected. The meals provided three times a day could equal the meals of three-star restaurants in the Michelin Guide in Paris. The nightly entertainments could not have been any better in the Moulin Rouge. There were special activities for teenagers so our kids were always busy and happy as well. There were lots of wealthy and "beautiful people" from many different countries in Club Med; at dinnertime, we often sat with some of them at the large round tables for ten people.

An apparently very wealthy couple who sat at our table started a conversation with us and found out that I teach physics and that we were living in Paris. I overheard the wife, who was loaded with expensive jewelry whisper to the husband, "not bad for a physics teacher." One afternoon the man was playing chess with someone and his wife asked me if I would play chess with her husband. She added that her husband is an excellent chess player and beats everyone in Club Med. I said, "I will try". The man was playing well and I was intimidated by the wife's arrogant attitude which made us feel that we didn't belong there.

Much to the disappointment of Michael who was watching the game and who thought that I was a super chess player, I lost a rook in the middle of the game. At that point, the lady looked at me triumphantly as if to say, "You have no chance." This made me decide to try everything to not lose the game. Eventually, I turned the game around and after 45 minutes, probably the best I ever played, I won. Michael was happy, but the lady burst out saying that it was luck and that we should play another game. We both agreed to play a revenge match. This time I was even luckier and won the second game in five minutes making the lady visibly upset. Money does not buy everything! In spite of the snobbishness of this wealthy lady, we had a super great time all through the week and we also met many nice people.

We were back in Paris the following week and life continued with more excitement for us. We went to lots of restaurants and tried all new French dishes. It was interesting to learn how our two children were handling their orders. Michael would always order the "plat de jour" the menu of the day, without any hesitation regardless of what it was; it was an easy solution and the cheapest usually. Suzika on the other hand could not make up her mind deciding among several dishes. Normally, Vera and I would help out by ordering one of Suzika's choices to have her not lose out if she got something she didn't like.

We also went to see Faust in the Opera Garnier; the Opera Bastille was not built yet. On another occasion, we went to listen to Rostropovich, the famous Russian cellist at the Theater Champs Elysees. We even went to the Lido on Michael's 16th birthday to watch the glamorous performers as he had requested. On weekends, we went sightseeing to Versailles, Chantilly, Fontainebleau, and other places, taking the RER train since we had no car.

It was nice to be back in Paris and we continued our full and exciting life in this beautiful city. We all loved being in Paris. At one-point Suzika asked me, "Dad, Paris is such a wonderful city, why did you go to the USA instead of coming to Paris when you left Hungary?" It was a reasonable question and I had to give a reasonable answer, " the reason I went to the USA was to be able to create the opportunity to take you to Paris and many more places." I think she got the message that nowhere else in the world has better opportunities for immigrants than the USA: it is the best place in the world to start.

When the French Open (for tennis) the Roland Garros was held in Paris, somehow both Michael and Susan were able to get tickets for this world-class event. It was a gloomy day until all of a sudden, a heavy rain forced many of the spectators to leave. Michael had the idea to stay at the gate and as people were leaving, he asked them to give him their tickets rather than throw them away. A little later the rain stopped and all of a sudden, several people wanted to enter to watch the games and Michael was able to sell the tickets he collected earlier. With the help of Suzika, they made the equivalent of several hundred dollars in French Francs.

After that, they went by Saint Germain des Pres, where a painter displayed his paintings, one of which Vera always admired every time we walked by. It is a surrealistic painting of people walking in the street in Paris on a rainy day. The kids bought it with their well-earned money at the Roland Garros and made Vera one of the happiest and proudest mothers in the world. We still have the painting displayed in our home.

Although most of the time we took the children with us to the restaurants, we made an exception when we went to the La Tour D'Argent, a three-star restaurant that claims to be founded in 1582 and frequented by Henry IV. No proof however shows the existence of the restaurant before 1860.

The restaurant is famous for its pressed duck and each duck is numbered. The guests receive a card with the number of their pressed duck printed on it. It was the most expensive and snobbish place we had ever dined in, but the duck was excellent! The waiters snub you if you order a bottle of wine cheaper than $200 (we were snubbed!) It is a beautiful restaurant with a view of Notre Dame. They also have one of the most elaborate wine cellars. However, in the last few years, it has lost its glamour as well as most of its stars. At any rate, we enjoyed much more the original little Le Bernardin which was only 100 yards from the famous La Tour D'Argent.

At one point, while Vera and I were running, I suggested to her that maybe we should buy a small apartment in Paris. We loved the city, it appeared that I would have the opportunity to work at Université Paris 7 and we would need to live somewhere. The possibility of renting out the apartment from time to time would bring some income also. Vera thought that it was a good idea, so we decided to look into the details of purchasing an apartment in Paris. Suzika of course was the happiest of us all, but I was also excited, remembering the saying by Professor Bolt at the last Acoustical Society meeting in Boston: "Why not both?" Why can't we live in the USA and enjoy Paris as well!

So, we were ready to learn what it takes to buy an apartment in France for people like us. First of all, we learned that foreigners have to put down 50% of the total price of an apartment as down payment! Second, the other 50% can be mortgaged provided one finds a bank to do it. But first, we had to find an apartment which we could consider. Prices of apartments were extremely high (and still are) even for a very small one-bedroom apartment. Compared to Knoxville the prices per square foot were astronomical. We looked at a few old run-down apartments in the 7th. By now we wanted to stay around Rue de Bac, we liked the area. None of the apartments within a reasonable price range that we looked at appealed to us.

We were at the point of giving up the idea of buying anything in Paris. Then one day we were jogging on Rue Vaneau when we saw some construction activity at the corner of Rue Vaneau and Rue de Babylone and a sign that one and two-bedroom apartments were for sale! After contacting the saleslady, we found out that the six-story building at 42 Rue Vaneau was a hotel before and the exterior of the building would remain unchanged. Inside new one and two-bedroom apartments would be constructed, two on a floor, each with a living room, bathroom, separate toilet, and kitchen. We also found that if we were interested, we would have to make a down payment of 5%, the equivalent of $8000 (for a one-bedroom apartment). The apartments would be finished in 9-10 months, around the spring of 1981.

We liked the plans and decided to do it. It was already the end of our stay in Paris and we were ready to sign the transaction for the sale. Our flight back to Knoxville was on a Sunday and we met the salespeople and the lawyers in their office on Friday at 11 in the morning. Alain Jungman joined us to help in the transaction which was conducted in French. We were informed about all the details of purchasing the apartment, the finances, and all the bureaucratic details of the French law. We had no second thoughts and wanted to finish the transaction. We had figured that we could afford the $8000 down payment and in nine months we would come up with the remaining 50% and the mortgage. To our surprise, at 1 o'clock without completing the closing, all the people involved got up and announced that they are going out for dinner. Furthermore, because it was Friday, they would not return before Monday. When we explained that we are leaving Paris on Sunday and were going back to the USA, they were sympathetic but would not give up their dinner. They suggested that we give Alain the power of attorney so he could take care of the closing, which we did.

The following year in 1981, we closed the contract and signed the loan for the mortgage in the bank. We furnished the apartment which we loved even though it was very small by American standards, 42 square meters which is equivalent to 452 square feet! But it had everything, a nice bedroom, a separate toilet, a living room, and a small kitchen. The apartment was on the 3rd floor (4th in the USA because the first floor in France is called zero!) We had two windows facing the corner of Rue de Babylone and Rue Vaneau. From our windows, we could see Matignon, the official residence of the prime minister of France.

42 Rue Vaneau, corner of Vaneau and Babylone in Paris.

I had a two-month appointment at the Université Paris 7 in May and June of 1982, and Vera and Suzika joined me later in Paris. Our apartment was rented so we had to find substitute housing. We found that the rental agency charges you an extra month rent for their service even for renting an apartment for just two months. But we had to accept the rule. We got a modern one-bedroom apartment in a high-rise building complex in the 16th Ar. near the Trocadero in Rue de Sablon. Our apartment was on the ground floor and through the window, we had a view of a beautiful garden. There was a big contrast between the 16th and the 7th Arrondissement. The 16th was much more modern and was known to house more of the nouveaux riches. After everything, we preferred the 7th but for a couple of months, we learned a different kind of lifestyle. The apartment complex was connected to a shopping mall with many stores and restaurants and often we had our breakfast in one of the small restaurants.

During our stay in Paris, we had several visitors. Everybody loves to come to Paris especially when they have "expert guides" to the city available. Vera's friend Zsuzsi Schwitzer came from Toronto with her husband and their teenage son. One evening we took them up to the top of Montmartre. On our way back walking through Pigalle, the young boy Ronnie wanted to see a call girl on the street and perhaps even talk to her. For whatever reason, to his great disappointment, none came by. Finally, a nice-looking blonde in high heels and mini skirt walked by, so just to please Ronnie I asked her in French what time it was. The nice blonde "girl" shocked us by responding in a deep bass voice.

Alex Vida, me, Vera, Zsuzsi (Vida) Schwitzer and Ronnie in a Paris cafe (1982)

A few days later my friend George Bozoki showed up with his new girlfriend Jayne. He rented a car and we took off to the Loire Valley to see the Chateaux and even stayed for a couple of days in Château **D'Ige**.

Chateau D'Ige in Burgundy

In the garden of the Château there were many fruit trees. On the pear trees each tiny pear was covered by a glass bottle. Later on, when the pear grows much larger the bottle will be removed and filled with alcohol. So, we learned the answer to the puzzle, "How do pears much bigger than the neck of a bottle get into a bottle?" We also found a superb three-star restaurant in the area. It was a wonderful trip together which we repeated many times later.

After finishing three marathons in Columbus and one in New York City, we decided to sign up for the Paris Marathon in 1986. By now after finishing four marathons we knew how to train for it. For six weeks before the event, we had to run every day 14 - 15 km. (8 - 9 miles) and once a week at least 30 km.

The first Paris Marathon, the Tour de Paris Marathon, took place in 1896. A big crowd gathered to watch 191 participants. It was run over a course of 40 km from Paris to Conflans-Sainte-Honorine via Versailles, and the organizers decided to award a commemorative medal to all runners who finished the race in less than 4 hours. The distance of 40 km was chosen as it is the distance separating Marathon from Athens. The current exact distance of the race is 42.195 km, the standard Olympic Marathon length. The present Paris Marathon dates from 1976. It is normally held on a Sunday in April (in 1988 it was on May 15) and is limited to 37,000 runners. It is organized by the Amaury Sport Organization and notable for the attractive route through the heart of the city of Paris, and for the food and drinks stations which include wine, beer, cider, oysters, oranges and even chocolate. In Paris, the spectators are not as enthusiastic as in New York but on the other hand, in New York, nothing more than water and Gatorade is given to the runners. Vive la difference!

The race starts on the Avenue des Champs-Élysées going downhill to circle round the Place de la Concorde before turning right onto Rue de Rivoli. The route passes the Louvre, then goes around the Place de la Bastille, and down Boulevard Soult to the Bois de Vincennes. A long loop of the Bois de Vincennes returns the route into the heart of Paris. The halfway point is reached at Rue de Charenton. From there the route now follows the course of the Seine, passing the Île de la Cité and going under the Pont Neuf, then through a series of tunnels. There is a large drink and foot massage station at Trocadéro, opposite the Eiffel Tower. The route continues along the Seine, before branching off east to eventually pass through the Bois de Boulogne, emerging for the final 200 meters to the finish line on the Avenue Foch.

As always, Vera finished the race ahead of me but we both felt very happy that we were able to complete it in a "foreign territory".

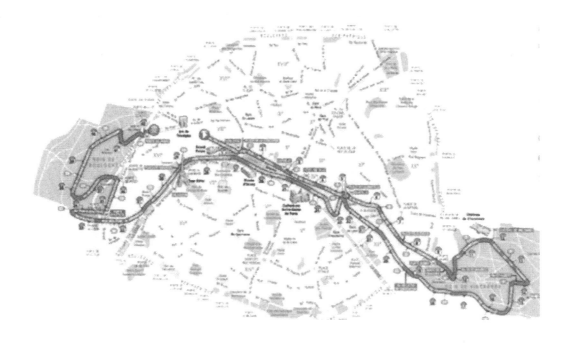

I arranged my Sabbatical leave from Ohio State University in the 1993/94 academic year to spend it at Université Paris 7. Paris by now was our second home and when we arrived at 42 Rue Vaneau in the middle of September it took us no time to settle in. Up until the summer our apartment was rented to an interesting American named Terry. We were convinced that he was working for the US Intelligence Services in some form or another. A robust 6'6" tall, weighing probably over 300 pounds, but with a smile of a young child. He owned two very expensive automobiles (one which was parked in our garage space in Rue de Sevres), had a large antique gun collection and at least 150 bottles of very expensive wine in our cellar.

Eventually, he moved out of our apartment but stayed in the building, renting an apartment twice the size of ours on the second floor. We let him continue to use the garage space and the cellar. We had very friendly relations with him and shortly after our arrival to Paris he gave us the keys to his apartment and told us to feel free to use the apartment in any way we wanted including the well-stocked refrigerator and freezer. He was a hunter and had lots of game in his freezer as well as expensive Russian caviar in the fridge. He took off from Paris not specifying for how long and where to. We never saw him again!

Our life in Paris got into a daily routine. We got up early to do our running usually up to the Tour Eiffel and back. After breakfast, I went to the Alliance Française where I started over again with French for beginners. We had about 23 kids from a dozen different countries in the class, most of them 18 to 20 years old college-age kids who came to Paris to study. I was the oldest and when we had to tell our age and I said soixante et un (61) some of the kids thought I was joking.

With my classmates in the Alliance Francaise in Paris (1994)

A cute girl from Hong Kong said "You are older than my grandfather". The next oldest person was a Russian woman Nina who was 36. Nevertheless, we all get along well, we often went out to have dinner in a cheap restaurant together, I was one of the gangs. Sometimes Vera joined us. I progressed well in my French, taking, second and third level classes as well where we had to give speeches on different topics and write long essays.

While I was taking French classes and working at the university, Vera kept herself busy taking culinary classes and preparing dinners every night for me and from time to time for our guests. She even took a class from the world-famous chef **Alain Ducasse**.

The most sophisticated dish in this book is the traditional French Cassoulet, which Vera has perfected through the years

Certificat de Stage

Je soussigné Alain Ducasse, certifie que Madame Vera Adler a suivi le stage « Desserts de réveillon » au sein de mon école de cuisine ADF, le vendredi 10 décembre 2004.

Paris,
le 10 décembre 2004

Alain Ducasse

Vera's Certificate from Alain Ducasse

Cassoulet

Serves 12

Ingredients for the Duck:

4 duck legs

Kosher salt

½ tsp thyme

3 cloves smashed garlic

Ground black peppercorn

Ingredients for the Beans:

1½ lb. Cannelini, Italian white beans. Soak overnight and drain.

6 oz. of bacon

2 peeled carrots cut in quarters

head of garlic halved crosswise

½ tsp. thyme

bay leaf

Freshly ground black pepper

Kosher salt

lb. fresh pork sausage (Sweet Italian, Toulouse, or unsmoked kielbasa)

Ingredients for the Pork Ragout:

1½ Lb. boneless pork shoulder (Boston butt), cut into 1in pieces.

4 g Kosher salt

Black pepper

2 tbsp. vegetable oil

1 large chopped carrot

4 garlic cloves finely chopped

½ tsp thyme

1 bay leaf

One 14.5 oz. can crushed tomatoes

6 cups chicken broth

Additional ingredients

2 cups fresh bread crumbs

¼ cup finely chopped parsley

Directions:

1. Preheat oven to 350 degrees

2. In a large roasting pan evenly scatter garlic, salt and pepper on the duck legs, sprinkle with thyme and put 2 tbsp. water in the pan. Duck legs should be skin side down. Cover tightly with foil and weigh down with a cast-iron skillet or a heavy baking dish. Bake it in the oven for 2 hours.

3. Remove the baking dish from the oven and remove skillet and foil.

4. Turn legs skin side up, cover dish with foil and bake 2½ hours longer.

5. Remove the legs from the baking dish and set them aside and reserve ¼ cup duck fat in a small bowl.

6. Remove the skin from the duck legs when is cool enough to handle and pull duck meat from bones, tearing them into 2 in pieces, and put aside.

7. Place the beans in a large pot with the bacon, carrots, garlic, onion, thyme and bay leaf. Pour in cold water to cover the beans. Season with black pepper and bring to a gentle simmer. Partially cover the pot and after 30 minutes season with salt. Keep cooking until beans are tender but not falling apart. Add additional water as needed.

8. Remove pot from heat and discard all the vegetables. Reserve the bacon and place it on a cutting board and when cool, cut into ¼ in pieces, and add back to the beans.

9. Sprinkle pork with salt and pepper. Heat oil in a large heavy pot over medium-high. Working in two batches cook pork turning until brown all over. Remove meat and reserve.

10. In the same pot place onion, carrot and garlic. Season with salt and pepper. Cook over medium heat until softened and lightly browned.

11. Return pork to pot and add thyme, bay leaf, tomato, and the broth. Bring to boil. Reduce heat partially. Cover pot and simmer gently for 2 hours.

12. Let the ragout cool slightly and skim fat from the pot.

13. Using a slotted spoon transfer bean mixture to the ragout add enough cooking liquid from the beans to cover.

14. Arrange the reserved duck skin in a single layer and cook over low heat, turning until both sides are crisps. Remove to a paper towel. Prick pork sausages with a fork all over and cook in the same pot, turning occasionally until brown all over and cooked through. Remove and cut the sausage into 2-inch pieces.

15. Add breadcrumbs to pot and brown until golden and crisp. Reserve the breadcrumbs in a bowl and add chopped parsley.

16. Rub the inside of a heavy Dutch oven with the cut side of the garlic. Ladle in one-third of the ragout mixture spread out in one layer. Top with half of the sausages and half of the duck meat. Then layer another ragout mixture on top and place remaining sausages and duck meat. Finally, top it with the last third of the ragout mixture. The liquid should come to the top to cover everything in the pot. Use remaining liquid broth if needed. Scatter 2/3 of breadcrumbs over the dish. This is the CASSOULET.

17. Preheat oven for 375 degrees and bake until golden brown until 25-30 minutes, remove from oven and use a spoon to break up crust, so the crust absorbs a little liquid. Smooth the surface.

18. Put the pot back into the oven for 25-30 minutes and another crust will form. Repeat the process 2 more times. Make sure you have enough liquid to moisturize.

19. Top with the remaining breadcrumbs and bake 12 minutes more.

20. Let rest at least 25 minutes before serving

21. Serve in bowls and crumble the duck skin over the top.

Blanquette de Veau

Serves 6

Ingredients for the stew:

3 lb. breast of veal, cut into 2in pieces.

6 cups of chicken broth.

1 large onion

2 carrots peeled and quartered

1 bay leaf

5 parsley stems

½ teaspoon thyme

1 celery stalk

Salt.

Ingredients for the pearl onions:

24 pearl onions.

½ cup stock from the stew

1/4 tsp. salt

1 Tbsp. butter

Ingredients for the sauce:

4 tbsp. butter

5 tbsp. flour

3½ cups of the cooking stock

2 cups of quartered mushrooms

1 to 2 tbsp. lemon juice

½ cup heavy cream

2 tbsp. minced parsley

Directions:

1. Place the veal in a pot and cover with water about 2 in, bring to simmer and cook for 2 minutes

2. Drain the veal and wash it under cold water.

3. Rinse the pot and return the veal.

4. Pour enough chicken broth to cover the meat. Bring to a gentle simmer, skimming any foam that comes to the surface.

5. Add all the ingredients listed under the stew. Taste for seasoning.

6. Cover partially and simmer for 1 1/4 hours until the meat is fork-tender

7. Strain the liquid from the pot to a container. Rinse the pot before placing the meat, not the liquid. Discard the onion, parsley, celery, and bay leaf. Save the carrots

8. Peel the pearl onions place them in a saucepan with half a cup of stock from the stew, add salt and butter. Simmer for about 30 minutes.

9. Arrange the cooked pearl onions over the meat. Add the carrots as well. Reserve the liquid from the pearl onion.

10. To prepare the sauce place the 4 tbsp. of butter in a saucepan and let it melt.

11. Stir the flour over low heat to the melted butter, stirring constantly for 2 minutes. Remove the saucepan from the heat and whisk in the stock

12. Bring the sauce to boil stirring, lower the heat to simmer and frequently stirring for 10 minutes.

13. Fold the mushrooms into the sauce and simmer 10 minutes more. Season with salt, pepper, and lemon juice to taste.

14. Add the cream to the sauce and pour this mixture over the meat.

15. Heat it until the sauce is thickened slightly on low heat.

16. You may garnish with chopped parsley and serve.

Tarte Tatin

You may use, apple, plums, peaches, apricot, or nectarine instead of pears.

Serves 6

Ingredients:

1 stick unsalted butter

1 pinch of salt

tbsp. of ice-cold water

8 pears peeled and quartered

¾ cup of sugar and ¼ cup of flour

Directions:

1. In a food processor, put the butter cut into small pieces add 2 tbsp. of sugar, the pinch of salt and start mixing by adding the flour. Add water as needed for the dough to form into a ball separating from the wall of the processor. The process can be done by hand instead of with a processor.

2. Wrap the dough in a plastic food wrap and refrigerate until the next step.

3. In a heavy bottom oven proof frying pan place the remaining sugar. There should be enough sugar to form a ¼ inch layer to cover the bottom of the pan. Cook on medium/low heat on the top of the stove until it turns into a reach medium-dark color. Don't let it burn. Don't stir it.

4. Remove the pan from the stove and place the quartered pears on the top of the caramelized sugar with the rounded side down in the pan in a nice pattern.

5. Take out the dough from the refrigerator and roll it out on a floured surface to the size to fully cover the pan.

6. With a fork prick the dough in order to ventilate during baking.

7. Bake in a preheated 350 degrees oven for 45 minutes to an hour until the top is nicely colored.

8. Let it cool to room temperature.

9. Flip over carefully by placing a flat plate over the pan.

10. If any of the pears is stuck in the pan, just place it on top.

11. Serve it warm with whipped cream or ice cream.

Liver Pate

Serves 12

Ingredients:

½ Lb. of fresh chicken liver

2 shallots

1½ stick of butter

1½ tbsp. of sugar

1 tsp. of dried thyme

½ tsp. salt

½ tsp. of freshly ground black pepper

2 tbsp. cognac

Directions:

1. Clean the liver from any fat, dry well with a paper towel.

2. In a small pot melt a quarter stick of butter.

3. Add the sugar and the roughly chopped shallots. Add water just to cover the shallots and a pinch of salt. Cook uncovered slowly until the shallots are caramelized and all the water is gone.

4. Heat another ¼ of a stick of butter and the thyme in a medium-sized frying pan and add the liver.

5. Cook the liver through until no visible blood is seen.

6. Add the cognac to the liver and continue cooking until the alcohol is gone.

7. In a blender mix the liver, shallots, salt and pepper and blend until the consistency is smooth.

8. Add the remaining 1 stick of butter and blend it all until it is smooth and silky, adjust the seasoning.

9. Serve with cornichon or with small pickles and white toasted bread cut into triangles.

10. Pour the liver mixture into a container that you will be serving from.

Coq au vin

Serves 6
Ingredients:

4 lb skin-on chicken leg quarters

Salt and pepper to your taste

1 tsp. thyme

2 bay leaves

A handful of fresh parsley

1 bottle of red burgundy wine

1 cup bacon cubed

5 large carrots peeled and chopped

1 large onion chopped

½ lb. pearl onion peeled

½ lb. of mushrooms sliced

½ lb. of mushrooms quartered

5 cloves of minced garlic

2 tbsp. tomato paste

¼ cup brandy

2 tbsp. olive oil

2 tbsp. of unsalted butter

Pinch of sugar

Directions:

1. In a large bowl put the seasoned chicken pieces. Add the thyme, bay leaves, and parsley. Pour the wine over the chicken. Toss until well coated. Cover with plastic wrap and refrigerate overnight.

2. In a large heavy-bottom pan cook the bacon cubes over medium/low heat. When the bacon is crisp remove it to a paper towel, leaving the excess fat in the pot.

3. Remove the chicken from the marinade, reserving the liquid. Dry the chicken with a paper towel until it is completely dry.

4. Heat the bacon fat over medium heat and add the chicken in batches and cook until well browned on both sides.

5. Remove the chicken and set aside.

6. Add the carrots, onion, sliced mushrooms, and garlic to the pot. Cook for 10 minutes until everything is lightly browned.

7. Stir in the tomato paste and cook for about three minutes.

8. Pour the brandy into the pot, scraping any browned bits about two minutes. Add the reserved marinade.

9. Bring to a boil for 15 minutes until the liquid is reduced to half.

10. Return the chicken and ½ the cooked bacon to the pot. Cover and reduce the heat to low and simmer for one hour.

11. Meanwhile, in a large skillet heat the oil and butter on medium heat. Put in the pearl onions add a pinch of salt and sugar. Cover and reduce the heat on the skillet to low and cook for 15 minutes, shaking the skillet to move the onion around. Uncover and add the quartered mushrooms on medium /high heat. Continue to cook until all soften, about 5-8 minutes.

12. Add the pearl onions and the mushrooms to the coq au vin

13. Sprinkle with chopped parsley and the reserved bacon and serve with crusty bread.

All our French friends were so impressed by Vera's cooking. They did not know that one could make foie gras or crème brulée at home! We started to have out-of-town guests also, from the USA, from Hungary and so on. Luckily, because we had access to Terry's two-bedroom apartment, we were able to accommodate several more people easily. In the beginning of November, we found a painter to paint our apartment that needed it after more than 12 years, but for the very high price of 10,000 Francs (about $2000) for a 450 square-feet.

The painter promised to have it done in one week. We decided to go to Bangkok for a little vacation during that time and stayed with the Halmais who had a nice large apartment there. The Burgers had already returned to Hungary. When we returned to Paris, we found to our surprise that the painting in our place was not even halfway finished. In the USA it is a one-day job. So, we moved into Terry's apartment and our guests the Nadais who arrived a few days later from the USA shared it with us. The painter usually arrived around 9 AM and after half an hour of work, he went to a brasserie across from our house, where he would drink with his bodies for several hours and then go home. It took him nearly a month to complete the job. Our consolation was that it looked good.

We enjoyed all the offerings of this exciting city. We went to the opera a lot. Paris has two Opera houses, the traditional Opera that Garnier founded in 1668 and the modern Opera Bastille opened in 1989.

Opera Bastille Paris

We even started to like Wagner. Parsifal, his last opera lasted 5 hours which gave you time to get your thoughts together. We also discovered new restaurants like La Os a Moelle, which always served marrow bones (moelle), or the chic L'Epi Dupin across from the Bon Marche, which had a very young imaginative chef and reasonable prices. The three-star restaurant L'Arpege near us on Rue Varenne was quite expensive and served a tomato-based desert. Today you could end up paying 400 Euros per person there. However, fortunately more and more young chefs who had good training in top restaurants nowadays have opened their own restaurants in Paris which compete well with the expensive ones.

In March we made our second skiing trip in France, this time with the Jungmans. It was quite different from going to Chamonix with the Club Med in 1980. It was a rather low-key setup where people skied in jeans rather than in colorful designer skiing outfits like at Chamonix. The slopes at **Var** in the Alpine foothills were more challenging and often you had to take the ski bar up the hill rather than a chair lift. We had a very good time. When we rented our skis and our boots from a little local store, the owner told us that he trusted us and that we could pay when we brought them back. Quite a contrast to the Colorado skiing experience where you have to give your credit card first before you get anything. We enjoyed the many Alpine dishes like *Tartiflette*, a potato-cheese, and-bacon dish baked in white wine, or the *Raclette*, a large block of cheese melted in a Raclette heater where you dip pieces of potato, ham, or other meats into the melted cheese. They also serve Fondues of various kinds which were much better than those we had in Switzerland.

Raclette heater

When we returned our ski equipment to the owner of the shop, he offered us a drink. It was a very friendly exchange.

At the beginning of April 1994, we took another vacation, this time to **Cannes** where we stayed in a rented apartment rather than in a hotel. We were again together with the Jungmans who knew their way around. I ran every day long distances in Cannes, I was preparing for the upcoming Paris Marathon which was scheduled for later on in April. Vera decided not to run this time. We loved the beautiful Riviera, the beaches, the lovely nearby towns in the **Provence,** and the medieval cities of **St Paul de Vance, Monte Carlo,** and **Nice.** Our favorite place however was the picturesque resort town called **Eze** on top of the mountain halfway between Nice and **San Remo.** It was a favorite hangout of Picasso.

Picturesque view of Eze

Although I ran every day and a few times even ran as much as three hours I was not as prepared for the Marathon as before. Plus, my heart was not in it because this was the first time I would run without Vera. I knew I could run 30 Km, about 19 miles, so I told Vera to wait for me at the Trocadero which was about that distance from the start, so we could go home from there. By the time I got to Trocadero and looked for Vera, I could not see her anywhere. So, I decided to finish it. Which I did in 4 hours 50 minutes.

The Acoustical Society of France held its yearly meeting in **Lille**, which is the fifth-largest city in France near the Belgian border. I stopped there a few times before on my way to Kortrijk, taking a train from Paris. Oswald usually picked me up in Lille and drove to Kortrijk. Once I missed my last train from Lille to Paris and had to stay overnight. This time Vera joined me at the meeting and we stayed in Lille for five days.

By now we had traveled quite a bit in France and enjoyed the many different terrains. Alsace was one of our favorites, particularly the 70 km drive in the wine country from **Strasburg** to **Colmar**, crossing the picturesque little villages, many with significant Jewish history.

Colmar Alsace

We liked **Burgundy** and the **Loire Valley** with its many Chateaux, and also **Lyon** with its two-rivers and its many fabulous restaurants. Normally we would rent a car to drive to our destination and on our return, we would drop the car off at the rental agency. We never felt the need to keep a car in Paris, not even for trips, because we enjoyed walking in this exciting city.

After almost twenty years of owning the tiny little one-bedroom apartment in 42 Rue Vaneau, Vera wanted to move to a larger apartment. I had no objection but I wanted to stay at the same address. In the seven-story building, there were seven one-bedroom and seven two-bedroom apartments plus a terrace apartment on the top floor. We put a letter in all the mailboxes in the building asking to exchange or to buy a two-bedroom apartment. Within a week we got two responses. We moved from the third floor (fourth in the US) to the fifth floor (sixth in the US) in 2002. The new apartment had a great view and was very spacious (by French standards).

Driving to Seville from Paris in 2002 our first stop was in **Vichy**, famous for its spas and its mineral water but more infamous for being the place where the Petain led French Government established a pro-Nazi apparatus during WW 2. From there we drove to the Massif Central, our first visit to this picturesque part of France. We loved **Rocamadur** which became one of our favorite places to which we returned several times and enjoyed their great cheese every time.

Our next stop was **Pau**, in the northern part of the Pyrenees, the birthplace of Henry IV. The -mile-long Boulevard des Pyrenees, has buildings only on one side and is open to the stunning view of the Pyrenees on the other side. I guess I should also mention that the cuisine of the area is probably the best in France.

From Pau, we drove to **St Jean de Luz**, a lovely sea resort on the Atlantic which is part of the *Pays Basque*, the Basque Country. Most people stay at the better-known **Biarritz,** but we found St Jean de Luz more to our taste. We also drove into the mountainous area nearby to visit the beautiful little villages in the **Pays Basque**. We sampled their unique cuisine which is somewhat similar to the Hungarian (stuffed pepper for example) and watched their folk dances and their colorful costumes during their festivals. The Basques are unique as is their "strange" language that is a non-Indo-European tongue like Hungarian, although there is no relation between them. Most of the Basques live in Spain and only a small percentage of them live in France. The French Basques are much less nationalistic than their Spanish brothers.

Back in Paris in early June 2005, we were happy to welcome Suzika with Richard Wilk, with whom she was going steady for the last several months. We thought that La Tour D'Argent would be a good introduction of the young man to Paris as well as to Suzika's parents. Ironically, Richard is not too keen on duck and foie gras, the specialty of this famous restaurant. Nevertheless, we had a great time together and Richard did not leave La Tour D'Argent hungry.

With Richard and Susan in the La Tour D'Argent in Paris (2005).

In March of the following year, we hosted Judy and Howard, Richard's parents in Paris. We became very close, spending Thanksgiving for the last two years with them and sharing lots of time with our new family in their home in Boston and in our home in Florida. In-laws rarely develop such a close relationship with each other. They are genuinely nice people and we enjoyed being with them whenever we had a chance. Our small apartment in Paris was sufficient to accommodate them and we had a very good week together in Paris.

Shortly after Richard's parents left us, Susan and Richard arrived bringing eight-month-old Hannah to her first visit to Paris. She had a ball from day one discovering her new environment.

Eight months old Hannah in our Rue Vaneau apartment in Paris. (2007)

We showed them our favorite spots in Paris. We went to the Louvre (It is never too early to start appreciating the arts!) and spent a whole afternoon up in Montmartre.

255

Near the Sacre Coeur in Montmartre (2007)

A few days later we drove to **Strasbourg** and from there did the seventy-kilometer drive through the wine country up to **Colmar**. Hannah had a great time.

Later on, in another trip in 2007, we drove from Spain, and our first stop in France was in **Carcassonne**, a historic fortified city. We reserved a B&B owned by some English people in the city but on our arrival, no one was around and the house was closed. We walked around in the medieval city for a couple of hours and finally, the English couple showed up and let us into their rather mediocre setup. They did not even apologize for being several hours late.

The entrance gate to Carcassonne France.

In contrast to our unpleasant experience in Carcassonne, we had the most wonderful reception in the Chateaux Puymartin, a castle between **Sarlat** and **Lez Eyzies** not far from **Perigueux**. When we arrived at the Chateaux-which was mostly converted to a museum, there were only two rooms for guests. - The owner, a young descendant of the original owners, left his group of visitors to accommodate us. We learned of the legend of the "White Lady" (La Dame Blanche) who was a prisoner in one of the rooms of the chateau for 15 years after her husband surprised her with her lover. The lover was killed!

The rooms were magnificent and the breakfast was served by the aristocratic hosts. The mother and son were very poor even though they were the owners of the castle. It was a historic treasure and the government would not allow them to sell any of its antiquities.

Chateaux Puymartin near Sarlat, France.

We ended our tour in Paris after stopping in **Saint Emilion**, a town famous for the wine, and also in **Bordeaux.**

We always wanted to bring Rachel to Paris many times when she was a little girl. Her parents finally let her come in 2008 when she graduated from high school.

With Rachel and Michael before her trip

A day before Rachel's arrival to Paris I was jogging near the Invalides and did not see a big concrete block in front of me (Vera said I probably was distracted by staring at someone in high heels.) and I fell bruising my shoulder, knees, and even my face. I was able to walk to the nearby Saint-Jean de Dieu clinic on Rue Oudinot bleeding from my face. I received excellent treatment at the clinic and was assured that I had no brain nor serious shoulder damage. Anyway, my face was all black and blue and when I picked up Rachel at the Charles De Gaulle airport, she was scared looking at me. The same day when we took her for a lunch to an outdoor café on the Champs Elysee, a couple who were sitting next to us could not look at me so they moved to another table. I started to wear sunglasses to avoid such unpleasant happenings.

Rachel enjoyed every moment of her stay in Paris. It was wonderful to visit everything with her and see the enthusiasm of this bright young granddaughter of ours and watch her discover our favorite city. She loved the museums, the restaurants, and our favorite nightclub "Aux Trois Mailletz", where the fantastic international entertainment starts at midnight and continues until six in the morning. We celebrated Vera's 65th birthday together in El Canto, a restaurant where all the waiters were opera singers. Rachel is very artistic and made a beautiful card for Vera's birthday. Vera still cherishes it.

Rachel's birthday card to Vera (2008)

Sanyi and Mari joined us in Paris for a few days celebrating Sanyi's 75th birthday. We spent several very nice days together. We went to see a light opera and also a group of singers from Cape Verde. They were singing the songs popularized by their country's famous singer named Cesaria Evora, who was discovered in Paris. We also took our visitors to our favorite night club, the Aux Trois Mailletz, where I showed off with my dancing performance on the stage.

Dancing in the Aux Trois Mailletz

In the beginning of July of 2012, Susan and Richard brought the girls to Paris. We signed them up in a summer Montessori School which was held in the American Church on Quai Orsai, a couple of miles from us. The school started at 9 in the morning and it lasted until 1 p.m. It was mostly playtime but the idea was that they would learn some French. Ironically, they made their friends with two little Italian girls and they probably learned more Italian than French. It was a great experience anyway.

Their parents left for an extended European vacation and we stayed with the girls. Every morning they got up around 7 and after breakfast of fresh croissants and baguettes from the bakery across the street, we walked around ten minutes to the bus station. They loved to hold their bus tickets and to validate them. Sometimes when there were no seats on the bus they had to stand. We had a ten-minute bus drive and another 10-minute walk to the school. After school, it was the reverse.

Often, they spent the afternoon with the two Italian girls. After many years they are still in touch. It was fun to spend time with Hannah and Talia in Paris, we took them to the parks, to restaurants, and they even liked to walk in the city. Once the parents came back, we had programs for all of us together. They all stayed in Paris for a month.

The Parisian school girls with their mother in Quai Orsai (2012)

In 2017 after spending a few days in Paris with Richard, Suzika, Hannah, and Talia, we were ready to drive south for a two-week vacation. Richard had to go back to Boston but he joined us a week later. Dayna, Suzika's childhood friend was also with us on our adventure. Driving about 400 km (250 miles) with seven passengers in a Ford S-MAX minivan, we arrived at our first destination, St-Denis du Pin.

Ford S-MAX

In this little village, we stayed at a pretty old Chateau called Domaine Rennebourg which our friends Françoise and Georges had recommended to us. The Chateau is owned by an old lady who is a descendant of a local branch of nobility.

The weather was very nice and we all went to the swimming pool to cool off after the long trip from Paris.

Hannah and Talia enjoyed the beautiful little theater in the Chateau where the next morning they showed off their dancing and singing. We were all delighted including the owner. We had a delicious continental breakfast, and after the show, we started our trip to Tonneins.

Breakfast at Domain du Rennenbourg 2017

The evening before our departure we went to a charming restaurant in the nearby village of Saint-Jean D'Angely and the next day we continued our adventure.

After dinner in St Jean

Tonneins on the River Garonne 2017

Tonneins, a little village with a population of 9000, is located halfway between Bordeaux and Toulouse. We stayed in Françoise's beautiful three-story house which is located right on the River Garonne.

We took the generous offer of Françoise to have her house as our base during our vacation. The most striking and inviting aspects of the house are the beautiful views of the river and the garden where we had all our meals. The house had all the amenities of an American home. We got to know the town very well by walking around to buy Talia's favorite treat, baguettes. While Suzika and Dayna drove to Bordeaux and Bergerac, we went to see a few French kids' films, which Hannah and Talia were able to handle easily since they had already seen them before in English. The highlight was the wonderful fireworks display on Bastille Day (July 14) which we all enjoyed watching from the garden.

We drove to **Capbreton,** a nice resort town on the Atlantic Ocean, where Françoise's family has a vacation home. The house is about a 10-minute walk from the beach and is very comfortable. We drove to a nearby very fashionable beach town called **Hossegor** that is full of little boutiques, nice cafes, restaurants and a big farmers' market. It is also considered one of the surfing paradises of the world. Close to the beach, we discovered the Canal Hossegor which connects Lake Hossegor to the ocean. We watched boys and girls jumping into the water from the bridge about 30 or 40 feet high. We would not let Hannah and Talia do the same.

We were only a short distance away from **Bayonne**, the capital city of Le Pays Basque near the Spanish border, so we decided to spend a day there. Bayonne is a very colorful city of about 50,000 people who speak both French and Basque, a very difficult language as challenging to learn as Hungarian. The Basque population is about 3 million, 10% of which live in France and the rest in Spain. After walking through the Old City, we visited a Museum of Basque history and culture. In the evening we went to listen to the Mozart Requiem in the beautiful Cathedral of Bayonne. After an hour, all the girls were saturated with this beautiful but rather heavy music and we left the cathedral to find young people dancing to Latin rhythm outside on the street. We participated. This was a nice finish!

After returning to Tonneins and saying goodbye to Daynika whom we missed right away, we went to a nearby restaurant in **Villeton** called La Chope et Le Pichet. The owners, a Belgian couple, who visited the town a few years earlier and fell in love with the area, renovated a house on the canal and made it a restaurant. It had beautiful surroundings with lovely trees and gardens.

In the restaurant La Chope et Le Pichet in Villeton

263

The girls performing

The day after Bastille Day we said goodbye to Françoise's beautiful home in Tonneins Richard joined us again and drove to St Jean de Luz, one of our favorite resorts in the Pays Basque where we spent a couple of days. We drove around in the Basque country enjoying the unique little villages like **Saint-Pée-sur-Nivelle** and **Espelette**. We admired the performances of the singers and dancers in their colorful costumes and tried their specialties like Tarte Basque, a tasty dessert. But what was most spectacular and what we admired most were their unique houses and the beautiful surrounding.

Saint-Pée-sur-Nivelle 2017

On July 19, we started our trip back to Paris, 500 km away. Richard handled the Ford very well. Halfway there, we stopped at another of our favorite spots that we were happy to share with our kids, Rocamadour, a very picturesque town perched on a cliff.

Rocamadour, Massif Central, France 2017

Happy family with a fake horse in Rocamadour 2017

Our last stop before Paris was at the best known chateau in the Loire Valley, **Chenonceau**. By walking through this beautiful castle, we imagined life as it was in the very romantic times of Henry II and Diane de Poitiers.

Chateau Chenonceau 2017

It was a beautiful way to finish our vacation. We all agreed to have a follow-up, which we did two years later in Israel, celebrating Hannah's Bat Mitzvah in 2019.

Our apartment in on the left side at the corner and our favorite restaurant, La Table D'Aki across the street in Rue Vaneau, Paris

One of the many dishes   *Our favorite desert*

The restaurant owner is Mr. Aki, a Japanese native who was the master chef in the Ambroise, a 3 star (Michelin's highest ratings) restaurant in *Place des Vosges* in the Marais. He opened his restaurant across the street from us in 2012, and we were probably his first customers. Every time we are in Paris we eat in this rather small but excellent restaurant. He is the only one who cooks because he doesn't trust anyone else. His dishes are just perfect. We send many of our friends to La Table D'Aki and he shows his appreciation with a bottle of good champagne as a gift. We dined here in October 2019 with our friends Oswald and Agnes Leroy from Kortrijk, Belgium. We hope the travel restrictions due to COVID 19 will end soon and we can go back to Paris and dine in Aki's restaurant.

19. BELGIUM

This was our first visit to Belgium and we planned to visit both the Flemish and the Walloon parts of the country and also go to Brussels, where Vera's aunt Stefi and her husband resided. The first thing I thought of while entering Belgium after leaving the French city of Lille is a little story by a Hungarian writer, Klara Feher. She wrote a book in Hungarian about the life of the immigrant entitled "Where should the Belgians line up?" The story starts at a military post where all the new draftees are standing in groups. The Sergeant makes an announcement: "All the Walloons should line up on my left and all the Flemish should line up on my right". The little Kovacs boy, whose parents had escaped Hungary and moved to Belgium only a few years earlier, steps to the front asking, "Where should the Belgians line up?"

I understood that we would be visiting two countries, separated by history, culture, and language. It seems that only the immigrants who mostly resided in the French part like Vera's aunt and the little Kovacs boy are the Belgians. As of today, the majority of about 60% is Flemish-speaking living in the North while the French-speaking people, about 40%, live in South Belgium.

Agnes and Oswald Leroy were waiting for us at the **Kortrijk** railroad station. They gave us a very warm welcome. We were taken to their home for a nice lunch. They lived and still live in a lovely single-family home with a beautiful garden, where two colorful peacocks were proudly walking. Our gourmet lunch was memorable in this magical setting. We stayed for a few days in a very comfortable apartment belonging to the University of Leuven in Kortrijk. We found the whole environment in Kortrijk to be very calm, comfortable and ideal living for a university professor.

Oswald would come home from the university for lunch and take a nap for a couple of hours of rest before returning to the university. Certainly, not the American style of a quick lunch at Wendy's and a dash back to work. Oswald worked on the theory of light diffraction through ultrasound with Professor Mertens who interacted with Professor Hiedemann of Michigan State University in the US.

Actually, for the next evening's dinner, the six of us (Vera and I, the Leroys and the Mertens) went to the Marquette, a very exclusive and probably very expensive restaurant. It was a royal treatment for us which we still remember after more than forty years. We were served foie gras, whole lobster, champagne and many bottles of great wines, French pastries and more, along with a very lively conversation and lots of humor. It was a very memorable evening and we felt that we had made a lifetime friendship with the Leroy family. Time has proven that the feeling was mutual.

Our next stop was in Brussels to spend a few hours with Stefi and her husband Jozsi. They left Budapest right after the war in 1945 and settled in Brussels where they were rather successful in developing a children's apparel factory. We both were happy to connect with them. Brussels is one of the most important international centers in Europe. It is the capital city of the European Union, headquarters of NATO, and the financial center of Western Europe. Until the 19th century, most people in Brussels spoke Flemish, a minor variation of the Dutch language. After the 19th century, the percentages rapidly changed and today more than 90 percent of Brussel's inhabitants are French-speaking. We visited Stefi some ten years later, but by then her husband had passed away.

Vera and Suzika with Stefi in the middle in Brussels. Belgium 1991

Grand Market, in central Brussels

One of the most known food chains all over Europe is Leon de Bruxelles, serving mussels in various sauces and with pommes frites (french-fried potatoes). Vera invented a lighter version, using cooked potatoes in the sauce instead of the French Fries on the side.

Moules Mariniere

Serves 4

Ingredients:

3 lb. mussels in the shells

3 cups of dry white wine

¼ cup of heavy cream

2 tbsp. butter

1 shallot

6 grape tomatoes halved

8 cloves of garlic mashed

2 potatoes peeled and cubed

A handful of chopped parsley

½ tsp. red pepper flakes

½ tsp. salt

½ tsp. freshly ground black pepper

Directions:

1. In a heavy pot melt the butter, add the chopped shallot, the mashed garlic, the tomatoes, and the spices. Sauté them for about five minutes. Add the wine and bring it to boil.

2. In a separate dish boil the cubed potatoes until cooked

3. Scrub the mussels under running cold water and then drop them into boiling water. Cover with lid for one minute, remove the lid and stir the content well with a wooden spoon. Put back the lid and cook for 5-6 minutes until all the shells open up.

4. Pour in the cream, test for seasoning. Add the drained cooked potatoes. Sprinkle with parsley and serve.

When we lived in Paris with the children in 1980, Oswald and Agnes Leroy invited us to Kortrijk, so we left from Paris changing trains in the city of Lille at the French-Belgian border. The Leroys had three children close to Michael's and Suzika's age. Anika, Vivian, and Pascal. So, we all had lots of fun connecting with a European family. We stayed in the Kortrijk campus housing of the University of Leuven but had all our meals together at the home of the Leroys. Michael and Suzika were both so impressed by the fact that Pascal Leroy learned six languages in his school. In addition to Flemish and French, he took German, English, Latin, and Greek. Certainly not the requirement for American schoolchildren.

We traveled together with the Leroy family to the nearby beautiful city of Bruges (Brugge in Flemish), frequently referred to as the Venice of the North. In addition to sightseeing and taking a boat ride among the intact medieval buildings, one of the most memorable moments was when Suzika played the piano after our lunch in a very nice restaurant in the town square in the middle of Bruges. She played Mozart's Turkish March and the Leroys are still talking about it after almost forty years.

Brugge the "Venice of the North" Flemish part of Belgium

In the last 40 years, we have visited Belgium several times, mostly in the Flemish part of the country to Ghent, Antwerp, and Leuven. We went to Brussels several times and also visited Ypres where one of the bloodiest battles of World War 1 was fought.

In June 2012, we went once more to visit Oswald and Agnes in Kortrijk and they took us to their vacation condo in Ostend on the North Atlantic on a very lovely 15 km Belgian stretch of beach between France and Holland. Interestingly, neither the French nor the Dutch allow construction along their beachfront so everybody from these two countries buys property in the Belgian area and as a result, there are thousands of condominium buildings along the coast. There is a boardwalk as well as an electric train that goes from one end to another of this very civilized resort. Our hosts took us to a fancy restaurant in the Casino for Vera's birthday. We always have a good time with the Leroys. Our friendship goes back more than forty years.

With Agnes and Oswald celebrating Vera's birthday in Oostende (2012)

20. POLAND

In the fall of 1978, I landed at the **Warsaw** airport. It was my first visit to Poland and the first visit behind the Iron Curtain other than to Hungary. Naturally, I had profoundly mixed feelings entering a country which was the cemetery of six million Jews but I also felt honored to be invited to the FASE conference. I took a taxi to the Forum Hotel where I stayed. The conference was held in the Forum a huge monumental building, called the Palace of Culture, built by the Soviet Union as a gift to the Polish people. It is a huge ugly boxy building that is the largest in Warsaw. The Poles have their famous riddle: "Where is the best place to be in Warsaw? The answer is: "In the Palace of Culture. Why? Because that is the only place where you can't see it".

Palace of Culture, a gift from Stalin, Warsaw Poland

Before the conference started, I signed up for a sightseeing tour of the city, and at the event registration desk, I learned that I was the only American. There were about 800 participants, mostly from the Eastern European countries who could not easily travel to the West, and quite a few Western Europeans, mostly from Germany.

On the sightseeing bus tour, most were Germans and when the bus driver started to describe the sights in English, the Germans asked him to speak German instead. The bus driver refused, saying that even though he knew the language he would not say a word in German because of their barbaric actions during the war. He made special efforts to point out the locations of the Ghetto mentioning that this was the place where our Jewish brothers fought the Nazis heroically. I was deeply touched to hear it and at the end of the tour, I thanked him and tipped him $20. (I was the only tipper).

My presentation went very well at the Conference. I gave a 30-minute talk and when I finished it they called me and asked me to give a second lecture which was not even planned. Fortunately, I had plenty of materials with me for a second lecture. There were a few Hungarians in the audience and they seemed to be proud of my performance. One of the highlights of the conference was a visit to **Zelazowa Wola** the birthplace of Chopin where we heard a wonderful piano concert of his works in the very house where he was born.

Zelazowa Wola, the birthplace of Frederic Chopin

After the concert, about 30 or 40 of us stopped for dinner in an inn across from Chopin's house. Most were Germans again but there were some French and other Western Europeans including my friends the Leroys from Kortrijk. The restaurant was too expensive unless you paid in western currency, so the Eastern Europeans did not come. The food was OK. They served *bigos*, the most common Polish dish of sautéed cabbage with stewed pork.

Restaurant Chopin in Zelazowa Wola

Bigos

Vera's version of Bigos, a typical Polish dish, sautéd cabbage with pork stew and sausage

Serves 6

Ingredients:

½ medium cabbage;

4 cups of sauerkraut;

1 can tomato paste;

½ lb. bacon sliced;

1 lb. pork diced (any parts that can be sautéd);

1 lb. Kielbasa sausage sliced

1 large onion diced;

2 cloves garlic minced;

1 bay leaf;

Optional salt and pepper to taste

Directions:

1. Cut your washed cabbage into thin slices and boil until tender in a pot.

2. Boil the sauerkraut in another pot in about 2 cups of water. Strain and keep the sour water aside.

3. Sauté your diced pork in a pan with some cooking oil (lard, coconut oil or butter are good), then set aside.

4. Sauté the bacon and sausage with the onion and garlic.

5. In a large pot, combine the cooked cabbage, sauerkraut, sour water, tomato paste, spices, and your cooked meats, onion and garlic.

6. Let simmer for about 1 hour. Serve

They had a very good three-man group playing folk songs. I enjoyed singing along and tipped the musicians like we do in Hungary. To the disappointment of the musicians, the other people of the group had different upbringings. I just grabbed the hat of one of the musicians and walked up to the guests one by one tapping on their shoulders and pointing to the hat for them to put in some tips. The musicians were very grateful! Oswald and Agnes still enjoy talking about the event.

I attended the Acousto-Optics Schools in **Gdansk** a couple of times before I came again in 1995 while Vera stayed in Paris. The School was organized by Tony Sliwinski, a professor of physics at the University of Gdansk. In a previous meeting, Tony invited about 15 of us to his tiny apartment for supper. I was so touched by his and his wife's Alina's hospitality that when I found out that he had never been to the USA, I decided to arrange a trip for him.

Not only did I invite him to visit Ohio State University all expenses paid, but I also contacted several other universities to send him invitations and cover part of his travel expenses. It was essential to make these arrangements for him because in the 1980s under the communist regime in Poland, the only way people could travel to Western countries was if everything was paid for in foreign currency.

Tony and I became very close friends and he invited me to every one of the Acousto-Optics Schools. In 1995 my lecture in Gdansk was entitled "Impact of Nonlinear Acoustics on Nondestructive Evaluation and Acousto-Optics". I liked to come to Gdansk, a seaport on the Baltic Sea. Gdansk was one of the Hanseatic cities, members of the Hanseatic League formed in 1393 as a commercial and defensive confederation of merchant guilds and market towns on the Baltic Sea.

The city of Gdansk, Poland

It was called Danzig by the Germans before WW 2 when they claimed the city as their own. It had a large German population and their attack against Poland started in this city. After the war and the defeat of the Germans, most of the German population was expelled from Gdansk. The conference was attended by my good friend Bill Cook, and in my lecture, I acknowledged the help I got from him at Michigan State University when I was a graduate student in 1958. Unfortunately, he passed away a couple of years later. He was a good guy!

From Gdansk, I took a train to **Krakow**, a city I always wanted to visit. It is one of the nicest medieval cities in Europe. It was especially interesting for me to visit *Kazimierz* the old part of Krakow which was established by king Kazimierz and where for centuries Jewish and Christian cultures lived side by side. Although most of the Jewish population of Krakow was murdered by the Nazis in nearby Auschwitz, there is a revival of Jewish life with a yearly Klezmer festival and other cultural events, such as courses on Klezmer music in the Music Conservatory.

The Jewish Quarter in Krakow

Vera and I came to Poland in 1998. I was invited to lecture again at the Acousto -Optics School in Gdansk. Before the meeting, we spent a few days in Prague with Steve and Marika. From Prague, we went to Krakow by train to spend a couple more days there. Vera had never been to Poland before and Krakow was my favorite city in Poland. From Krakow, we took a day tour to Auschwitz, an exterminating camp where more than one million Jews and others were murdered in gas chambers from 1942-45. Vera's mother was one of the inmates there who survived working in an ammunition factory. Unfortunately, Vera's 11 years old brother Lali was one of those gassed in Auschwitz.

Auschwitz-Birkenau Concentration Camp

The following day we had to take a train from Krakow to Warsaw where we had to get a plane from Warsaw to Gdansk. When we arrived at the Warsaw airport, we were shocked to find that all flights to Gdansk for that day were canceled. My lecture was the next morning so there was no way I could get there in time. We went to the office of LOT, the Polish airline to explain the situation and asked them to call Tony Sliwinski in Gdansk and explain what happened. Within fifteen minutes we were told that someone would drive us to Gdansk.

So, we were taken in a large Mercedes on this 300-mile trip and I was able to give my lecture thanks to the people at LOT. I am not sure if the airlines in France or the USA would have given this courtesy. After the conference, we came back to Warsaw this time by plane and spent a couple of nice days there. In the Warsaw opera, we saw a grandiose performance of Tchaikovsky's *Mazeppa*, during which at times had at least three hundred performers on the stage.

National Opera Warsaw Poland

Our visit to the home of Mordechai Anielewich in the old Ghetto was a memorable part of our time in Poland.

At the home of Mordechai Anielewics,   the leader of the Warsaw Ghetto Uprising 1998

In 2014 Vera and I together with our friends Françoise and Georges came back to Poland for a few days after a trip to Lithuania. We were so impressed by the way Warsaw changed in the last few years. It looks more like Manhattan with its high skyscrapers, while thirty years earlier it looked like a city in a third world country. An important sign of progress was the newly built Museum of the Jews of Poland.

Downtown Warsaw 2014

S5. MAINE

In 1978, while visiting Montreal, we decided to spend a vacation in **Ogunquit**, a little resort town on the Atlantic Ocean in Maine. There we met my friend Poncike (George Karpati) with his family. We had a wonderful week in Ogunquit where our children enjoyed the beach and we all loved the restaurants with their great seafood. Poncike, my childhood friend from Debrecen, was the best man at my wedding and I was the best man at his wedding.

Poncike was the most brilliant person I've ever known. When he passed away unexpectedly in 2009, the front page of the Montreal Gazette showed his picture with the title "Giant in Neurology".

Ogunquit Maine

Poncike and I with our wives and children on the right in Ogunquit Maine (1978).

In 1993 the meetings of the Quantitative Non-Destructive Evaluation, QNDE, which for many years took place in La Jolla, were held in Bowdoin College in **Brunswick**, Maine. It was quite a contrast to be in a small liberal arts college established in 1704 in New England as opposed to the huge modern University of California campus in La Jolla.

Bowdoin College Brunswick Maine

Sanyi and Mari joined us this time in Maine and we enjoyed the bargain meals at Cook's place: 3 lobsters for $15! We had 3 each.

With Sanyi and Mari at Cook's place Maine 1993

S6. OHIO

Vera was doing quite well in her two stores in Knoxville so she decided to open a third store further north in **Cincinnati**, Ohio. We made several trips each year to New York fashion shows to order merchandise from the US and foreign manufacturers. Upon the return from one of these New York shopping trips, we stopped in Cincinnati and selected a location in a newly built mall called North Gate Mall. The same day we signed a lease for another store three times larger than the one in West Town Mall. The opening was scheduled for the fall of 1974 and the construction and design was handled by Arnold Schwarzbart, the same architect who had built our store in the West Town Mall.

Susane Suede and Leather Fashion in Northgate Mall, Cincinnati (1974)

During my stay in Cincinnati, I discovered a fantastic restaurant, called **Mozart**. It stayed open quite late so I could go there after closing the store at 9 PM or sometimes even later. It was located in Vine Street, in a slightly rundown area downtown. The restaurant owner was an interesting character, a jazz pianist with a Che Guevara beret, and a Ph.D. in psychology. Often, he and I were the only ones left after 10 PM sitting at separate tables. For the next 10 years or so, while Vera had the store in Cincinnati, I ate there almost all the time when I was in Cincinnati. I always ordered the same thing. I started with a veal terrine, followed by a bib lettuce salad with gorgonzola cheese. The main course was their special, fettuccini prepared in cream sauce, shredded carrots, shrimp, and lobster. It was a wonderful meal! They also baked round loaves of their own crispy Italian bread. Normally, I would stay till midnight, since I started eating so late. The owner and I rarely talked although we greeted each other.

A few years later, Vera almost opened a restaurant together with him in Columbus, but it did not work out. I also took Michael to eat at Mozart when he joined me in Cincinnati during Christmas breaks. Suzika also came there a few times with me. Mozart was probably the first and the most memorable of the many gourmet restaurants that I have known through the years. I will always remember being there.

In 1980 I got an offer from Ohio State University which I could not refuse: A full professorship in the College of Engineering in two departments, Welding Engineering and also in Engineering Mechanics, double my

University of Tennessee salary, and the responsibility of starting a new Ph. D. program in Non-Destructive Evaluation (NDE). So, we moved to **Columbus**, Ohio in September 1980. We bought a nice bungalow in Canterbury Village near the Scioto River in Upper Arlington, in the western part of Columbus.

Our home in Canterbury Village, Upper Arlington, Columbus.

We both were active in Ohio. At OSU I developed a Ph. D. program in the teaching and research of NDE with the involvement of several faculty, postdocs, and graduate research assistants. Vera opened her fourth store, the second in Ohio in the Ohio Convention Center.

 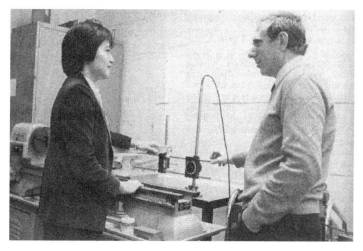

Non-Destructive Evaluation Laboratory at Ohio State University, Columbus

Susane Suede and Leather Fashion in the Ohio Convention Center

286

Michael enrolled in the Upper Arlington High School, where he joined the band as a tuba player. Suzika attended Jones Junior High School and won several first-place awards in state competitions in Spanish. She also jogged daily like the rest of us.

Michael in the Upper Arlington HS   Suzika is leading in a 5K race

In the second month of our stay in Columbus, there was an open house for the faculty of the College of Engineering hosted by Dean Glower. At that reception, we met several faculty members who came from Hungary in 1956. They were happy to meet Vera and me, and shortly afterward we were invited to the home of one of the professors for dinner where several other Hungarian couples were also invited. Pretty soon, we met about 12 to 14 couples from Hungary who settled in Columbus in or after 1956. It was an active group known for socializing, inviting each other for dinners, parties, barbecuing, and rotating New Year's Eve celebrations in the members' homes.

I am singing with Almost Kovacs in the home of Ivan Halasz.

We were welcomed by most of the Hungarian couples who were all in our age group and started to have a very active social life. Vera by then had become a real gourmet cook with her cooking classes in Paris and was recognized as one of the best cooks among the Hungarians. She made a wonderful variety of French and Hungarian dishes at dinner parties for 10 or 12 people in our home.

A dinner party in our home in Canterbury Village (the mid-1980s)

We participated in our friends' children's weddings which were always full of music, dancing, and good food.

Vera and I are dancing at a wedding in Columbus cheered by our friends.

Both Vera and I felt confident that after more than twelve years of long-distance running, we were ready to try to run a marathon. The history of the Marathon goes back to 490 BC when a messenger of the ancient Greek army named Pheidippides ran 42.195 kilometers from Marathon to Athens, the equivalent of 26 miles and 385 yards, to announce that the Greeks had won the battle against the Persians. Today's Iranians are still angry over the continuing historical reminder of their defeat. Upon his arrival to Athens, Pheidippides screamed *nenikekame* "we won", and then he collapsed and died!

Not knowing this detail about the ending of Pheidippides' Marathon run, we decided to give it a try. We learned that for about six weeks before the race, one should run at least 70 miles a week and not less than 18-20 miles at least once a week. We also found that a group of people starting at the Jewish Community Center on College Street would run the recommended 18-20 miles every Sunday for several weeks before the race. We showed up at the Center the next Sunday morning where about 15 - 20 men mostly in their mid-thirties were ready to start training with a run into German Village close to 10 miles from the Center and back. The pace of between seven and eight minutes per mile was pretty fast for me. However, I tried to keep up with the group but by the time we arrived at German Village, I was out of breath and knew that I would not be able to run back to the Center.

Vera on the other hand was smiling while keeping pace with the rest of them. I told her that I was bailing out and she should wait for me at the Center. I started to run slower but soon realized that I was unable to run back, so I found a taxi. Luckily, I always carry some cash with me, just in case, and was able to get back to the Center to meet Vera there. While waiting, I met a man and a woman in their thirties, arriving at a much slower pace to the Center. After talking with them, I learned that they also were preparing for the October Marathon but because the group was just too fast for them, they were training separately.

So, I found the solution to my problem! In Physics, we know that $d=rt$ (distance = rate or speed multiplied by the time elapsed). We typically ran at a speed of 10 minutes per mile but the distance is the same, so what if takes longer? For the next 5-6 weeks Vera trained with the fast group and I trained with the couple.

It was quite exciting to see the thousands and thousands of runners lining up at the start in downtown Columbus on a beautiful Sunday morning on October 16, 1983. Ten times more people lined up along the streets as spectators. After kissing goodbye to Vera, who started out with the men she had trained with, I joined my partners as the race started and we were keeping our pace while we kept on talking to each other. At each mile, there was a water stand where volunteers handed out some water in paper cups to the runners. Sometimes we could even get Gatorade.

It was one of the most exciting events of my life. About a mile or so before the finish I saw Suzika who joined us in the run and told me that she was quite worried about me since her Mom (Vera) already finished the race a long time ago and she did not know what happened to me. Finally, my partners and I arrived to the finish line and hugged each other for finishing our first marathon.

Vera at the finish in the Columbus Marathon (1983)

I learned that while my time was 4 hours and 25 minutes, Vera completed her run in 3 hours and 30 minutes, averaging eight minutes per mile, a remarkable achievement. She placed third in her age group and qualified for the Boston Marathon! My time was 10 minutes per mile but I was overjoyed that at age of fifty I could finish the Marathon. The following year after training a little harder I finished in 3 hours and 45 minutes which was 8.65 minutes per mile. This was the best time I ever had in the six Marathons I ran. Five were with Vera, three in Columbus in 1983, 1984 and 1985, one in New York in 1986, and one in Paris in 1988. I ran one more alone in Paris in 1994.

I am finishing the Columbus Marathon (1984) with my best time

Michael took over the leather store from Vera and changed the name from Susane Suede to Adler Luggage and Suzika attended Tufts University in Boston.

These siblings are happy to be in Canterbury Village with us.

In 1987 Vera and I decided that we would not run the Columbus Marathon because Michael wanted to do it and we wanted to cheer for him. It was quite a beautiful sunny day in early November when a large group of runners among them Michael started the Marathon run in High Street. We cheered him on all the way making sure that we got to the various milestones of the race. At the finish, not only Vera and I but several of our friends were waiting for his arrival holding with several "Go for it Michael!" signs. When he crossed the finish line, our joy was probably even greater than when we finished the challenging race ourselves. Parents are parents!

Michael finishing the Columbus Marathon 1987

In the spring of 1988 when Michael took over the management of Vera's leather store, a beautiful young girl named Annie was working in the store. They fell in love and by the time we returned from our Balkan trip a wedding date was set. The wedding was scheduled in the lovely Great Southern Hotel on October 22nd, 1989. It was a beautiful event with more than 200 guests. Most of our relatives lived too far away in Israel and Hungary to attend, so our family was represented only by Vera's mother, Suzika, and my cousin's Agi's family from Knoxville. But we were rewarded by many of Vera's and my childhood friends who came from all across the USA and Canada with their families. Michael's best man was Steve's son Robi. We also invited all our friends from Columbus. Many of our friends whom we had met through our professional activities also accompanied us. I was very happy to see Bill Cook, my old friend from my student years at Michigan State University.

The evening before the wedding, Vera arranged a dinner reception in our home for about 70 out-of-town guests. Our friends, Mary Juhasz and her husband John, who both had a Ph.D., took care of all the cleaning and service for the event in our home. We were very grateful. The wedding ceremony was conducted in the traditional Jewish manner by Rabbi Garry Huber, from Temple Beth Tikva, in a Chupa set in the Hotel's hall. Before the ceremony, a five-piece chamber orchestra which was arranged by our late dear friend, the cellist Judith Ebner, played classical music from Haydn, Wagner, etc. After the ceremony, we had a very nice reception with many delicious dishes. During the dinner there were a few speeches, the most memorable words were those of Suzika who represented our family. The best part of the wedding was the traditional Jewish dancing to the music of the 6-piece local band. We lifted both the groom and the bride sitting on their chairs. The dance went on for close to an hour until everyone tired out. As always, I performed my Russian Cossack dance in the center of the circle. Afterwards, the band played ballroom dance music including a Hungarian Csardash. It was the first wedding among the children of our childhood friends and everybody enjoyed it.

Vera and I walking Michael to the Chupa. (1989)

Michael and Annie at their wedding in Columbus (1989)

Vera opened a costume jewelry store called "Illusion', across from Michael's store in the Convention Center, it was an instant success and Vera was much happier selling jewelry than selling leather goods. A couple of years later she opened her second Illusion store near Ohio State University in the Lane Avenue Mall.

Vera in her new store Illusion 1990.

Rachel with Vera in our pool, Canterbury Village, 1992

Rachel, with her mother's grandparents in front of our window overlooking the ravine 1992

In the spring break of 1993, we were ready to go to Keystone for a skiing vacation, but before our flight, we had a department meeting. I was already dressed in a colorful sweater for our trip. In the middle of the meeting, the door opened and President Gee entered the conference room with a couple of photographers and holding an apple. He came directly to hand me the apple saying, "You have been selected as the 1993 Distinguished Scholar". The award is the highest recognition of Ohio State University given each year to faculty members. I was of course speechless and overjoyed especially when Dr. Gee told us that my award was the only one for the College of Engineering faculty. Somewhat later I got a congratulation letter from the State of Ohio Senate for receiving the award along with a $20,000 check.

Before leaving the room, Dr. Gee said, "This is the ugliest sweater I've ever seen". It was a great pleasure to go to Colorado right after the meeting. Actually, I liked the sweater.

The award. (1993)

Celebrating with my friends, from left, Stas, Gabor, John, and Peter.

In July 1995 we moved to Florida. The day before our departure, Mary and John gave us a nice going-away party in their home where several colleagues and friends saw us off with their goodbyes. We were touched. The hardest part was to say goodbye to our little granddaughter, Rachel, and to her parents. But we knew that we would see her often. The highlight of coming back to Columbus was to come for Rachel's graduation ceremony first in 2015when she received her BA in Social Work from Ohio State University and a year later in 2016 when she got her MS.

Leaving Columbus 1995

Rachel at her graduation ceremony, receiving her MS from OSU 2016

S7. COLORADO

Joe and Ibi Koenig, the most sports-minded couple in our group in Columbus, had a motorboat and I learned from them how to water ski on the Scioto River. The following spring Vera and I joined them in Snowmass Colorado for a week-long skiing trip.

Vera and I with Ibi and Joe Koenig in Snowmass Colorado (in the 1980 s)

Both Vera and I became reasonably competent skiers. For the following 20 years we have continued to spend a week of skiing with the Koenigs in Keystone, Colorado where they had a condo, and thanks to their generosity we were their guests. Normally we would fly from Columbus to Denver and from Denver take a shuttle to the condo in Keystone. The Koenigs spent there three or four months a year, and on our arrival, they welcomed us warmly. We took a bus in the morning to the slopes and with rental ski equipment enjoyed our daily four or five hours of skiing. Keystone is close to 8000 feet high and has excellent slopes, some as high as 12,000 feet, for all levels of skiers.

We went out to the local restaurants a few times but most often we ate very good home-cooked Hungarian food. At one restaurant on top of a Lodge, close to the highest elevation in the area, there was a band playing some country and western music. We noticed that no one was dancing. Being adventuresome and never shy to initiate dancing anywhere, Vera and I went to the floor to soon find out that dancing is not easy at 12,000 feet. After a few minutes of struggling, we lost our breath and understood why nobody was dancing there.

Keystone Colorado

In Keystone Colorado, 1993 *Skiing in Keystone Colorado*

Skiing in Breckenridge, Colorado (2003)

We started to take Rachel skiing with us. First, we took her to the nearby Breckenridge and the following year we took her to Taos, New Mexico. It was fun to watch her progress.

I also went a few times to lecture at the University of Colorado in Boulder. Colorado is one of the prettiest states in the United States

S8. MASSACHUSETTS

In 1979 I was nominated to become a fellow of the Acoustical Society of America. The nomination read: "For his contribution to ultrasonic spectroscopy". It was quite an honor. To be a member of a scientific society, one just needs to join and pay membership fees. To become a Fellow, one needs to be nominated and voted on by a committee. The ceremony of the new Fellows' award was scheduled for the June meeting of ASA in **Boston**. Our family had never been to Boston. I had been there for one day in 1965 on my way to New York to pick up our VW which was shipped from Germany. I stayed with the Doolittles, a young couple, with whom we shared an apartment in Göttingen.

The ASA event in Boston was a good opportunity for all of us to see this historic city. The kids had to be at the New York airport a few days after the ASA meeting, so we had to plan around a long vacation again. First, we drove to Washington DC, which was on our way driving from Knoxville. In Washington, we spent a few days visiting all the important historical sites which was very educational for all of us. In addition to Michael and Susan, we took Edina along on this trip, the daughter of my cousin Agi. In Washington, we stayed at an apartment rented by Smarijahu Golan from the Technion who was out of town but was kind enough to let us stay at his place.

In Boston, more accurately in **Cambridge**, we stayed at the Hyatt Regency for a week. It was near MIT where the ASA conference was held and where I had two presentations. I regularly attended these and many other conferences, but the highlight of this meeting was the plenary awards session where the new Fellows get their awards. For me, it was even more rewarding and educational to listen to the acceptance speech of Richard Bolt who got the Gold Award, the most prestigious award of the society. Richard Bolt was a professor at MIT and part-owner of the well-known consulting firm *Bolt, Beranek and Newman*, involved mostly in concert hall acoustics.

Among other things Bolt said, "In my professional career, I was at the point that I had to decide whether to stay in academics or get into the business world. Then I solved that puzzle: *WHY NOT BOTH?*". I liked that! From then on, I often used Bolt's advice. Enjoy both the USA and Europe, be in academics and in business at the same time, etc. I was often open to new ideas, though I did not always follow them.

We enjoyed Boston very much. We all jogged along the river and went to the *Legal Sea Food* restaurant; at that time there was only one in Boston, they serve very good clam chowder, but today there must be hundreds throughout the US. We also ate brie at Faneuil Hall and enjoyed watching the chess players at Harvard Square.

Faneuil Hall Market Boston, Massachusetts

Clam Chowder

Serves 6

Ingredients:

2 tbsp. unsalted butter

1 medium onion, finely diced

1 white part of a leek finely chopped

3 tbsp. all-purpose flour

2 cups chicken stock

2 (10-ounce) cans chopped clams in juice

1 cup heavy cream

2 bay leaves

1-lb. potatoes, cut into 1/2- inch cubesA handful of chopped Italian parsley.

Salt and freshly ground black pepper

Directions:

1. Heat the butter in a large pot over medium/high heat

2. Add the chopped onion and the chopped leek and sauté until softened, mixing often. Stir in the flour and distribute evenly. Cook at low heat for a few minutes.

3. Add the chicken stock, bay leaves, potatoes, and the juice from the clams (save the clams). Bring to boil and lower the heat to medium-low and cook until the potatoes are fork-tender, about 20 minutes stirring often.

4. Add the clams and the cream mix it well and cook for another 5 minutes.

5. Add the parsley and season to taste before serving.

We all had a great time. We didn't know yet that Susan who was only 12 years old at the time, had decided to settle in Boston someday. After she graduated from Upper Arlington High School, we took her around to various universities where she was accepted, like the University of Michigan, Washington University in Saint Louis, and Tufts University in Boston where she eventually enrolled.

In 1985, we flew to Boston for a parents' orientation at Tufts University in Medford, where Suzika was a freshman. Oded, Sanyi and Mari's son joined us for the short trip. There were several events for the parents to participate in. One was a briefing by the Provost of Tufts, Sol Gittleman a scholar of Yiddish literature. To the well dressed and affluent audience at the very expensive Tufts, he said,

"Many of you are descendants of immigrants from Eastern Europe who came in the early 20th century to the United States. You probably were told that your ancestors were very wealthy and prosperous back in the old country. I have news for you: nobody came here who was successful back there, so don't kid yourselves!" I liked that guy.

We came to Boston many times to visit Suzika or friends after she graduated, and we are still coming after more than 35 years. We usually stayed at the Charles Hotel near Harvard Square.

Harvard Square Cambridge Massachusetts.

By May of 1989, we went to Suzika's graduation at Tufts University. She graduated cum laude. Michael and Vera's mother also attended the happy occasion, and to celebrate the beautiful occasion we all had a super graduation dinner at the Charles Hotel in **Cambridge**.

Suzika, the celebrity, Vera's mother, Michael, Vera, me and Margarita at Tufts University graduation ceremony (1989)

After her marriage, Suzika settled in **Newton** Massachusetts and we are so happy with her beautiful family. Massachusetts is a great state and now we have even more motive to go there 3 or 4 times a year.

Richard and Suzika with Hannah on right and Talia on left in Newton, Massachusetts.

Hannah and Talia now bigger than in the previous photo in front of their house in Newton, Mass.

21. CZECH REPUBLIC

I flew Budapest-Prague-London on British Airways in 1982. When the plane landed at the airport in **Prague,** it was clear that I'd be the only one to leave, and that the rest of the passengers who were mostly Hungarians would continue to London. Through the window of the plane, we could see an armed soldier waiting for me and a few of the Hungarians cried out, "The man is doomed, they will never let him leave this country".

Czechoslovakia, (after 1993, the country was split into the Czech Republic and Slovakia) was probably the most indoctrinated communist country in the Eastern bloc ever since 1968 when the Soviets invaded the liberalized country led by Dubcek. I walked out of the plane which was a few hundred feet from the terminal and as I walked into the terminal, I was followed by an armed soldier. Although I had an American passport, a visa, and a letter from the organizing committee of the conference, it still took about 25 minutes and many questions before they let me leave the airport.

I took a cab to one of the best hotels in Prague where I stayed throughout the conference. It was very comfortable except for the single towel in the bathroom which was not much larger than a handkerchief and which was made out of some rough material that did not absorb water. Oddly, among the many shortages in Prague, there was a towel shortage.

I had the afternoon free so I thought of buying a booklet about Prague. Unfortunately, none of the stores had any English language books of any kind, plenty in Russian! Luckily, during the conference, we had an English-speaking guide so I had a chance to enjoy many interesting aspects of this beautiful, ancient city.

The conference was mostly attended by scientists from the eastern bloc, a few from Germany and France, and one or two from the States and Canada. In contrast to the Hungarians and Poles whom I met earlier in the conferences in Hungary and Poland, the Czechs were not too friendly with westerners. You could tell that they were afraid of being observed by secret service people. It was a very sad time in Czechoslovakia.

The level of the conference which was held at the Charles Technical University was very good, at least as good if not better than the one in Brighton, England. I had the opportunity to take a sightseeing tour with a guide to better appreciate Prague which is one of the oldest cities in Europe, established more than 1100 years ago. The Moldau River goes through the city and is crossed by many interesting bridges, of which the most colorful is the Charles Bridge, which was built in the 14th century. It is adorned with Gothic statues and is the most popular point in Prague for tourists and local artists, musicians and vendors.

Charles Bridge and the castle in Prague

The Prague Castle including the Royal residence and the many churches is so huge that the tourist would need to spend days to see everything but of course we could only see the high points during the couple of hours we had. I was especially glad to visit the old town to see the *Altneue Synagogue* (the new old synagogue) that was built in 1270 in the Gothic style. It is the oldest functioning Synagogue in Europe and is the only Synagogue I ever have seen with a clock and tower.

The clock arms move counter-clockwise because Hebrew letters read from right to left. A story goes that when the Swedes were trying to attack Prague in the 17th century, they gathered at 6 o'clock in the evening and planned to attack at 7 p.m. They waited for the clock on the Altneue Synagogue to move to 7 from 6, but to their surprise, it moved to 5 and their plan of attack was messed up. This great tale may or may not have happened!

The Tower clock with Hebrew letters in the Old-New Synagogue in Prague

Twenty years later, we returned to a quite different Prague with Vera and with our friends Steve and Marika Szasz. By then, it was one of the most visited cities of Europe after Paris, London, Rome, Madrid and Berlin.

After spending a few days in the city, we visited the picturesque town *Karlovy Vary* (Karlstadt in German) 130 miles from Prague. Karlovy Vary is known for its many spas and thermal baths. It is also the home of Moser, the very famous crystal factory. We visited the Moser museum where there was a cut crystal cup specially made for Stalin on display! Karlovy Vary has a lively cultural life with a yearly film festival and other artistic events.

Karlovy Vary Czech Republic

We saw the work of Czech artists in other art museums besides the one in the Czech Republic. When we visited an exhibit in the Museum of Arts in Saint Petersburg, **Russia**, we met Matusek a Czech sculptor from Brno, who was exhibiting his works of beautifully carved wood. We really liked one piece, "Dead Can Dance". He said he could not sell it during the exhibit but he would contact us after he finished there. Sure enough, we got a letter from Matusek telling us that if we paid for the shipping, he would send the large heavy carving to us and if we liked it, we could send him $1500, otherwise, we could send it back. We have it displayed in our living room; we call it "Even the Dead can Dance".

July 2020 I was supposed to go to a Conference in Prague but because of COVID-19, the Conference postponed until 2021.

Carved wood sculpture by Czech artist Matusek.

22. NORWAY

Vera and I made a trip with Alain Jungman, my colleague at Universite Paris 7, and his wife Liliane to Sandefjord, Norway to attend the meeting of the Federation of the Acoustical Societies in Europe. We traveled with them in their car which Alain drove to Hamburg, Germany and from there we took a boat to Copenhagen. The short overnight trip in stormy weather was enlightened by a very good band of musicians who turned out to be Hungarians. The next day we took another boat trip to Norway and again the people in the band were Hungarians. We spent a couple of days in **Oslo** and we experienced our first visit to a Scandinavian city.

The city was very homogenous with all attractive Nordic-looking People. Even the break-dancers on the street were freckled, light-skinned, light-haired boys. A special note was that it was not unusual to see a pretty young girl riding her bicycle topless.

I joined the singing with the Salvation Army in Oslo (1984)

The Frogner Park was a huge area full of statues of very large men and women workers which looked like works of socialist realism, the Soviet-style kind of art. Everything was very clean and orderly in Oslo but without much flavor, much like the food in the restaurants.

Frogner Park, Oslo Norway

When we took off to our Conference in **Sandefjord** we found much prettier scenery on the way. Sandefjord is a small resort spa city on the sea and we enjoyed spending time swimming after the lectures at the conference. To our great surprise, at the conference, we met a couple originally from Hungary who settled in Norway in 1956. According to the man who was an acoustician, it was very challenging to learn Norwegian. Certainly, having to deal with the two complex languages of Hungarian and Norwegian must have been difficult. The most interesting part of our trip began just after the conference when we drove to the area of the impressive fjords and glaciers. Although Oslo was not special, we still think that **Norway** is one of the prettiest countries we have ever been in.

Alain, Vera, Liliane and me sailing in Norway 1984

Vera and I at the glaciers in Norway (1984)

We stayed in bread and breakfast places mostly in small towns. They were cheap even though rather spartan. The showers had a coin-operated gadget that controlled the flow of hot water, and sometimes while we while taking a shower and were all soaped up, the hot water would stop until we put more coins in the meter.

We passed ten days driving and taking ferries all the way north. While driving through a small town we were stopped by the police because Alain was driving 10 km above the speed limit. We had to go into the police station where we were informed that the fine was the equivalent of $150, a huge amount of money in 1984. We tried to reason with the policeman but he did not understand what the issue was. If you do something wrong, the law requires you to pay for it! You either pay or stay in prison for three days. I paid! Moving on, we were rewarded by a very nice visit to Bergen a very pretty colorful city. In the open fish market, we had a cured salmon sandwich on dark rye bread that was so good, we are still looking for another one even half as good.

At the fish market in Bergen, Norway (1984)

Salmon Gravlax

Serves 8

Ingredients:

2 one-pound salmon fillets with the skin (2 lb. total)

1 tbsp. black peppercorns

1/4 cup kosher salt or finely ground sea salt

2 tbsp. sugar

3 tbsp. vodka

1 bunch of fresh dill

Directions:

1. Remove any pin bones from salmon with needle-nose pliers or tweezers.

2. Put peppercorns into a small Ziploc bag and crush by rolling them with a wine bottle or pressing them with a heavy skillet. In a small bowl, combine salt, sugar, and crushed peppercorns.

3. First, wash both sides of the salmon with the vodka.

4. Spread the salt, sugar & ground pepper mixture evenly over one fillet.

5. Place half of the dill over the first filet and place the second fillet on top of the first one so that the flesh side of both fillets are touching, and the skin is outside.

6. Place the rest of the dill over top. Place it in a large freezer Ziploc bag. Get as much air out as possible, and zip the bag.

7. Put the bag with salmon in a Pyrex or other shallow baking dish, place a cutting board on top of the salmon, and put a weight (around 8lbs) on it. I use a few canned goods in a cast iron frying pan.

8. Refrigerate for 3-4 days turning the bag with the salmon over onto the other side every 12 hours.

9. After 3-4 days, get the salmon out of the bag, scrape off some of the dill and peppercorns, and dry the fillets with paper towels. Once cured, the salmon will stay in the fridge for a week tightly wrapped in plastic. Can also be frozen for a few months. Defrost in the fridge for 24 hours before serving.

10. To serve, slice very thin at a 45-degree angle scraping each slice off the skin. Sprinkle with chopped fresh dill and serve.

We also visited the place in Bergen where Edward Grieg was born and listened to his beautiful *Peer Gynt* in his house.

Vera at the home of Grieg in Norway (1984)

On our way driving back to Oslo, we stopped in a restaurant where a large band was playing jazz music. The Jungmans smiled and said jokingly, "Finally we have some musicians who are not Hungarians". At one point the pianist started to sing" mellek *utcan hogyha vegig megyek rajta*" a well-known Hungarian song from the 1950s. We approached them and found that they all were Hungarians. At that time, there were so many Hungarian musicians and so few opportunities in Hungary that they were all over. From Oslo, we took another boat trip back to Copenhagen where we stayed a few days.

23. DENMARK

Coming back to **Copenhagen** from Norway we stayed for a few days in an economical simple bed and breakfast place that was OK for us since it was clean and we're not spoiled. We spent a whole day in the well-known Tivoli Garden, which was created in the 19th century and is probably the oldest amusement park in Europe, After Euro Disney, it is the second most visited amusement park with close to 5 million visitors.

Tivoli Garden Copenhagen, Denmark

Coming back to Copenhagen 15 years later in 1999 for another Ultrasonic Conference, we thought we could afford to be less economical so we settled in the elegant D'Angleterre Hotel. One should have a good time whenever and anywhere it's possible and we did.

Hotel D'Angleterre Copenhagen

The street next to the Hotel D'Angleterre is the busiest shopping street in the city and while I attended the conference, Vera enjoyed shopping at *Ecco* which has the best Danish shoes. We walked a lot, took a boat tour on the North Atlantic, and visited the signature landmark of the city, the statue of the Little Mermaid, *Den Lille Havfrue*. It is modeled after the fairy tale of the same title by Hans Christian Andersen.

Den Lille Havfrue Han, Little Mermaid Copenhagen

When we were on the way to the airport, we were informed by the cab driver that there is a big difference between the Danish and the Swedish people even though both of them are Scandinavians. He said proudly," We Danish work to live and the Swedish live to work". We heard the same story from the French people at

Metz across from Saarbrucken when they compared themselves the same way to the Germans. Things are changing and people are the same and we all love to live and live to love.

24. JAPAN

Our first trip to Japan in 1987 was also our first trip to East Asia. Because of the long 22-hour flight we got first-class tickets from Los Angeles to **Tokyo** on Air Japan. It was super comfortable with excellent service and meals, both Western like foie gras and steamed whole lobster, as well as Japanese, like sushi and sashimi, etc. So, when we arrived at the Tokyo Narita Airport, we were quite rested.

A friend of mine Katsahiro, who worked in Oak Ridge National Lab for several years before he returned to Japan was waiting for us. He was chief scientist in a national institute in Tokyo. During our 90-minute bus trip to our hotel in the middle of Tokyo not too far from the Imperial Palace, my friend briefed us on the best way to spend our planned five day stay in the city. Katsahiro invited Vera and me out for dinner and he also arranged a visit to his institute for me.

With Katsahiro in Tokyo (1987)

Our hotel was nice and clean and after we rested for a few hours, we went jogging as always to learn about the city. We ran around the beautiful garden of the Imperial Palace as well as through some of the very busy streets of Tokyo.

Ropongi district Tokyo

We met Katsahiro for dinner at a very fancy restaurant called Seryna. I remember the name because it sounded like the name of one of my favorite aunts, Serena. We took a taxi to the Roppongi district and were so impressed by the cleanliness of the interior of the taxi and the gloved cab driver. Katsahiro ordered for us and we had the most amazing meal with shabu-shabu, Kobe beef, abalone salad, and various exotic fish cooked on a hot stone. I could just guess that he spent a fortune for the three of us. A Kobe shabu alone runs around $200.

Bento box in Seryna restaurant, Roppongi district Tokyo

The next day I visited Katsahiro in his institute while Vera was wandering around the big city. I could tell that in many ways Japan was much ahead of the rest of the world in technology. I mentioned to him that I had lost contact with Ryo Sugihara, a professor friend of mine at the University of Nagoya who spent his sabbatical at the University of Tennessee in the late 60s. Within minutes he handed me the telephone and Sugihara was on the line. Thirty years ago, one could not do that in the USA.

Sugihara was very happy to hear from me and invited us to nearby Nagoya the following week when I had my conference in Toyohashi. I had another contact in Tokyo, an engineer named Shimada who was in my lab at Ohio State University for a year. He took us around Tokyo showing us some of the highlights of the city. We took the metro everywhere which was very convenient. We went to a park with Shimada where about 30 or 40 young men dressed like Elvis Presley were playing the guitar and singing his hits.

Vera and I got to know the city a little and learned even more in 2004 when we returned again. We participated in a Geisha ceremony which was quite interesting. We also went to a Kabuki theater, where only men performed in the traditional fashion. The play lasted for nine hours and it was all in Japanese so we left early. It was amazing to see that Tokyo is full of the most impressive French pastry shops where nicely dressed sales girls welcome the customers. We walked a lot in this fantastic city about the size of five Manhattans with multiple Times Squares in Ginza, Asakusa, Akasaka, Roppongi, and so on. All in all, we were very much impressed by Tokyo. Before leaving for Toyohashi, we took a bus ride to a mountainous resort town called **Nikko** about 100 miles from Tokyo.

Nikko, Japan (1987)

It was quite a challenge for the bus drivers on the high mountain road which had as many turns as the letters in the alphabet. Unfortunately, we saw many wrecked cars in the valley. Despite the fright, it was well worth it to make that one-day excursion. Nikko is famous for the many shrines and springs.

Shrines in Nikko Japan

From Tokyo, we took a train to **Toyohashi**. It was somewhat of a challenge since we had to change trains, and while in Tokyo all the signs were in both English and Japanese, in the smaller cities this was not the case, not even at the railway station. For this reason, it was hard for us to get around but we made it to Toyohashi a small city near where the Toyota automobile is made.

The conference, which attracted several hundred people was a big event for the city. The reception which was held in the City Hall was very spectacular with a band playing western music and with excellent buffet-style food. At one point when Vera was walking with an empty plate, looking over the choices, the mayor of the city to please her put a whole lobster on her plate, not leaving any room for anything else. The whole reception was televised and the next day when Vera went into a nearby shop the people recognized and greeted her, recognizing her from the TV broadcast as the only western woman at the conference.

In the conference, I talked about the porosity measurement technique. Ryo Sugihara and his wife picked us up at our hotel and took us to a restaurant in Nagoya, where a whole room was reserved for only the four of us. We were seated on the floor Japanese style eating their exotic food. We were very close friends with the Sugiharas while they were in Knoxville. Ryo who was a plasma physicist shared an office with me at the University of Tennessee Physics Department. The secretaries with their Tennessee accents had trouble communicating with Sugihara who spoke English with his special accent. Often a secretary would come into our office and say something like, "Can you tell Professor Sugihara that his airplane ticket is ready to be picked up?" I would turn to Ryo and say," Ryo, your tickets are ready", translating from English to English.

Sugihara's wife was a home economics professor in Japan and an excellent cook. We already had our first exposure to various Japanese foods like tempura, sukiyaki, and more in their home in Knoxville. On this visit to Japan, we had a nice time with them in the restaurant although their English was a little rusty after twenty years. Also, like all the Japanese people we knew, they mixed up the letters R and L. So, they called Vera, "Vela" and me "Rasro".

Chicken & Shrimp Tempura

Serves 4

Ingredients:

1 tbsp. Sriracha hot chili sauce

¼ cup of soy sauce

¼ cup honey

1 egg

1 cup of flour

1 cup of cornstarch

1 cup of water

2 cups of corn oil

1 tsp. salt

9 large shrimp deveined

1 lb. chicken breast cut into long strips

1 carrot peeled and sliced

1 red pepper cut into thin slices

1 broccoli with florets and stalk cut into 4-inch pieces

Directions:

1. Before frying the ingredients, make the sauce and set aside. In a small bowl mix the chili sauce honey and soy sauce.

2. In a large bowl mix the beaten egg with the flour, cornstarch, salt, and cold water. Set aside.

3. Heat oven to 225 degrees. Line a large plate with paper towels and set aside. Line a baking sheet with parchment paper and set aside.

4. In a large wok or heavy pot heat the oil over medium heat to 375 degrees. Dip the vegetables into the batter and cook in the hot oil for 3 minutes turning once until golden brown. Drain on the paper towel plate then transfer to the parchment-covered pan and put it in the oven to keep hot.

5. Dip the shrimp into the batter and cook in the hot oil for 3 minutes turning once until golden brown. Drain on the paper towel and add to the vegetables in the oven to keep hot.

6. Dip chicken strips into the batter and cook in the hot oil for 5 minutes, turning once until the coating is crisp and golden brown. Drain on the paper towel.

7. Add to the vegetables and shrimps and serve with the sauce.

Despite our not knowing each other's language, as we learned through the years, with nice people you can always understand each other and have fun! From Toyohashi, we went to Osaka, the second-largest city in Japan to visit two friends with the same first name, Akira Nakamura who had been on sabbatical at the University of Tennessee where we worked together in nonlinear acoustics, and Akira Matzinawa who had been on his sabbatical at Ohio State University in our department. Both Akiras were professors at the University of Osaka. We had nice visits with the Nakamuras in their home, the only Japanese home we were invited to while in Japan. The Matzinawas took us to a very fancy Chinese restaurant.

We stayed in a very nice hotel. One morning when we went for our long jog, we lost our way and even though the hotel was a very tall building, we could not see it because of the hilly terrain of Osaka. Luckily, I carried a matchbox with me from the hotel to remember its name. When we showed it to a cute young woman who was walking by, she started to run with us in high heel shoes without hesitation until our hotel became visible. The Japanese are the politest people we have ever met. We visited a beautiful modern ceramic museum in Osaka. When we entered the museum, we saw that there are two sections: one with Chinese ceramics and the other with Korean ceramics. Are there Japanese ceramics?

One evening we were walking in a neighborhood in Osaka and overheard some singing from a bar. When we entered, we saw a bunch of happy people singing and reading the words from a screen. They welcomed us and asked us to join in with the singers. Since we could not read Japanese, they put on a song with English words. It was the Beatle song "Yesterday" which all of them knew how to sing but we didn't. This was the first time we encountered karaoke.

Another time when I was busy at the University of Osaka and Vera was walking with Mrs. Nakamura, a bunch of uniformed schoolchildren approached Vera. They thought that she was some famous movie star and standing in line in an orderly way, they asked for her autograph. She got a big kick out of that and enjoyed that it a great deal.

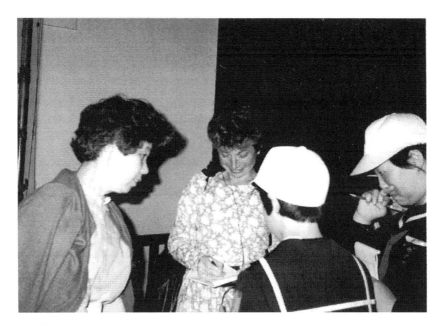

"Famous" Vera signs her autograph to schoolgirls in Osaka (1987)

Osaka is a busy city with the biggest crowds I have ever seen. On the sidewalks, everyone walks in the same direction. If you want to turn around, you have to go across the street to the other sidewalk where everyone walks in the opposite direction.

A busy street in Osaka, Japan

We also were astonished to see a huge mall with about a thousand stores built at least ten stories below the Osaka railway station. The Nakamuras took us over by train to beautiful and spectacular Kyoto, the ancient capital city of Japan. We would renew the pleasure when some years later we came back to Kyoto for the 18th ICA meeting.

For my second trip to Japan in 1991, I flew from Bangkok to Tokyo and took a train to Karuizawa, a very picturesque resort town about 100 miles from Tokyo. The conference was rather small with only about 100 participants. I talked about our recent nonlinear acoustics work for the evaluation of adhesive joints. It was a very relaxing few days in Karuizawa and it certainly was a big contrast between a small well-kept Japanese resort town as opposed to the bustling crowded Bangkok with its nearly 10 million inhabitants.

Karuizawa, Japan (1991)

Our next trip with Vera was to the 18th ICA meeting in Kyoto Japan in 2004. This was our second trip to Kyoto and my third visit to Tokyo. We decided to spend an extra week in Tokyo to learn as much as we could about how to get around in this fascinating city without any help from our Japanese friends and after one week, we knew Tokyo very well. In Kyoto, our friends, the Matzinawas, who spent a year in Columbus in the 1980s, invited us to a very elegant restaurant. Unfortunately, Akira passed away shortly after our visit. He was a great man!

Private Residence in Kyoto

With the Matzinawas in Kyoto (2004)

In 1996 I was walking with Janos on the street in Budapest when I heard someone yell," Rasro, Rasro". It was Akira walking toward us with several Japanese people. The International Welding Society had a meeting in Budapest that year. When we left Akira and his colleagues, Janos commented "You know everybody!" My dear friend Janos also passed away a few years later in 2009. The bad thing about getting older is that many of your friends are no longer around!

25. HONG KONG

In 1987 we stayed in the Regent Hotel, an elegant 5-star hotel on the waterfront of Hong Kong. Today it is called the Intercontinental Hotel. This was before the Chinese Government took Hong Kong back from the British in 1999. Hong Kong was a very dynamic place with elegant stores and people. At night however, we noticed a bunch of young couples sleeping on the waterfront probably with no other place to sleep. So, we saw that the wealth of that rich city was not shared by all. For the three days we enjoyed their super restaurants, but also walked around some of the steep streets leading to the less affluent neighborhoods and resisted the attacks of the tailors running toward us with their measuring tapes offering a good deal on a made-to-order suit in a couple of hours.

Hong Kong

26. TAIWAN

Taiwan is an island in the Pacific known originally as Formosa which belonged to Japan until 1945 when it became part of the Republic of China. After World War 2, the Communists took control of mainland China and it became the People's Republic of China. At that time, the Government of the Republic of China under the leadership of General Chiang Kai-shek escaped with several millions of their followers and relocated in **Taipei.**

During the process, they transported many of the mainland arts and crafts and other museum pieces to establish the National Museum of China in Taipei which is much nicer than the one in Beijing. For many years until the 1970s, the Republic of China of Taiwan represented all the Chinese people in the United Nations. Slowly the People's Republic of China, under the leadership of Mao Tse-tung, received the recognition of more and more countries and replaced the Republic of China in the UN. Today there are only maybe a dozen or so countries in the world who recognize Taiwan as the representative of the Chinese people. It has a population of about 25 million, more than half of whom consider themselves Taiwanese and the others consider themselves Chinese. Interestingly, it was always reported that Taiwan became the second strongest economy in Asia next to Japan after Chiang Kai-shek moved in with his followers. One of my Taiwanese colleagues always commented, "Big deal! Before Chiang Kai-shek, we were number one".

We settled into a semi-decent hotel in the middle of Taipei which was arranged for us as their guests by the National Taiwan University. It was certainly not like the Regent in Hong Kong but it was OK. Vera and I were picked up by one of the professors and taken directly to the university faculty club for lunch. We were welcomed by half a dozen professors and the head of the department of solid mechanics who was a Purdue Ph.D.

Soon after we sat down around a round table. A very huge bowl of some assorted fragrant Chinese dishes was placed in the center of the table. Everyone started at once to take food with their chopsticks and after eating what they had picked, they dug into the bowl again. Vera and I who were not used to eating from a community bowl just set there sipping our tea. The Purdue guy must have remembered the way people eat in the States. He asked everyone to stop eating and said something to the waiter in Chinese who then came back with some plates and a serving spoon. After that, everyone continued eating from the same bowl with the new procedure but we apologized saying that we are not hungry.

From left: Huang, his wife, Vera, me, and Chang in Taipei (1987)

In the afternoon I gave a one-hour lecture to a rather large audience. Upon returning to our hotel Chang and Huang, two former students from the University of Tennessee were waiting for us. They were very eager to entertain us and took us to a very nice restaurant. We all enjoyed talking about old times in Knoxville as we were walking home from the restaurant which was not too far from our hotel. It was a nice evening and the city certainly looked very safe.

I walked ahead with Huang and about 50 yards behind us Vera walked with Chang. All of a sudden as we walked by a well-lit barbershop, two young girls in sexy clothes came toward us asking me, "How would you like a haircut?" Huang in a high-pitched frightened voice screamed toward me, "Professor Adler, they don't really give haircuts!" I smiled at the girls and pointed to Vera who had almost caught up to us, saying "There is my barber". We all had a good laugh.

The father of my student, Shaio-Wen Wang, was a famous senator in the Taiwanese Senate. He contacted us through an English translator since he spoke no English and asked us to join him and his wife for dinner at a restaurant. The restaurant was probably one of the fanciest we have ever been in, and Senator Wang, a very kind jolly gentleman with his wife and the very well-dressed good-looking translator were the only ones there with us. He reserved the whole restaurant for the five of us. They had at least 7 waiters bringing one dish after the other of the most delicious Chinese food we ever experienced. We counted over 14 (fourteen) courses.

With Senator and Mrs. Wang in a Taipei restaurant, Taiwan 1987

We had a wonderful time with Shaio's parents. They were wonderful hosts and the next day when I had to go to the University, Mrs. Wang together with the translator took Vera for shopping and had lunch together with them.

Vera with the English translator in Taipei Taiwan (1987)

A few years earlier I had arranged for a green card (permanent residency in the USA) for Shaio and offered her a position in the NDE group. A little after our return from Taiwan, Shaio married a chemist also from Taiwan and they moved to Philadelphia. Both of them got jobs in the Navair Material Research Lab. Unfortunately, due to an unknown cause (probably some chemicals which they used for their study of adhesives) both of them died shortly after their little girl turned 1 year old. Such a tragedy for a really beautiful person. Shaio was a special person and an excellent scientist who worked with me for over 7 years. We all miss her.

Before leaving Taipei, we visited the Chinese National Museum located in a beautiful park in Taipei. As I mentioned earlier most of the Chinese treasures including the museum pieces were moved from the mainland to Taiwan by Chiang Kai-shek. It was an amazing collection of Chinese craftsmanship. There was a huge ivory piece containing several concentric spheres, and on the surface of each sphere, a whole miniature city was carved in exacting detail. Doubtless, it took a large family several generations to complete this masterpiece. Our visit came to an end with a banquet organized by the University in our honor. We all drank a lot of heavy Chinese schnapps and many of the professors got drunk and made fun of the Japanese people whom they considered inferior. They think their cultural heritage is superior to the technical advances of the Japanese.

National Museum of Taiwan Taipei

S9. HAWAII

I was involved in co-organizing a joint American-Japanese session in the 1989 meeting of the Acoustical Society of America in Honolulu, Hawaii. Vera and I had never been to Hawaii, so we were looking forward to our trip. A week before the conference we arrived in Maui, one of the nicest of the eight islands of Hawaii. We stayed at the beautiful Sheraton Resort Hotel and Spa and drove around Maui exploring its natural beauty.

Sheraton Resort Hotel Maui

Hana, an area about a couple of hours of driving from our hotel is truly the last undeveloped area of Maui, with seven natural pools and waterfalls. We also happily found out that near our hotel there was a 10K race in which we both participated, and not surprisingly Vera got her first price trophy.

Vera wins first place 10k race in Maui, Hawaii, 1989

From Maui we took a plane to the Big Island also called Hawaii, the largest island in the USA. It is known for its many volcanoes, one of which is the largest active volcano on earth. All in all, the experience of the natural wonders of these two islands was much more memorable than the Hawaiian food.

The Acoustical Society of America meeting on Oahu Island in Honolulu was one of the largest ever. It was attended by over 1300 people and there were close to 1000 presentations. The 1960 meeting in Providence, Rhode Island where I gave my first presentation, had only 680 people and 172 presentations. The Honolulu conference was attended by many Japanese people since it was a joint conference. I nominated Mack Breazeale for the prestigious Silver Medal and during the banquet, I gave a speech describing his professional activities. I think he enjoyed it when I said, "Mack put the University of Tennessee on the map".

As always with the Acoustical Society of America meetings, we had a performance during the banquet. This time in Hawaii there was hula dancing but to my disappointment, the dancers were mostly very heavy girls not like those in the Hollywood movies. As they say in French, "a chacun son gout", there is no accounting for taste!

27. SERBIA

From Lake Balaton in Hungary we drove with Alain and Liliane Jungman to Szeged a town bordering on Yugoslavia, which became Serbia a few years later. We crossed at **Subotica** an old Hungarian town which was called Szabadka before Yugoslavia took over the whole region of Vojvodina. This was my first visit to Yugoslavia and I was quite excited because I had lots of respect for this country and its leader Yosif Broz Tito.

Tito was the idol of my childhood because he not only fought the Nazis with his partisans but in 1948 he was the first to turn against Stalin's dictatorial rule of an East European country. I was too young in 1945 when many older members of the Hasomer Hacair volunteered to build damns near Sarajevo, but I learned the marching songs, like *"yeden, dva, yeden dva omladina Titova"*, (one-two, one-two, we are the youth group of Tito). I thought for a long time that Yugoslavia was an ideal, harmonious confederation of the seven South Slav Nations; Serbia, Croatia, Slovenia, Montenegro, Macedonia, Bosnia-Hercegovina, and Kosovo. Only a few years later did we find out otherwise. I knew that there were some problems and the reality of the country used to be summarized as: *"Yugoslavia is a country with seven nations, five languages, four religions and only one Yugoslav: Tito"*. But in August 1989, we had a very peaceful trip through the country to **Belgrade,** the capital of Serbia where we stayed in the Sava Center hotel complex, the place of our ICA conference.

Sava Center Belgrade Serbia

Belgrade is right on the Danube River and is a very colorful city though far from the beauty of Budapest. The Conference was well attended and we had several presentations from our group. Vera and I attended several concerts, went to restaurants and enjoyed the nearby fishing villages. We wanted to visit Dubrovnik in Croatia on the Adriatic Sea. We took a plane for this excursion but because of the stormy weather, the plane could not land in Dubrovnik and the pilot took us back to Belgrade.

When we returned to the Sava Center where we had left most of our luggage, we found out that we could not even get close to it because after our ICA meeting finished the whole center was blocked for the next few days. There was a meeting of the leaders of the Third World Countries and Muammar Gaddafi arrived with his wives, children, and camels. So we slept in another hotel and took another flight to Dubrovnik; this time the plane landed successfully.

28. BOSNIA-HERZEGOVINA

During the Conference, we drove with the Jungmans to **Sarajevo** via **Banja Luka** in Bosnia Hercegovina. Sarajevo used to be called the "Jerusalem of the Balkans". In the same neighborhood, there were mosques, orthodox churches, catholic churches, and synagogues. I considered Sarajevo the most spectacular city I had seen in a long time. Its impressive features are the nearby mountains where the 1984 winter Olympics were held, the old town with the Muslim influence dating from the Turkish occupation, the visibility of a sizable Jewish culture, and the influence of the Austro-Hungarian monarchy. The unique combination made it a very exciting city with nice people and good looking young girls and boys who were indistinguishable as Serb or Croat or Bosnian. I could not imagine what tragedy was coming to this multicultural city a few years later.

Sarajevo Bosnia-Hercegovina

29. CROATIA

After our unsuccessful earlier attempts, we took another flight to **Dubrovnik**; this time the plane landed successfully. Dubrovnik is probably the most popular tourist attraction on the Adriatic Sea in the interesting region of Dalmatia. We enjoyed staying there for a couple of days and liked it so much that years later we took an extended vacation to the area with our friends.

As time went on all our friends felt that we should take more vacations together so in 2006 we decided to go to the Adriatic Sea, maybe one of the most beautiful parts of Europe. We hired a minivan and the owner of the travel company, Arpad Kiss, drove us from Budapest to Croatia.

From left: Shira, Poncike. Marika, Steve, George Bozoki, Jayne, George Burger, Scarlett, me, and Vera. (2006).

It was well worth it to come back to spend a couple of days in Dubrovnik. The scenery, the cultural offerings, the galleries, the excellent restaurants, and the beach all work together to make it one of the most visited places in Europe.

Dubrovnik on the Adriatic Sea

The historic Jewish presence in the city is evidenced by a 13th Century Synagogue built well before a large number of Sephardic Jews came from Spain after the Inquisition. It is one of the oldest Sephardic Synagogues in Europe.

13th Century Sephardic Synagogue in Dubrovnik, Croatia

When we visited the Synagogue there was an exhibit by a famous Croatian painter Jovan Obican and we bought one of his prints, "Jewish Wedding".

Jewish Wedding by Jovan Obican

While we were in Dubrovnik, I started to have stomach aches like what had happened a few times in the previous six months. After a couple of hours, it went away. A couple of weeks later I had to have emergency surgery in Paris for a strangulated hernia.

Our next stop on the Adriatic was the elegant large resort town **Split**, which with its quarter-million inhabitants is the second-largest city in Croatia, as well as having the best looking girls.

Split on the Adriatic, Croatia.

Opatija or Abbazia as it was called before Yugoslavia took over in 1947 used to be the resort town of the most privileged in Europe before World War 1. Franz Joseph Hapsburg the emperor of the Austro-Hungarian Monarchy used to spend six months there during the winter. In 1920 Italy took over the city, and many less expensive accommodations allowed the middle class to enjoy it. When Yugoslavia split up, Opatija became part of Croatia. We all had a wonderful time there.

Opatija on the Adriatic, Croatia

We crossed over to Italy to visit Trieste and Venice before continuing into Ljubljana, Slovenia, and then to Zagreb, the capital of Croatia, our last stop on this trip to the former Yugoslavia before we all returned to Budapest.

30. MONTENEGRO

In 1989, Vera and I rented a car in Dubrovnik and drove to Montenegro through some difficult rugged mountainous roads.

Near Kotor, Montenegro

Because of the cheap gasoline and the slippery road, my car slid into another one next to me. Luckily no one was injured but a police car showed up at no time, and the official asked for our passports and told us to follow him. We did not feel comfortable giving up our passports so Vera insisted on sitting in the police car and I followed them to **Kotor,** a city in Montenegro. We were taken to a courthouse to the circuit judge. Fortunately, they assigned us a Hungarian speaking lady to interpret the trial. We were fined 200,000 dinars or a few days jail term for reckless driving. I thought I would have a heart attack until we found out that it was only twenty dollars which we gladly paid. From Kotor, we drove to a very pretty resort town called **Sveti Stefan**.

Sveti Stefan, Montenegro

31. SLOVENIA

After driving through Croatia in 2006 with our friends, we went to **Ljubljana**, the capital of Slovenia, surrounded by mountains. We spent only one day there but had the impression of a very clean city with very disciplined people. We stayed in a beautiful spa hotel and when we were told that we could not wear swimming suits and that we had to go "au naturel" only three of us took advantage of the super clean pools, Vera and I, and then George Bozoki joined us. The other seven preferred to wander around outside the spa.

Ljubljana on the river, Slovenia

After the Spa, we took a tour of the city and had a good view of Ljubljana from the Tower in the grandiose Ljubljana Castle.

Ljubljana Castle, Slovenia

In the evening we sat down in an outdoor restaurant and experienced their local dishes which were not too different from Hungarian cuisine. We had meatloaf with hard-boiled eggs in the middle, called *Stefani Pecenka*, and also *pogaca* (in Hungarian pogacsa) a biscuit-like roll with cheese or cracklings.

All ten of us had a great vacation in 2006 and decided to have a follow-up. Unfortunately, it would not happen, Poncike, George Bozoki, George Burger and Scarlett are no longer with us. Very sad but lots of beautiful memories.

Slovenian Meatloaf

Serves 8

Ingredients:

1 lb. ground meat of your choice, pork, beef, or chicken breast

1 medium-size onion chopped

2 slices of white bread

eggs

½ cup of breadcrumbs

1 tsp. Hungarian paprika

1 tsp. salt

½ tsp. black pepper

Mazola corn oil

hardboiled eggs

Directions:

8. Preheat the oven to 350 F.

9. Fry the chopped onion in a pan until the onion is transparent. Remove the onion from the oil.

10. Place the ground meat in a large bowl

11. In a small bowl mix the eggs well and add the paprika, salt and pepper

12. Soak the sliced bread in water and squeeze out the water

13. When the onion is cool add to the ground meat. Add the egg mixtures and the softened bread. Mix all ingredients well with your hands.

14. Place half of the meat mixture on a greased baking sheet and form a rectangle approximately 4in wide and long enough to lay the boiled eggs out end to end

15. Lay the hardboiled eggs in a row in the middle. (You can cut off the ends of the eggs if you want big slices of egg throughout)

16. Cover the eggs with the remaining meat and shape into a loaf.

17. Place the baking tray in the oven, add a little water and cover with foil.

18. Bake for 1 hour and then remove the foil and cook for a further 10 – 15 minutes or until brown.

19. Remove from the tray. Cut into slices and serve hot or cold.

32. GREECE

We had never been in Greece before so in 1989 we thought that since it was so close to Yugoslavia, we could not miss the opportunity. We signed up to join a one-week tour with an American group who were flying from New York to Athens. We took a short flight to **Athens** from Belgrade and upon arriving at the Athens airport we took a taxi to our hotel which was located downtown. On the way, I asked the driver about the taxi fare which I had checked previously and knew that it was supposed to be around $20.00 to $25.00. I was concerned when the cab driver pushed the tariff-meter into his glove compartment without answering me. It was even more suspicious that when we arrived to the hotel, he pulled his cab behind the hotel rather than to the main entrance.

It was pretty late, around 10 PM, and very dark. We were shocked when he showed us the meter reading at $95.00. I told him that it was ridiculous and that we would not pay that much. He got really angry and threatened to drive us back to the airport. When I offered him $35.00, he took our luggage out of the trunk and drove away. Unfortunately, we left a very nice painting that we purchased in Dubrovnik in the trunk. To add insult to injury, we had to walk quite a distance around the hotel to get in. This was our introduction to Greek taxis. We also learned later that the cabs can pick people up from the street even if you are already in the cab, and that the sharing of the fares in such cases was complicated.

The hotel was nice though, and it was conveniently located in the middle of the city. The rest of our tour group was to arrive in two days, so with our jogging and walking, we had a head start on learning about the city before they arrived. The city was quite polluted in 1989 but it improved after the 2004 Olympics. We visited the Archeological Museum first, which is probably the best in the world or maybe the second best after Cairo. We hired a private tour guide named Helen who was a very classy and knowledgeable woman who taught us a lot about Greek history.

Next, we visited the local Jewish Museum and learned that there were three periods when Jews came to Athens: after the Exodus, after the destruction of the second temple, and during the rise of Fascism in other parts of Europe. The museum is located in Plaka, the most touristy area known for its many restaurants with loud Greek music and its very "welcoming" pushy waiters who try to convince you of the superiority of their establishments.

Restaurants and nightspots in Plaka, Athens

After our self-guided exploration, we went on the official city tour of Athens later with our group. The most impressive feature was the Acropolis. It is located 500 feet above sea level and the name means the highest point in the city: *Kron* highest point, and *Polis* city. Many of the remains of important buildings go back to 6 BC. For most of the other people in our group, it was a challenge to climb up to the top.

Acropolis. Athens

After a couple of days, our group left Athens and for the next five days, we traveled by boat and by bus all over Greece. One of the most spectacular visits was to **Delphi** with its ancient theater built in 400 B.C. which seats over 5000 people.

Our group in Greece. Vera and I are squeezed in on the right. (1989)

Entertainment on the boat in Greece (1989)

The theater in Delphi, Greece

What impressed me most about Delphi was the acoustics of the theater. No matter where you sat, you could hear a small coin dropped in the middle of the stage. It puzzles me why modern architectural acoustics cannot duplicate the design of the ancient Greeks even with the most powerful supercomputers.

We enjoyed our visit to the beautiful Greek islands. In Mykonos we wandered into the home of an old lady who offered us her freshly baked bread, We also went to Rhodes, one of the largest of the Greek islands in the Eastern Aegean Sea. We returned to Greece several times in the next fifteen years to visit other islands like Santorini and Crete.

In 1995 Vera and I went to Crete, the largest of the Greek Islands when I was invited to a meeting there which was organized at the Technical University of **Chania**. The meeting was rather small, I gave a presentation on ultrasonic wave propagation in *Biot Solids:* two-phase materials, that is, solids filled with fluid, for example, bones.

Chania, Crete

We enjoyed the many good restaurants where we ate grilled fish and octopus almost exclusively. During the conference banquet, we were entertained by a group of young Greek dancers, who got us involved in the dancing and who taught us several Greek dances.

We made a tour of the capital city of Crete, **Heraklion**, and there we learned quite a bit about the advanced technology of ancient Greece. Their irrigation system was so advanced that when a modern Swedish Engineering firm visited there, one engineer said the Cretans would not be allowed to install the ancient system now because the Swedes had a patent on it! A few years later in 1999 we returned to Chania for another conference and afterwards visited the stunning island of **Santorini** with its two main towns, Fira and Oia and their beautiful white and blue houses, hot springs, and fantastic restaurants.

Oia, Santorini, Greece.

We enjoyed several of the Greek Islands but our favorite place in Greece was the elegant city of **Thessaloniki** or Saloniki, the most European city in Greece. It is the second-largest city in Greece with more than one million inhabitants. The cafes, the food, and the architecture all resembled Central Europe more than Greece. It used to be called the Jerusalem of the Balkans, because of its very rich Jewish history going back to 50 BC. When St Paul was traveling through the world trying to convert the pagans to Christianity, he was not too successful with the Jews in Thessaloniki. During the Ottoman era, 60% of the population were Jewish, mostly Sephardic who emigrated from Spain after the Inquisition. When Vera and I visited the Jewish museum in Saloniki and asked the director which part of the city was the Jewish quarter, he said, "The whole city".

Thessaloniki, Greece

33. THAILAND

On a Sunday in 1991, we celebrated Rachel's 1ˢᵗ birthday in our home. The next day I had a flight to **Bangkok,** Thailand on the way to Karuizawa, Japan to the 5ᵗʰ International Symposium on Nondestructive Characterization of Materials.

Before my flight to Bangkok, I attended a dinner reception which was held at the United Hungarian Church of Knoxville to honor Arpad Goncz, the president of Hungary. I felt a lot of respect for President Goncz, a scholar who fought for a democratic Hungary all his life. So, after his speech and a bunch of heavy Hungarian dishes I took my flight to Bangkok.

My friend George Burger was stationed in Bangkok as the representative of the Hungarian X-Ray equipment manufacturers for the five Southeast Asian countries. So, it was a convenient stop for me on the way to the conference in Karuizawa. It was late evening of the following day when I landed at the Bangkok Airport. George was waiting for me with his Thai chauffeur who drove me to his beautiful apartment building in a fashionable part of Bangkok. It was a very modern building with a huge beautiful garden and an Olympic size swimming pool which was kept spotlessly clean by two Thai attendants. George and his wife lived in a four-bedroom four-bathroom beautifully furnished apartment.

The apartment complex where the Burgers lived, Bangkok, Thailand

He had a three-year assignment before his retirement. Before coming to Bangkok, he was the director of Medicor's X-Ray division for many years. In Bangkok, they had a full-time chauffeur named Yaya as well as a full-time maid who learned Hungarian and Hungarian cooking. The next morning, I did my usual running and discovered that as soon as I left George's secluded area, the city was full of poor houses, open sewers, bad roads, and lots of stray dogs. However, the people especially the young girls, were neatly dressed and everybody looked clean and friendly. About thirty minutes after I started my run, I got caught in a torrential tropical rainfall. I got soaking wet and the floating garbage from the flooded streets came up way above my knees.

Flooded Street after a heavy rain in Bangkok, Thailand

Once I was back at the Burgers' I had to drop off all my clothes and sit in a tub for half an hour. Otherwise, I had a few great days in Bangkok and the surrounding area. I came back to Bangkok with Vera in December and spent New Year's Eve there also with the Burgers. On this trip, we visited the unique, colorful floating market, and when we jogged we made sure not to run too far from George's neighborhood.

Floating Market, Bangkok, Thailand

With Vera in Bangkok, Thailand 1991

The visit was partially business also. Vera had discovered that almost all the cubic zirconium jewelry that she sold in her *Illusion* store was manufactured in Thailand. Therefore, while we were in Bangkok, with the assistance of George and his engineer from Hungary, Marci Halmai who spoke Thai, we found several sources. Most of them were located in single-family homes where the whole family made beautiful costume jewelry of all kinds.

Because of the contract with the owner of Illusion, Vera had to purchase her goods from them. But we were able to buy cheaper directly in Thailand than the owner could in the USA. So we formed a company: *LV Imports*. The Illusion Company would place orders for various styles and colors etc. and LV Imports, with the help of George and Marci who got a commission for their services, became the supplier of all the Illusion stores. For the next few years, it was a lucrative although complicated venture because of the legalities involved in purchases, shipping, and customs, etc. The irony was that Vera had to continue to buy her merchandise from Illusion, the same goods that she sold them herself.

We had a very nice time in Thailand. For we went to the beautiful seaside resort of **Pattaya** about 60 miles from Bangkok where we spent New Year's Eve. George drove us from Bangkok to Pattaya and on the way, he was stopped by the police for speeding. I had bad memories from Norway and Montenegro and had no intention of spending time in a Thai jail. Luckily, George knew his way around Thailand after spending years there. He just pulled a banknote from his pocket and handed it to the policeman who saluted us as we drove away!

Pattaya, Thailand

We returned to Thailand two more times, in 1992 and, 1994. By that time the Burgers had returned to Hungary and we stayed with Marci and Agnes Halmai in their elegant condo in Bangkok.

34. CHINA

Beijing looked very peaceful on our arrival in September 1992 for the ICA meeting. It was already three years since the Tiananmen Square massacre in 1989, when over two thousand demonstrators, mostly students, were killed by the people's army. We were in peaceful Belgrade at that time in 1989 participating in the 13th ICA meeting. By 1992 things changed in both countries: Yugoslavia was in the middle of a bloody civil war and China was quiet. The siege of Sarajevo lasted several years with several thousand casualties, and you have to wonder what if the locations of the ICA meetings were exchanged.

In Beijing, we stayed in the elegant Kunlun hotel where on each floor a tall attractive girl in uniform assisted the guests in the elevator. At first, I thought that the same girl ran up and down from one floor to the next because they all were the same height and all looked the same! Another unexpected aspect of the hotel was that every afternoon an opera singer entertained the guests in the tea room.

The conference was well organized and in addition to the over 500 Chinese Acousticians, there were about 1000 visitors from 15 countries. In 1992 there were very few cars in Beijing and the streets were jammed with thousands and thousands of bicyclists. So, when the conference organized a bus tour with about 12 buses for the participants, a police car drove in front of the buses and a policeman with a loudspeaker instructed the bicycle riders to get out of the way.

It was quite spectacular to visit the Forbidden City and many other indispensable attractions, but the highlight for us was to climb the 5000 plus steps to the Great Wall. One of the greatest wonders of the world, it was built through many centuries, starting about 2000 years ago. It is said that it is the only structure on earth that is visible from outer space.

Great Wall near Beijing, China

Several of the visiting scientists, who had been with me at Ohio State, were very eager to entertain us and show us their very exciting city. Kunyu Wu, a professor at Shenyang University who worked with me for a couple of years, took Vera and me to the famous Peking Duck restaurant, a 7-story building serving duck in various ways on each floor. Vera was very much impressed by the many delicious dishes and asked Wu to arrange a visit to the kitchen. After a rather lengthy discussion in Chinese which sounded more like an argument between Kunyu Wu and the waiter, he turned to Vera saying, "Mrs. Adler, you don't want to go to the kitchen. It is very dangerous because you may slip on a duck skin." After that Vera was not too curious about Chinese kitchens. By the way, we thought that American Chinese food is far better than the original, although the food at Peking Duck was an exception.

Peking Duck Restaurant Complex Beijing, China.

During the summer of 2014, I had an invitation to a *New Advances in Acoustics* conference planned to be held in **Shanghai** during the week of the end of January and the beginning of February 2015. I was asked to give the keynote lecture of 45 minutes. I accepted the invitation and all expenses were covered by the conference organization and by the Emeritus Academy research grant at Ohio State University. I had to convince Vera to go with me on this trip because she hates long flights. Rather than flying from Clearwater to Shanghai, which would have taken 22 hours, we took a flight to Paris where we stayed for ten days and then took an Air France flight to Shanghai from there. This was only a "short" flight of 11 hours on a jumbo plane with 520 passengers. We came to Shanghai several days before the start of the conference to have enough time to learn about the city.

We stayed at the Guang Dong Hotel, where the conference was held, and with the help of the concierge who was among the few people who spoke English, we hired a private guide with a car and chauffeur on the first day of our stay. Our tour lasted 10 hours starting with the most spectacular view of the People's Square in the center of Shanghai that is about a 15-minute drive from our hotel. Everything that we have ever seen in big cities, like Tokyo, Hong Kong, or New York looked insignificant compared to the skyscrapers here. They have built over 5000 skyscrapers in Shanghai in just in the last twenty years. It amazed us to see a vibrant city of 26 million inhabitants living in a futuristic environment. They had just completed the Shanghai Palace, which with 140 floors is the world's second-highest building after the tallest is in Dubai.

The most significant construction of the People's Square was the Shanghai Museum, which we visited on our own the next day. Our guide also took us to the most famous Buddhist Temple in Shanghai, the Ying'an Temple. A young lady who spoke excellent English translated some of the quotes of Confucius written on the wall. To me, the most striking was: *"Studying without thinking is confusion, and thinking without studying is laziness"*.

We also learned the secrets and beauty of the Chinese tea drinking ceremony. Next, we went from the temple to the old French Quarter where the Europeans used to live. Today, it is probably the only place in the world where elegant restaurants and boutiques are side by side with the headquarters of the Communist Party. Interestingly, most of Shanghai shows very little signs of the Communist regime, not like what we observed in Beijing over twenty years earlier. We were told that there are nine thousand billionaires in Shanghai! Even if that is in Yuan at 6 to the dollar, it is not too bad.

Shanghai (2015)

From the French Quarter, we went to visit a silk museum and a pearl museum, and after a late lunch we ended up at the Bund, a spectacular view of the Huangpu River, a lower branch of the Yangtze. Many condominiums were built around the river and the average price per square foot runs around $4000, and many apartments sell for over $15,000,000. At the moment, there are no apartments in Shanghai that can be found below one million yuan. Our guide lives outside the city and travels two hours each way to and from work. When we asked our guide how she commutes to the city from her home? Her answer was by **BMW**, bus-metro-walk.

The Bund on the Huangpu River, Shanghai, China

After our one-day tour, we felt comfortable enough to explore the city on our own. The next day we went to the Jewish Refugee Museum, located at the Moshe Ohel Synagogue. During World War 2, thirty thousand Jewish Refugees were admitted to Shanghai from Austria and Germany. It was the largest number of any country in the world where Jewish refugees could find safety from the Nazis. They were settled around the area of Moshe Ohel, which was called little Vienna because of the many cafes and restaurants established by the refugees. We were pleasantly surprised to find out that the Hungarian Honorary Consul Pal Komor, whose grandfather's name was Kohn, was instrumental in arranging entrance visas for the refugees. Of course, the Chinese Government had the principal role in accepting the refugees.

Our next stop was the Shanghai Museum where we spent several hours learning about the ancient craftsmanship of the Chinese people going back to 6000 BC. The museum has over 120,000 pieces and is certainly one of the most impressive museums we have ever visited.

Shanghai Museum in the People's Square

The following day we went to the Yuyuan Garden and the Bazaar area. This old part of Shanghai was a big contrast to the skyscrapers that we admired around the Bund. It is made up mostly of well-kept buildings of old Chinese architecture with thousands of little shops and restaurants. We wanted to eat some dim sum dumplings that Shanghai is so famous for and we settled into one of the many restaurants. The restaurant was called *Lu Bo Lang* and while eating a variety of dim sum which we were not crazy about, we found out that it was the most famous restaurant in Shanghai when we saw pictures of the Clintons, Queen Elizabeth, Fidel Castro and many other celebrities who had eaten in the restaurant. A few days later we came back for a full dinner and ate abalone which was OK, but not great.

Lu Bo Lang Restaurant in Shanghai

My best meals during our nine-day stay in Shanghai were the scrambled eggs or omelets served at breakfast in the hotel. However, Vera's homemade sweet and sour pork would win prizes in Shanghai!

On our last day in Shanghai, we went on a day tour organized by the Conference. After spending a couple of hours in the historical museum in the Pearl Tower we went shopping. Shanghai's designer stores can easily compete with the ones in Paris.

Sweet and Sour Chicken (or Pork)

Serves 6

Ingredients:

1 cup orange juice

½ cup of cider vinegar

¼ cup honey

1 tbsp. chili powder (optional)

1 Tbsp. ground cumin

2 lb. chicken legs, bone in and skin on.

1 orange peel cut into Julian pieces

1 Tbsp. olive oil

Salt and pepper

Directions:

1. In a large zip lock bag mix orange juice, vinegar, honey, chili powder and cumin. Add all the chicken and refrigerate for 24 hours.

2. Take out the chicken pieces and the orange rinds from the marinade. Wipe them very dry with a paper towel. Reserve the liquid

3. In a heavy bottom pan add olive oil and heat medium-high. Add the chicken and the orange rinds. Sear them until well browned on all sides. Season with salt and pepper.

4. Add the marinade to the pot and cook on slow simmer until the chicken is very tender and well coated with glaze. If needed, add a small amount of water.

5. Serve on a platter decorated with fresh orange slices.

35. SWITZERLAND

We took the TGV from Paris to **Geneva**, Switzerland where we met Steve and Marika Szasz. I had a conference in Vienna and they wanted to join us. For the following 15 years, they came with us to eight of my conferences all around the world. Since none of us had ever been in Switzerland before, we thought it was a good opportunity to travel across the country to get to Vienna. We rented a car and drove through all the interesting parts of Switzerland. From Geneva, we took a short trip to nearby **Chamonix**. It was quite different to see the mountains in the summer than during our winter skiing vacation in 1980. From there, we continued through the cities of **Lausanne** and **Montreux,** the fashionable hang-outs of the film crowd.

Montreux, Switzerland

These cities are in the French part of Switzerland. After we left them, we traveled through many long tunnels to the mountains of Interlaken, where we took a train to the heights to see hundreds of beautiful ice carvings.

Train to Interlaken and ice carvings

Afterward, we stopped in the pretty little town of **Zermatt** before crossing into Italy.

Zermatt, Switzerland

Driving along the **Lake Como** area we endured a terrible rainstorm before we found a wonderful hotel which we remember for its great service and view of the lake after the storm.

Lake Como, Italy

Our next stop was in **Lugano**, my favorite city in Switzerland with all the charms of its Italian influence. The food here certainly was the best we found anywhere in the country.

Lugano, Switzerland

From Lugano, we drove across the picturesque countryside to **Lucerne,** where the Kapellbrücke the oldest wooden covered bridge in Europe was built. It serves as the city's symbol.

Kappelbrucke in Lucerne

From Lucerne we drove to **Zurich,** the elegant German speaking city and the largest banking center in the world. All through our weeklong stay in Switzerland, we developed the routine that Vera and I would get up at 7 AM to jog around the city and after an hour or so, we knew which areas were worth visiting. By the time we finished our breakfast with Steve and Marika, we were ready to give them a city tour.

Zurich, Switzerland

From Zurich, we drove toward Austria. Looking back on our visit to Switzerland, we thought that it is a beautiful country to visit only once!

36. LIECHTENSTEIN

We drove across tiny Liechtenstein, a German-speaking country with 37,000 inhabitants and probably the smallest country in the world. It is one of the few microstates in the world (others are Andorra, San Marino, Malta, Monaco and a few more) It is located in the Alps between Austria and Switzerland. We were disappointed to not come across any border patrol to stamp our passports.

Vaduz castle, Liechtenstein

37. MONACO

Monaco is a well-known microstate with a population of around 40,000. Over the years we have visited its main city of **Monte Carlo** several times. From Eze in France, it is only a few kilometers and we could not resist the temptation to visit the Grand Casino although we did not play. Another time in 1999 when we drove from Paris, first to Cannes and through Saint Remo to Rome, we also stopped for a few hours to have a cup of coffee and visit the Royal Palace of the Prince of Monaco. It is a very rich country and a favorite of investors because of its very liberal tax policy and its refusal to report financial transactions to the authorities of other countries.

Grand Casino Monte Carlo   *Monte Carlo, Monaco*

38. LUXEMBOURG

Driving back from Germany to Paris in 1999, we stopped overnight in the city of **Luxembourg,** the capital of Luxembourg, a small country of 60,000 inhabitants, bordered by Germany, France, and Belgium. In this small country, they use three different languages, Luxembourgish, French, and German. The city of Luxembourg was selected as one of the four capitals of the European Union along with the other three cities of Brussels, Strasbourg, and Frankfurt. We arrived late to the city and were happy to find a hotel without a prior reservation.

Hotel Alfa, Luxembourg

39. CHILE

In 1995 we made a trip to **Chile**, where I had a conference, the *2do Encuentro Internacional de Acústica en Chile*. Steve and Marika joined us on our trip. The meeting was held in **Valdivia**, in the South of Chile. We spent a week in this lovely city.

Valdivia, Chile

According to some archeological findings, people lived in this area in 12,000 BC. The conference was held at the University of **Valdivia** and all the lecturers except me and two other Americans were Spanish speaking. My presentation was in English and was translated into Spanish, as were the questions and answers of the discussion. The area near the conference site had received many Central European immigrants and had excellent pastry shops.

An Austro-Hungarian pastry shop in Valdivia, Chile

I am still trying to find an Esterhazy Torte as good as the one I had in Valdivia. One evening, all four of us were invited for dinner by Dr. Leo Beranek the world-famous acoustician who was the owner of the large acoustic firm in Boston. Leo passed away at the age of 102 when he was still active until his death and is certainly a role model for many of us in the acoustical community.

We had a nice visit to the Lake region of Chile, one of the most interesting places we have ever visited. On top of the snow-covered mountains, there are crowds of people skiing, while below others are swimming in the warm water of the lakes.

Lake Regions in Chile.

I took advantage of the chance to enjoy one of the waterfalls. We were fascinated by the variety of this beautiful country, probably one of the most beautiful we have ever seen. We continued our exposure to Chile by flying to **Santiago**, the capital.

Santiago, Chile, The Andes Mountains are 17,783 feet high.

Santiago, Chile

We stayed in a very elegant hotel where we requested an English-speaking guide to drive us around and give us a tour of the city, but unfortunately, their regular guide was ill and his substitute knew only three words of English:" your name is ..." So, for example, when we arrived the palace where Pinochet attacked the government of Salvador Allende, our guide said, "your name is ..." and related the rest of the event in Spanish. Of course, we already knew the end results: Pinochet established a brutal dictatorship in Chile where he ruled for 17 years. Still, we enjoyed the beautiful city and the surrounding Andes Mountains, which reach 17,783 feet near Santiago. Steve was impressed by the quality of the architecture in the city.

In Santiago with Steve and Mary 1995

Santiago has excellent restaurants and each evening we experienced their gourmet food. We also enjoyed their colorful entertainment, dances, and music. The only negative was that they were smoking cigars everywhere which dampened our mood considerably.

Folkloric entertainment in Santiago Chile

Before leaving Chile, we took a tour to **Vina del Mar** and **Valparaiso** on the Pacific Ocean. In Vina del Mar, we ate in a beautiful restaurant on a cliff facing the ocean. I was tempted to take a dip in the water and put on my swimming trunks which I always have with me. As I walked toward the water, a bunch of young kids were fascinated by me because the weather was a little on the chilly side for swimming. They followed me and applauded as I walked into the ocean while Vera and our friends enjoyed the show.

Vina del Mar, Chile

40. PUERTO RICO

During one of our holiday gatherings, we all decided that it was high time to take a leisurely vacation together with our childhood friends and wives. We chose a 12-day Caribbean cruise on the Royal Princess cruise ship. By then, Suzika had been transferred over to Go Ahead, a division of EF, a company that dealt with travel. She became vice president of marketing and sales, so we got a real good deal on this cruise.

Our tour started in **San Juan, Puerto Rico**. We flew in from Tampa, had a short visit in the city, a long dinner in a nice restaurant, and a few hours' sleep in a hotel.

San Juan, Puerto Rico

The **Royal Princess** turned out to be a high-class ship, with real gourmet cooking in their several restaurants. We had Las Vegas-style entertainment every evening and after the shows, we enjoyed dancing to the music of very good bands.

Royal Princess Cruise Ship

But the most important part of the cruise of course were the stops on the many Caribbean islands where we spent most of the day sightseeing before we returned to the boat.

41. ST. THOMAS

Our first stop was **St Thomas** noted for its beautiful St John's beach and for being the birthplace of the famous impressionist painter Jacob Abraham Camille Pissarro, credited by many as the father of the Impressionist movement.

St Thomas by Pissarro

We visited the house where he was born into a French-Jewish family, and although we did not purchase any of Pissarro's paintings, we bought a painting that was closer to our budget from a young woman who had a gallery in the house.

42. MARTINIQUE

The next island was **Martinique** which belongs to France and where you can find all the stores of Paris. It was the birthplace of Napoleon's wife Josephine, who obviously was not the favorite of the locals because they beheaded her statue in the main square in 1991. It was a symbolic act from an anti-colonial group. When Vera mentioned "Poor Josephine" to our local tour guide, the guide responded, "What do you mean poor? We are poor, not her".

Statue of Josephine in Martinique

43. GRENADA

Every day we landed on a different island. In **Grenada,** we took a tour of the famous rainforest, an area of continuous rainfall.

Rainforest, Grenada

44. VENEZUELA

We stopped at **Caracas, Venezuela** where we were shocked by the extremes in the people's standard of living. On the one hand, there were the most luxurious multimillion-dollar homes owned by billionaires, and on the other, thousands and thousands of homes were built illegally without electricity and water on the slopes of the mountains. During heavy rains, many houses without proper foundations would slide down the hills. It was a very sad sight to see the abandoned and destroyed homes. The crime rate was extremely high in Caracas and a number of our fellow travelers were robbed while walking in the city even in the elegant downtown area with its many nice stores.

Our guide, a young medical student, clearly a leftist, said that while the rich sent their billions to Florida, the people were preparing themselves for a takeover. It happened and unfortunately like in many countries in Eastern Europe when a socialist system is established, the poverty for the majority of the people may even get worse.

A poor neighborhood in Caracas, Venezuela

45. CURACAO

We enjoyed our visit to **Curacao**, which in the 17th century received a large number of Sephardic Jewish Immigrants from Holland who had first left Spain after the Inquisition and then moved to Portugal. Once Portugal followed the brutal example of Spain, the families moved to Holland. We visited the old Synagogue in Curacao, which was built in 1651 and is the oldest synagogue in the Western hemisphere.

Mikve Emanuel-Israel Synagogue, Curacao

Colorful Beach Homes, Curacao

46. PANAMA

After several days at sea, we finally arrived at the **Panama Canal**, one of the most monumental engineering constructions of mankind. The canal connects the Atlantic Ocean to the Pacific. The construction was started by the French in the 19th century but eventually was built by the Americans who completed it in 1914. It is about 50 miles long but its width in some parts is only 200 feet which limits the access of very wide ships. It was fascinating to see the Royal Princess, probably one of the larger boats to pass through the canal, maneuver with only a few inches of room on either side.

The Panama Canal

The Locks of the Panama Canal

47 MEXICO

After passing through the Panama Canal, we headed to our final destination: **Acapulco, Mexico**. It was a disappointment. The town itself is not any more attractive than Tijuana. However, there were beautiful homes and a gorgeous view of the ocean in the mountainous areas outside the city which is what attracts many tourists.

Highs and Lows of Livings in Acapulco, Mexico

It was our custom through the years that after a week in La Jolla for the QNDE meeting, we frequently visited **Tijuana** to enjoy their many restaurants or to just walk around and enjoy this colorful city.

Street entertainment in Tijuana, Mexico

The only other part of Mexico we know is Cozumel. In 2000 at Thanksgiving we took a cruise with Suzika who was single at the time, along with Michael and his family. Aunt Suzika shared a room with Rachel on the Carnival boat. After stopping in Key West, we landed in Cozumel where we spent a day scuba diving.

Scuba diving in Cozumel, Mexico.

During the last 10 or 15 years we have taken several Caribbean cruises with friends and family and most of the time we stopped in Cozumel. In 2013, we took along three of my cousins, Edi and Vera from Israel, and Agi from Knoxville. It was a pleasurable family reunion.

From Left, Vera my cousin, Vera my wife, me, Agi, and Edi Caribbean Cruise, 2013

48. RUSSIA

When we arrived at the **St Petersburg (Leningrad)** airport in June of 1997, a car was waiting for us. It was sent by Professor Kulakov of the Radio Engineering and Electronics Division of the Russian Academy of Science which organized the four-day meeting on Advances in Acousto-Optics. Vera and I came from London where we had spent a few days sightseeing together with Steve and Marika who joined us again at the meeting.

The driver of the car was a scientist and a member of the Institute. While he was driving us to the hotel, he explained that after the fall of Communism in the Soviet Union much less money was dedicated to research than before and many researchers had to work part-time. He was very happy that he was assigned to drive us around during our stay as this earned him his full salary.

As we were riding from the airport on a very wide boulevard, we were impressed by the well-kept elegant buildings. After a few days, we found out that the route on this boulevard was chosen to impress foreign visitors with a positive first impression of the city. Behind the elegant edifices, there were many unimpressive little buildings. It was like the story of Potemkin village. In the 18th century, Grigori Potemkin who wanted to impress Czarina Catherine built a fake village near the Dnieper River in Crimea.

Our hotel which belonged to the Institute and was conveniently close to the conference site was a typical example of boring gray Stalinist architecture. However, the rooms were OK and we had meals three times a day in the hotel restaurant. The bathroom had a nice hand-held shower which was long enough to be pulled all the way to flush the toilet when it malfunctioned.

It was fascinating to see a leftover from the Soviet era: the two ladies sitting in front of the elevator on each floor. They probably used to keep an eye on who was going in and out of the rooms, but now they probably were kept on the payroll to keep the unemployment rate low.

The conference was rather small, maybe 100 people mostly Russians, and by now I knew quite a few of the people who were students or faculty of the Acousto Optics School in Gdansk. St Petersburg was fascinating with its many historic buildings. The Winter Palace where the Bolshevik Revolution started in 1917 now housed the world-famous Hermitage museum. The city was built during the rule of Peter the Great, who overcame the opposition of the old nobility of Russia and was able to bring in Italian architects to give the city its unique combination of styles.

St. Petersburg, Russia

Winter Palace, Saint Petersburg Russia.

I still thought of the city as Leningrad, which was named after Lenin when he died in 1924 but in 1992 it was renamed, St Petersburg. During the Second World War, the city was under siege by the German Army for almost three years. The city was named Hero City after the war, one of the four Hero Cities along with Stalingrad, Odessa, and Kharkov.

We appreciated the many cultural offerings of the city. In addition to the Hermitage, we went to an exhibit in the Museum of Arts.

We also had the good fortune to get tickets to the Kirov-Marinski opera, whose conductor and music director was Gregoviev who remained there for many years.

Kirov-Marinski Theater, St Petersburg, Russia

We had heard a lot about the famous Saint Isaac Cathedral, the largest Orthodox cathedral in the world, and were eager to visit it. The cathedral which was built in the 19th Century served the city until the Bolshevik revolution when it was changed into the Museum of Religions and Atheism. The Soviets installed a large Foucault pendulum hanging down from the tower of the cathedral/museum, which demonstrated the rotation of the earth. After the fall of Communism, the cathedral was re-consecrated by the Orthodox Church, and the pendulum was removed, so unfortunately, we could not see it on our visit which was a great disappointment. Surely, Galileo also was disappointed.

We visited many of the palaces outside the city; the most impressive was the Palace of the Czarina Catherine, built in the 18th century around 25 km from St Petersburg. When the four of us arrived in a limousine, we saw a band of old soldiers in uniform welcoming the visitors. One of them shouted *Amerikanski* to us and they started to play "Yankee Doodle Dandy". Besides the music, the palace was even more impressive than Versailles.

Palace of Czarina Catherine, Tsarskoye Selo (Pushkin) Russia

After the conference, we were ready to take an early morning train to Helsinki. We said goodbye to the fellow who was driving us around during our stay. We thanked him for being such a good guide. He begged us to let him take us to the railway station at 5 in the morning rather than take a taxi. He explained that this way he would get full salary for an extra day! These were hard times for scientists in Russia.

My next visit to Russia was to a meeting in **Moscow** in August of 2002. This time I and my friend and colleague, Stas, went from Paris to the 16th conference on Nonlinear Acoustics that was held at the famous *Lomonosov University* in Moscow. The university is the oldest in Russia, established by Lomonosov, a scientist, mathematician, and politician in 1755. It was called Moscow State University until 1940 when it was renamed after its founder. It is rated as the best university in Russia and one of the leading institutions in the world.

Lomonosov University, Moscow, Russia

Stas and I arrived on a flight from Paris and upon our arrival, we were supposed to fill out a form declaring the total amount of foreign currency that we brought in with us. But there was no one around to receive the form so we just left it on the counter. We then exited the airport in a taxi to our hotel near Arbat, a traffic-free pedestrian street which was the most fashionable street in Moscow in the 18th century.

When we checked into our hotel, we were told that we had to put down 120 rubles, about $15 at that time to cover telephone expenses. If it were used up, the operator would tell us that we needed to pay more. I called Vera who was in Paris and we talked for about ten minutes with no interruption. Afterwards, I figured that I still had a lot more money left in my telephone account so I called my children in the USA and spoke a while with them also.

The next day, around 6 in the morning I woke up to a ring of the telephone and to someone who said with a heavy Russian accent, "Mr. Adler, you are in big trouble because you did not pay for your telephone usage". I was very concerned and tried to explain that I had made the calls with no interruption in my conversation and that I would go down to reception and make the payment. That is when the man on the phone started to laugh. I recognized Stas's voice and realized that it was he who had pulled the joke on me. We had a great time in Moscow, largely because he spoke Russian and we got around everywhere easily.

We visited the Kremlin, where they were selling two kinds of tickets. There was one line for foreigners where the price of the tickets was $20 and another line for Russians where the tickets were $4. Stas bought two Russian tickets and he walked through giving the tickets to the ticket taker but when I tried to do the same, he looked at Stas asking "*kto on?*", who is he?" We had to go back and stand on line for the foreigner's ticket. Anyway, it was well worth it!

The Kremlin

Kremlin means "fortress inside a city". It is a huge fortified complex in the center of Moscow. It was the residence of the Czars, and during the Bolshevik period, it included the residence of Lenin and later on of Stalin. It is the "White House" of the Russians but with the difference that there are also many churches and castles inside the large area.

We walked quite a bit on Arbat street, sampling the very good Georgian restaurants instead of the less attractive Russian fare. Nevertheless, we still like a good Russian Borscht.

384

Borscht

Serves 6

Ingredients:

1 lb. pork or beef or combination

6 garlic cloves crushed

bay leaves

14 cups water

4 beets

4 potatoes

1 medium-size onion chopped

1 cabbage shredded

2 carrots grated

1 red pepper cubed

2 tomatoes chopped

1½ tbsp. vinegar

2 tbsp. sugar

Parsley, dill, salt, and pepper

Sour cream

Directions:

1. Cut the meat into small pieces. Crush 4 garlic and 4 bay leaves to season the meat and put everything into a ziplock bag to marinate for few hours in the refrigerator.

2. Wrap the beets in an aluminum foil and roast for 45 minutes in the oven at 400 degrees.

3. In a large cup bring 14 cups of water to boil

4. Rinse seasoning from the meat and add to the boiling water. Lower the heat to low medium and cook for about 45 minutes, until the meat is tender.

5. Peel the potato and cut into small cubes and put in a bowl of cold water.

6. Shred the cabbage and set aside.

7. Chop the onion and saute it in 2 tbsp. butter in a large frying pan.

8. Peel the carrots and shred into the onions. Add two more tbsp. of butter.

9. Grate the cool beets and add to the onion and carrots.

10. Add the cubed pepper and the chopped tomatoes to the frying pan. Add 2 cloves of crushed garlic. Turn the heat down to low/medium.

11. If the meat is cooked, add the potatoes and cabbage to the broth. Cook 15 minutes.

12. Transfer everything from the frying pan to the broth. Add vinegar, salt, pepper, sugar, parsley, dill, and 2 bay leaves. Correct to your taste.

13. Cook another 15 minutes and serve with sour cream.

Arbat, pedestrian street, Moscow, Russia

We went to a night club called Prague, for an excellent performances of Gypsy songs and dances. It was full of old Russian Mafiosi with their gorgeous young models on their arm. When we left, two taxis were waiting in front of the club. Our hotel was quite far, so we decided to take a taxi. We had heard that taxi drivers would cheat you and that you better ask in advance how much the trip would cost. So, when Stas asked the driver "how much?" we were told it was $12. When we were getting into the cab, the driver told us to change to another one. When we got to the hotel, the driver asked for $50. Stas told him that the other guy had quoted $12. The driver said, "That was the other driver, not me". It was a setup. It can happen anywhere. We were ripped off in Athens, Prague and Budapest also.

The conference was at a very high level and I enjoyed listening to the presentations more than I usually do. After the conference, they gave us a tour of their laboratories and I was quite impressed by the quality of their doctoral students.

When we got to the airport, we were asked to show our stamped forms showing how much currency we brought into Russia. Since there was no one around to help us when we arrived, we just left the forms on the counter so our forms were never stamped. When they asked Stas how much money he had, he told them that he had $500. They took him away to another room to interrogate him about how he got the money. When I tried to follow him, they sent me back. Then they asked me how much money I had. I was smart enough to learn from Stas's experience and avoided trouble. I pulled out $30 from my left pocket although I had $800 in my right pocket.

It was over twelve years after the end of the Soviet regime but it was still stressful. They made Stas change his dollars to traveler's checks which cost him some money but we happily left the airport and flew to Paris. It still was a great trip.

49. FINLAND

We took a sleeper car from St Petersburg in 1997 to be able to rest a few hours before getting to **Helsinki**. When our train stopped at the Finnish border, we observed a very strange scene. A short fat woman soldier, a border guard burst into our car shouting in Russian and pulled off the blankets and looked under the beds. We found out later that she was looking for restricted Russian Icons being smuggled out of Russia. In a short time, she realized that we had no prohibited Icons and left us alone.

Arriving at the Helsinki railway station, we looked for evidence of something that we were taught as students years back in Hungary. We were told that Hungarian and Finnish make up the Finn-Ugric language group and that there are many similarities between the two languages. So, we did a little research. "Exit" in Hungarian is "kijarat" so we looked for something similar. I noticed a sign which said "Ulgang" but it was in Swedish similar to the German "Ausgang". Since Finland was under Swedish rule for hundreds of years all signs are in both Finnish and Swedish. Next to "Ulgang" we saw a sign with "Ulos" not even close to "kijarat".

Finnish is not an easy language and easily competes with Hungarian in difficulty. We tried once more to test the similarities of the two languages: Steve told us that the Hungarian sentence "*kicsi halacska uszik a vizben*" (little fish swimming in the water), is exactly the same in Finnish. So, at the first opportunity we had, we asked a young waitress in a restaurant if she understood" kicsi *halacska uszik a vizben*" she looked us like we were crazy. Even when Steve tried to demonstrate a swimming fish with his hand, it did not further the research at all. So, we gave up the comparative study of the Finn-Ugoric language group. I later was told that if someone were to write a Ph.D. dissertation comparing the Hungarian and Finnish languages, a few words would exhaust the study.

The city of Helsinki is a clean modern city. The structure that most impressed us was the unique underground church called *Temppeliaukio.*

Temppeliaukio Underground Church Helsinki, Finland

50. SWEDEN

Apart from our disappointment in Finn-Ugric linguistic research in Helsinki, we had a nice visit to the city on the Baltic. We took a cruise from Helsinki to **Stockholm** on the luxury boat Silja Serenade, certainly the most impressive ship I have ever sailed on. It was like a city on water, with stores, restaurants, entertainment, plazas and promenades, an unforgettable 16 hours of wonderful experiences

The Silja Serenade Helsinki to Stockholm

We spent a few days in the exciting colorful city of Stockholm despite the fact that when we arrived at our hotel one early morning after our run, we were surprised to see broken glass outside the restaurant next door. Apparently, people get out of hand after drinking. All through our visits in the northern countries, we found that people drink a lot to keep warm. We heard that if you have a guest at your house and put a bottle of alcohol on the table, they will not leave until the bottle is emptied. But during the daytime everywhere in the city the streets were very clean and people were very polite and helpful. Nevertheless, the evenings could be rather colorful.

Late Evening in Stockholm, Sweden

We visited the museum dedicated to the *Vasa*, a large ship which was built in the 17th Century and which because of poor design, sank only a few hundred meters from the port causing the deaths of several hundred people. They were able to bring the ship up to the surface 300 years later to restore it and make it a museum. There is also a Jewish Museum in Stockholm where we bought an excellent CD of Klezmer music.

51. AUSTRALIA

We had our customary large Thanksgiving celebration with our friends in 1997. Sanyi bacsi and Ica neni had also come to Florida from New York to be part of the more than 25 people who enjoyed the turkey and trimmings. This year was special because we also celebrated Sanyi bacsi's 90th birthday.

I did not suspect that Vera and my kids would take advantage of the opportunity of the presence of my friends and families here to organize a surprise party for my 65th birthday on the following day. I woke up to find our house full of signs and presents with birthday wishes. My kids' generous gifts were especially treasured. I got a nice watch from Michael, and Suzika gave us two tickets for a two-week vacation to Sydney and New Zealand with all the hotel arrangements paid.

Sydney Australia. The famous opera house of the city is on the left.

We landed in the beautiful city of Sydney in the Spring of 1998. Our first impression was that this is one of the most livable and beautiful cities you could hope for with its excellent climate, beautiful beaches, busy downtown, and thriving cultural scene. What else do you need? The only problem is that it is too far! From what? From everything?

Anyway, we had no desire to move there, so we just enjoyed our one week stay. There are many very good restaurants where we ate lots of fish and seafood. It's also a nice place to run, which we did every day. Once we ran through the whole city of Sydney to the famous Bondi Beach. The beach was about 5 miles from our hotel. We stayed at the beach all day, enjoyed the nice water, had a good seafood lunch, and then ran back to the hotel.

We had a chance to see *Swan Lake* in the Sydney opera house. We thought that the opera house which is one of the highlights of Sydney looks a lot better outside than inside. We visited several museums and also made an excursion to the Royal National Park which is about an hour's drive from the city, where we had a chance to see a Tasmanian devil. It is not as cute as in the cartoons. After seeing it, Vera started to call me that on the occasions whenever I would lose my patience.

52. NEW ZEALAND

From Sydney, we took a plane to **Christchurch**, New Zealand for the second half of our visit. Everyone who knew that part of the world had always told us that New Zealand is probably the most picturesque country in the world. It is certainly true that New Zealand with Norway and Chile are the leaders as far as natural beauty. Christchurch is the largest city on the southern island of New Zealand and we had a good tour on the one day we spent there.

Next, we took a 10-hour bus ride through the countryside to **Queenstown** stopping briefly at the Cook National Park. We decided to extend our stay in Queenstown from one to three days because we enjoyed it so much. We still think about the city as our favorite place in New Zealand. It is a small mountainous town that is part of the Fjord Land National Park area. It is full of excellent restaurants and about 50 bars for all tastes. We had probably the best rack of lamb and salmon ever. Our four-hour bus drive through the National park was breathtaking. However, it was topped by the two-hour boat ride on **Milford Sound**, which was recently rated as one of the most spectacular sights in the world.

Vera in Queenstown New Zealand (1998)

Milford Sound, Fjordland, New Zealand

From Queenstown, we flew to **Auckland**, the largest city in New Zealand which is located on the North Island. We took a day tour of about three hours by bus from Auckland to Rotorua, a place mostly known for its geysers and hot springs. We also visited a nearby Maori village where we learned about their history and enjoyed their cultural offerings.

Maori Cultural performance, New Zeeland

From Auckland, I called up Avri Koves, an old friend who lived in **Wellington**, the capital city of New Zealand. Avri and I became close friends on our way to Israel in 1949 even though we spent only a few months together. In Hatzor, he was upset when we decided to leave the kibbutz. I met him some ten years later in Montreal where he resided after immigrating from Israel a few years before. We walked through the streets of Montreal in the evening trying to catch up on the happenings of our lives over the last ten years. It was morning by the time we said goodbye to each other. I never saw him again. Although we talked on the telephone in New Zealand, I had no time to stop in Wellington. I heard from friends that he passed away recently.

53. EGYPT

In the summer of 2000, we made a trip to Israel with George Bozoki and his wife. They were celebrating their tenth anniversary and asked us to join them in Israel. We stayed again at the Yamit Hotel in Tel Aviv. Our cousins Sanyi and Mari together with Agi who was also George's cousin, and Avishai, her husband, treated us to a wonderful week of vacation in a resort on the Red Sea in Egypt. This was our first visit to any Arab country, and we had a wonderful time.

The hotel accommodations, as well as the food, was much better than we expected. This part of the Red Sea is much nicer than it is at Eilat. The snorkeling was even better than in Hawaii. The people of Egypt were very friendly and we decided to make a more extensive tour the following year including Cairo, Alexandria and other parts of Egypt. Unfortunately, the second Intifada started a few months after our visit and we decided to postpone the trip. We never made it! Tragically, my dear friend George passed away in 2009.

Avishai, George, Jayne, me, Agi, Sanyi, Mari, and Vera in Sinai, Egypt (2000)

394

Snorkeling Paradise, the Red Sea in Egypt

54. PORTUGAL

Suzika arranged another tour for us, this time to Portugal for ten days in 2003. After arriving on a flight from Paris to **Lisbon,** we met the people in the hotel with whom we would spend time together for the next 10 days. We were immediately taken by the colorful old part of Lisbon.

Street in Lisbon, Portugal

It was an interesting group with a variety of backgrounds. We met a Russian history professor from San Francisco, and a medical doctor with a Hungarian wife and other diverse companions. Our tour guide was a Spaniard not Portuguese but he was excellent. While in Lisbon we went to a night club where we heard performers singing Fado songs, a melancholic style that we liked so much that we bought several CDs of the most famous Fado singer Amalia Rodrigues. We stayed for three days in Lisbon, a very colorful city. In central Lisbon, there is a moving memorial to Lisbon's Jews.

"In memory of the thousands of Jews victims of intolerance and religious fanaticism, who were murdered in the massacre begun in this area on April 19, 1506".

It is heartening to see the growing awareness of past evils. We can only hope that this consciousness remains firm all over the world! *(Photo and comment: Frank Gerace, childhood Shabbos Goy, Brooklyn, NY, 1942)*

From Lisbon, 25 of us drove north in a comfortable air-conditioned bus. Our first stop was in Fatima about 100 miles north of Lisbon, where the story goes that in 1917 three children met with a miraculous lady. It is believed by many that a visit to Fatima can cure all kinds of illnesses.

Our next stop was in Coimbra where one of the oldest universities in Europe was established in 1240. Next, we drove to **Porto**, the second-largest city in Portugal where we also spent a couple of days. We visited the leading distillery of port wine in Porto but were not too impressed. You can get a better-tasting one for $15 in Costco, so for Port, you don't have to come to Porto. But it is a lovely city!

We enjoyed Portugal very much. Our tour guide filled us up with tons of information about Portugal which for over 600 years was a great world power. The Portuguese were the first to go to China and Japan. It is said that they discovered that there was no ready phrase in Japanese to express thanks or to say "thank you" before their arrival. It is said the Japanese learned the word "Obrigado" from the Portuguese, which became their own "Arigato". There are many other examples in both directions; the one I really like is" tempero" in Portuguese for seasoned fried food that is derived from its Japanese equivalent "tempura".

We also learned from our guide that after the Inquisition a very large number of Jews who did not want to convert to Christianity in Spain came to Portugal. Unfortunately, because of the pressure from their neighbors, the Portuguese also forced the Jews to convert, but with less ferocity. Many of the Jews also became

Marranos in Portugal but only formally as they continued to practice their traditions secretly. Some estimate that about 25% of the Portuguese including a past president, have some Jewish roots.

One of the Portuguese Marranos, Captain Arthur Carlos de Barros Basto, had learned of his Jewish roots from his grandfather when he was a young boy. He became a celebrated and highly decorated officer in WW 1. He later turned toward Judaism and changed his name to Abraham Israel Ben-Rosh. He decided to locate Jews who for years were hiding their identity from the outside world but who practiced some aspects of Judaism secretly at home. He traveled across the country and succeeded in helping hundreds of descendants to return to Judaism openly.

The military authorities of Portugal did not approve of Abraham's actions and charged him in court with false accusations. He was discharged from the Army despite all his decorations and heroic deeds in WW 1. He was referred to as the Portuguese Dreyfuss, the French officer who was charged and falsely convicted of treason at the end of the 19th century. During the 1930s, Abraham helped relocate many Ashkenazi Jews from Eastern Europe to Portugal. With the aid of another crypto-Jew, who moved from Porto to Shanghai, Abraham was also instrumental in establishing a synagogue in Porto.

Synagogue Kadoorie Mekor Haim in Porto

We continued our travel to Evora, where Vasco da Gama the Portuguese navigator lived. Da Gama was the first European to reach India to link Asia to Europe. In Evora one also finds a most unique Chapel: *O Capel dos Ossos*, the Bone Chapel. The walls and ceilings of the chapel are made of human bones. Our last stop was in Estoril, a very upscale seaside resort nearest to Lisbon which is called the Portuguese Riviera.

We had a very interesting vacation, thanks to Suzika. Once, when I mentioned to a French university professor that my daughter had arranged several trips for us including one to Australia, he said, "I'm lucky to get a metro ticket from my daughter". On the other hand, Suzika never gave us a metro ticket!

In 2018 I was invited to an Ultrasonic Conference held near Lisbon in **Caparica**, a resort town with the most visited beaches of Portugal. It was a beautiful setting in a nice hotel just walking distance from the beach. It was a small but well-attended conference with participants from many countries.

Lecturing in Caparica, Portugal 2018

Attendees at the Ultrasonic Conference, Caparica, Portugal 2018

Relaxing entertainment by colleagues in Caparica, Portugal

We took a day tour to the historic Belem, part of Lisbon famous for its museums and the tower of Belem. A famous pastry called *Pasteis de Belem*, a special custard tart is their specialty, orinially created by monks in Belem,Lisbon. We also enjoyed the beaches in Caparica. I had another invitation for 2020 at the same place but COVID 19 decided otherwise.

Vera's homemade Pasteis de Belem

55. HOLLAND

When we arrived in **Amsterdam** from Paris in 2004, it was a challenge to get to our prearranged lodging because of the city's elaborate canal system. After driving around for over an hour and a half we realized that there was no way we could pull our car up to the house, so we parked our car as best we could and dragged our two large suitcases along the canals. Normally, for the short 3-day trip that we had planned for Amsterdam, we would only take very small suitcases but this time we had tickets to fly back to Florida from Amsterdam. Our biggest challenge was to carry our suitcases up to the third floor in a narrow steep typical Amsterdam building. This was our first trip to Holland although, on our way to Göttingen in 1964, we landed in **Rotterdam.** We spent a very pleasant three days jogging, walking, and enjoying the beauty of the historic areas of Amsterdam, the lovely center of culture,. We visited the Rijk Museum, the Rembrandt House, the Van Gogh Museum, and even swung by their unique red light district.

A typical Canal street in Amsterdam, Holland.

After the inquisition in Spain, a large number of Sephardic Jews settled in Holland, and later even more came from Portugal. The so-called Portuguese Synagogue which was established in the 17th century still exists. Among the most notable of the exiled Jews was the Spinoza family, whose famous member was Baruch Spinoza. He was the noted philosopher who was born in Amsterdam but eventually was expelled from the Jewish community for his criticism of the bible. Almost three hundred years later, Anna Frank, a Jewish girl, captured the attention of the world with her diary which was discovered after she was murdered during the Holocaust in the Bergen Belsen concentration camp.

We visited her home in Amsterdam.

Anna Frank pokes her head out from her hiding place in Amsterdam 1942

56. IRELAND

Even though I have no ties to Ireland and none of my family members are Irish, somehow, I have always admired these people and their strong attachment to their history. Once when I was attending the Alliance Française in Paris, on St Patrick's day I dressed up in all green: shoes, socks, pants, shirt, and so on. From then on, the owner of the café where we went during a break has called me Patrick.

In 2005, we signed up for a two-week bus tour to Ireland and saw most of the important parts of this beautiful country. Vera and I took a flight from Paris to **Dublin** where we met the rest of the group who came from the States.

Dublin, Ireland

We had a good tour guide who taught us a lot about the history of Ireland. We learned how St Patrick in the 5th century introduced Christianity as well as the Roman alphabet, and in more modern times how Ireland in 1922 achieved independence from England after the 10-year War of Independence. I found similarities between them and the Hungarians. Their strong temperament as well as their struggles against major powers brought the parallels between these two countries to my mind.

I am not much of a beer drinker but you don't get away from Dublin without sampling Guinness. We learned that the perfect way to pour takes 119.5 seconds! Our tour guide even asked us to write a limerick including the word Guinness as many times as we could. So, I just wrote four lines, repeating Guinness 5 times in each line:

Guinness, Guinness, Guinness, Guinness, Guinness

Guinness, Guinness, Guinness, Guinness, Guinness

Guinness, Guinness, Guinness, Guinness, Guinness

Guinness, Guinness, Guinness, Guinness, Guinness

It certainly rhymes!

Best place for Guinness in Dublin, Ireland

Although I was concerned about eating the Irish stew because I feared the taste of mouton, it was quite delicious with lean lamb meat. Their salmon is even better. The Irish countryside is beautiful because of the lush green landscape, fruit of the abundant rains. We were fascinated by watching a delightful unique show of how shepherds direct the sheepdogs with different whistle tunes to herd hundreds of sheep. What skill! We climbed **Dunmorehead** of which is the westernmost part of Ireland and Europe.

Dunmorehead, the westernmost part of Ireland

We visited the cities of **Galway** and **Cork,** as well as **Kerry** and other counties. Near the city of Cork, we visited the famous Blarney Castle, a historic medieval stronghold, where the "kissing stone" is revered by the believers of the legend. According to legend, kissing the Blarney Stone, a carboniferous limestone rock in the castle, provides the kisser with the gift of fluent, elegant speaking and writing. This kisser is still waiting 15 years later for the result.

Kissing the Blarney Stone   2005

Blarney Castle, Ireland

57. BERMUDA

Our main event of 2005 however, was the trip to **Bermuda** where we were invited in September by Richard. He was lecturing regularly on hip arthroscopy to local orthopedic surgeons in Bermuda and invited us together with his parents to spend a week vacation there. *Arthroscopy* is a minimally invasive surgical procedure on a joint, routinely the knee, in which examination and sometimes treatment of any damage is performed using an arthroscopic device. At that time, Richard was among the few orthopedic surgeons applying it to the hip.

Bermuda, a British *Overseas Territory*, is an island in the Atlantic about 1000 miles north-east of North Carolina. This was our first visit there. We felt an instant attraction to Judy and Howard, the parents of Richard. The four of us had a wonderful time together exploring the beauty of the island and enjoying the excellent local restaurants. After a couple of days when Richard proposed to Suzika, one could not find four happier parents anywhere in the world. Richard is everything that we hoped for as a husband for our daughter.

From left, Howard, Vera, Richard, Suzika, me, and Judy in Bermuda 2005

S10. ALASKA

We scheduled a trip to Alaska with Sanyi and Mari for May 2007. We met them in Vancouver, where we had just been a few months before, and we sailed on the very luxurious Holland American *Ryndam* for seven days.

Sailing with Ryndham in Alaska (2007)

Alaska is comparable to Norway or New Zealand in terms of the natural beauty of the magnificent glaciers. I took a helicopter to the top of the frozen mountain (although the rest of the group chickened out) and up there drank the purest water ever from a tiny creek.

The views out the windows on our train trip from Yukon into Canada were breathtaking. Even more surprising was to see the carving on a rock of *Debreceni VSC*, my home town's soccer team, one of the best in Hungary.

In Alaska, seen from the train from Yukon to Canada

Mari and Glaciers in Alaska (2007)

Sanyi, Vera and me on our Alaskan tour (2007)

When we got off the boat in **Anchorage**, we rented a car and spent a couple of days driving around. It was another great trip spent together, except for our being attacked by giant mosquitos!

58. CORSICA

With Ponci and Shira we took a short trip to Corsica in 2007. From Paris, we flew into **Ajaccio**, Napoleon's birthplace, and rented a car with insurance coverage. We drove around the difficult roads of Corsica that are similar to those of Sicily and enjoyed the views. We went south to **Bonifacio**, a very nice town close to the neighboring Italian island of Sardinia.

Cliff of Bonifacio Corsica a view of Sardinia

There were teams of wild pigs everywhere on the side of the road. Most of the sausages which we enjoyed were made from these boars. The food in Corsica was kind of a mixture between Italian and French. Ajaccio is certainly full of Napoleon references.

He is visible everywhere in Ajaccio

Just as I was ready to return our rented car, as I was driving through the parking lot gate, I made a sharp turn and hit the side of the car on the gate. They put an 800 Euro charge on my credit card even though I had insurance. I called up American Express and they took the charge off immediately. American Express always backs you up and is the only card I deal with! Sadly, this was our last trip together with Ponci.

59. PERU

We took a 12-day tour with Joe and Ibi Koenig to Peru in March 2009. Joe provided many of the photos in this chapter. Margarita also joined us to explore the many wonders of this exotic country. The territory which is Peru today was the seat of ancient cultures, such as the Norte Chicos in 3500 BC, considered the oldest civilization in the Americas, as well as the better-known Inca Empire which had the largest extension in Pre-Columbian America.

Our first stop was **Lima**, the capital of Peru with a population of over 9 million that was founded by Pizarro who led the Spaniards to conquer the Inca in 1535. Our group of about 35 had a welcome lunch at the beautiful La Rosa Nautica restaurant built on a pier in the ocean.

La Rosa Nautica restaurant, Lima, Peru Vera is on the pier 2009

After our lunch, we spent the afternoon sightseeing in Lima, visiting many historic sites and colonial neighborhoods.

Lima, Peru 2009

412

In the evening we had dinner at one of the best seafood places in Lima, *Astrid y Gaston*, a recommendation of Suzika who worked in Latin America for many years. The food and the ambiance were excellent, although we had a little too much ceviche for a while. Actually, in nearby Sarasota, Florida, there is an excellent Peruvian restaurant, called *Selva* where we eat often.

Astrid y Gaston restaurant, Lima, Peru

A couple of days later we flew to Cuzco, the ancient capital of the Incas. On our arrival at the Cuzco airport, we were entertained by the local musicians. We love Peruvian music, so we bought several of their recordings. We did not stay in Cuzco but took a 70 km bus trip to **Ollantaytambo**. We returned to Cuzco another day.

Ceviche

Serves 2

Ingredients:

½ Lb cooked shrimp

1/4 red onion thinly sliced

1 half minced jalapeño pepper

1 small chopped red pepper

1 small cucumber chopped into small pieces

1 Stick of chopped celery

Juice of one lime

A handful of finely chopped cilantro

Directions:

1. In a bowl combine shrimp, pepper, cucumber, jalapeño pepper, onion, cilantro and mix well

2. Pour lime juice over the mixture, refrigerate at least for 30 minutes and serve

We were entertained at the Cuzco airport on our arrival, 2009

Taking the bus from Cuzco, we stopped to take a look at the city from the mountain top and were welcomed by the locals.

Llama with her friends and a view of Cuzco from above

Ollantaytambo was a ceremonial and religious center and the royal estate of Emperor Pachacuti of the Inca Empire. It is close to 10,000 feet above sea level.

Ollantaytambo, Peru

It was also a stronghold of Inca resistance during the Spanish conquest in the 16th century. When Cuzco fell to the Spaniards, Ollantaytambo was the temporary capital of the Incas.

Ollantaytambo, Peru

From here we took a train to one of the seven wonders of the world **Machu Picchu.**

Taking the train to Machu Picchu

In 1983, UNESCO designated Machu Picchu a World Heritage Site describing it as "an absolute masterpiece of architecture and a unique testimony to the Inca civilization".

Machu Picchu is located in the Cuzco region on an 8000-foot-high mountain ridge. Most archeologists believe it was built as an estate for Emperor Pachacuti in the mid-15th century and was inhabited for about a century until the Spanish conquest. The Spaniards never discovered the city and it was hidden for more than 300 years until 1910, when an American historian from Yale, Hiram Bingham, called the world's attention to its existence.

Some sources claim that an English missionary and a German engineer had located the place 40 years earlier. Since then, there have been many repair and restoration projects. The Incas' very unique architectural and construction methods have withstood climate change for hundreds of years, The Incas did not use any mortar to secure the fitted stones together but polished the surfaces of the stones to have mirror-like surfaces which allow inter-atomic forces to do the job of ensuring adhesion and structural strength.

In Machu Picchu with Ibi and Joe, 2009

City Plan Machu Picchu

Fascinated by the views in Machu Picchu 2009

After two days of enjoyable but somewhat challenging mountain climbing, we decided to take a leisurely spa adventure at the unique natural hot spring spa that was walking distance from our hotel in **Aquas Calientes**.

Scenic Route to the city of Aquas Calientes　　　　　*Aquas Calientes Spa*

From Machu Picchu, we took a train back to **Cuzco** which has a population today of close to 400,000, and formerly was the capital city of the Inca Empire from the 13th to the 16th century. The Killke people occupied the region from 900 to 1200 AD, before the arrival of the Incas who built Cuzco in the 12th century. When we arrived to the city, there was a holiday celebration, and thousands and thousands of people were celebrating all over the city, including the military, the clergy, and everyone else including us.

Celebration in Cuzco, Peru, 2009

The Sacsaywaman, a citadel that we toured for a whole day, is another wonder of the area that is only a couple of kilometers from the center of Cuzco. The walled fortress complex was constructed by the Killke around 1100 AD. The Incas later expanded and occupied the complex in the 13th century by building with large rocks, some weighing as much as 30 metric tons (60,000 lbs.). It is still a mystery how they were able to move such large stones from as far as 10 miles away. It is estimated that it took more than 20,000 people and roughly 70 years to complete. The Spaniards soon destroyed 80 % of the citadel. Just a year before our visit in March 2008, archaeologists discovered the ruins of an ancient 2,700 square-foot temple, a roadway, and an aqueduct system at Sacsaywaman.

Saksaywaman citadel, Peru

Some stones are close to 10 feet high.

In the evening we went to a restaurant in Cuzco for entertainment by the locals and to sample typical Peruvian food, like *rocoto relleno*, a stuffed spicy pepper not too different from the Hungarian *toltott paprika*

Peruvian dancers in Cuzco, Peru, 2009

Rocoto Relleno (spicy stuffed peppers)

Continuing our tour toward **Lake Titicaca** our bus stopped at **Andahuyalas,** a town at 10,000 feet above sea level. After wandering through their colorful market and buying some sandwiches, we sat down for a drink in a small restaurant.

In Andahuyalas, Peru, 2009

We were climbing higher and higher. The local sign shows that we were at 4,338 meters (14,238 feet) above sea level.

Luckily we had trained in Keystone Colorado during our skiing trips. But many other people in our group started to feel dizziness due to the altitude and were offered coca leaves to chew to adapt to the altitude.

We stopped at a local farm where the very friendly people offered us some of the potatoes they roasted in their stone oven. Peru has thousands of different kinds of potatoes of all kinds of shapes and colors.

Roasting a variety of potatoes at a farm in Peru

We stopped at **Sillustani** to visit the unique pre-Inca cemetery on the shore of Lake Umayo where important people of the era were buried in the tower-like *Chulpas*. The common people were buried underground, a custom continued by the Incas as well.

Chulpas, burial towers in Sillustani, Peru

By late afternoon we arrived at our destination near Lake Titicaca. From our hotel, we had a view of the lake which is shared with Bolivia and is the largest in South America. At 12,507 ft is the highest lake in the world.

Lake Titicaca, Peru, elevation 12,507 ft the highest altitude lake in the world

The next morning we had an exciting boat trip on the lake where we visited several of the man-made floating islands. There are over seventy of these floating islands on Lake Titicaca, where people live, hunt, fish and grow essential crops. The islands are of various sizes and shapes and 40 - 60 people live on some of them.

Floating Island on Lake Titicaca, Peru.

We learned about their daily activities, habits and culture from the residents of the Islands. For example, when there is a serious disagreement among them, sometimes they might cut the island in two or three to continue living in peace separately.

Enjoying the experience of the floating island on Lake Titicaca, Peru, 2009

Sailing on Lake Titicaca in an indigenous reed boat, 2009

We landed at a small town with a population of 2000 on **Taquile Island** about 30 miles from Puno. We had to climb even higher and by now at 14,000 feet even we were not refusing coca leaves. We had a nice lunch of quinoa soup and fresh fish from the lake along with a mixed salad.

Path to the top of Taquile Island, at Lake Titicaca

Waiting for our dessert and coca leaf tea, 2009

The next day we flew south and stayed for a couple of days in the beautiful new Hilton Hotel, in the **Paracas National Park** by the ocean. All the important sightseeing spots which we planned to visit in the next couple of days (Nazca, Ballestas Island, Pisco) were a short drive from the hotel.

Hilton Hotel at the Paracas Resort, Peru

The next morning, we drove to the nearby airport where we were taken in passenger planes to fly over the Nazca Desert and observe the remains of the **Nazca** civilization, the **NAZCA LINES.** The Nazca people were a prehistoric civilization that lasted over 1000 years until 800 AD. There is no written account of Nazca history and for the last 100 years, archeologists and other scientists have tried to solve the mysterious existence and interpretation of the Nazca lines. Although the conquistador Pedro Cieza de Leon published a book about their existence in 1553, he mistook them for trail marks. In modern times, the Peruvian archaeologist Toribio Mejía Xesspe spotted them first in 1927 and reported his discovery to a scientific conference in 1939.

The Nazca geoglyphs are lines etched into the desert sands. Radiocarbon dating has established the date of the making of the Nazca lines at around 200 BC. Because of the isolation and the dry climate of the desert they have survived more than two thousand years. We bought the book "Mystery of the Desert", written by a German-born Peruvian mathematician, Maria Reiche, who summarizes the results of many investigations and theories about the lines, concluding that the direction and connection of the lines relate to astronomical and cosmological observations.

The lines depicting animal figures show us some of the animal world at the time of the Nazca, but provide little insight into their meaning. It is a continuing research effort and just recently a Japanese team using artificial intelligence scans have discovered lines that represent humanoid figures among the Nazca lines.

Nazca lines as seen from the airplane on both sides of the road

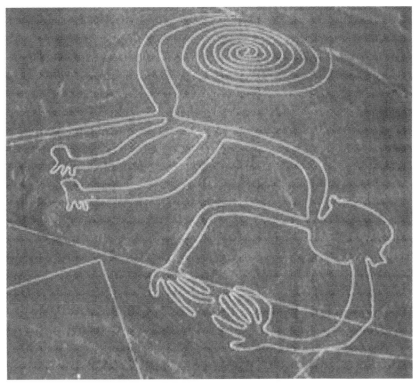

Nazca lines etched in the Nazca Desert,

After Nazca, we took a boat ride to the **Ballestas Islands,** a set of small Islands in the Paracas region, close to our hotel. On our way to the islands, we observed another type of geoglyph, the Paracas Candelabra, a prehistoric geoglyph on the hills of the Paracas Peninsula at Pisco Bay. It is estimated to date back to 200 BC, although many believe it is much older. With a large, branchlike appearance, the purpose and meaning of the Candelabra remain unknown.

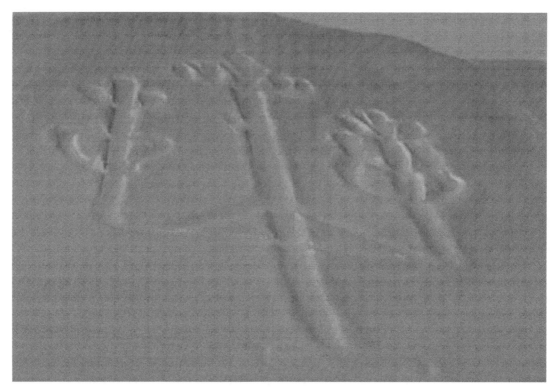

Paracas Candelabra, Peru

The Ballestas Islands are marine rock formations inhabited by beautiful rare birds and huge pelicans at least 4 times the size of their Florida cousins, as well as penguins, sea lions, and many other species. It was a fascinating trip for nature lovers.

Ballestas Islandés, Paracas Región, Perú

Pelicans on Ballestas Islands, Peru

Sea Lion on the Ballestas Islands, Peru

Our last visit to the area before we returned to Lima and from there back to Florida was to a Hacienda where we had a nice lunch and learned about the process of producing the national drink, Pisco, a yellowish brandy distilled from Muscatel grapes.

An expert explains Pisco production

Pisco Distillery

As we left, we toasted our hosts and each other, saying *Adios* with a **PISCO SOUR**.

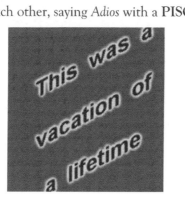

Classic Peruvian Pisco Sour

This drink accompanies a toast in many languages:

Khali kaq kachun, egészségére לחיים, في صحتك, salute   à votre santé, salud ypa, 乾杯, 건배, cheers Στην υγειά σας, prost

Ingredients:

1½ oz. Pisco

1 egg white

1 oz. lemon juice

¾ oz.simple syrup: (½ cup of water bring to boil and stir ½ cup of granulated sugar and stir until sugar dissolves).

Directions:

1. Vigorously shake and strain contents in a cocktail shaker with ice cubes. Pour into glass.

60. HONDURAS

We started the year by taking a Caribbean cruise with our friends the Nadais and the Sarkadis. They visited us every year ever since we moved to Florida and we thought we'd add a new experience. So, we took a Carnival boat together for four days, starting at Port Tampa.

Sailing on the Caribbean with Carnival 2010

After our first stop at Key West, we landed at a Honduran port, we decided to take a private tour with a taxi rather than the one organized by Carnival. Were we ever lucky! The six of us squeezed into a run-down taxi, whose driver assured us that he would drive us around and take us to one of the best places for lunch. We didn't know that we were in an area with the highest rate of murder and kidnapping in the world.

A poor area in Honduras

We were shocked by the worst poverty we had ever seen. When we arrived to our not very attractive destination and saw the shady characters, we all started to be concerned. We were offered to buy some uninviting food which, because of the scary surroundings, none of us had the desire to taste. After paying a ridiculously high price for the meal for the driver, we felt rather fortunate when the cab driver dropped us off at the port unharmed. We were much happier with the organized tour on our next stop.

61. GUATEMALA

The best part of our tour was that we were together, enjoying our friendship in the ship's luxurious setting where we forgot the slums of Honduras. To this day our fellow travelers' visits to our home continue but we miss the presence of Gabi, a very kind and good friend, who passed away in June 2011.

Dining with the Nadais and Sarkadis in the Carnival, 2010

From left, me, Vera, Gyuri and Myra Sarkadi, Eva and Gabi Nadai, Caribbean 2010

62. LITHUANIA

In May 2011, we signed up for a tour to the Baltic together with Joe and Ibi Koenig as well as with Margarita. Our first stop was in **Vilnius**, the capital city of Lithuania the largest of the three Baltic countries with a population of around three million people. We stayed in a hotel next to the National Drama Theater, known for its dramatic statue of the Three Muses.

The National Theater of Vilnius, Lithuania with the 3 Muses. Vera is the 4th one.

Walking in the old city we spotted a Hungarian Restaurant.

Old Town in Vilnius   Hungarian restaurant in Vilnius

I always wanted to visit Vilna, now it is called **Vilnius**, which used to be called the Jerusalem of the North. Vilna was the world capital of Talmudic learning for many centuries. The Gaon of Vilna, a famous Rabbi lived here in the 18th century. In fact, Jews have resided in the city for over seven hundred years.

Synagogue in Vilnius, Lithuania

Between the wars, Vilnius (at that time under Polish rule and known as Wilno) was a bustling international center of modern Yiddish culture and scholarship. Renowned scientists, teachers, writers, sculptors, and musicians made their homes here. Jewish secular and religious institutions flourished, including *Der Yiddisher Visenshaftlicher Institut* (Scientific Institute). In the 1920s and 1930s, Vilnius was selected to be the headquarters of the Institut which published countless scientific works. Albert Einstein, Sigmund Freund, and Marc Chagall were honorary members of the board. Ninety-five percent of the Jewish population of Vilnius, close to 90,000 were murdered during World War 2, among this number several thousand were massacred by the local population.

Our tour guide was very knowledgeable in the Jewish history of Lithuania and was very instrumental in showing us important sites, like the Jewish Museum, the Ghetto areas, and the statue of the Japanese consul Sugihara who saved thousands of Jews from the massacre by providing them visas. This was a very meaningful part of the tour for us.

437

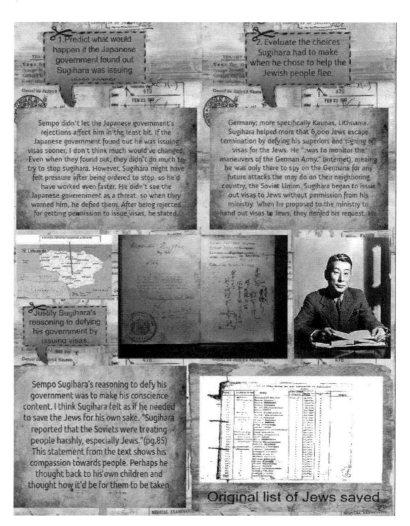

Sempo Chiuene Sugihara, Japanese Ambassador in Lithuania saved thousands of Jews during the Holocaust

From Vilnius, we drove to **Trakai,** which was the capital of the western part of the **Grand Duchy of Lithuania.** Under the leadership of Gediminas, in the 14th Century, the Grand Duchy of Lithuania was the largest European country. It extended from the Baltic Sea to the Black Sea and included Belarus, Ukraine, part of Poland, and part of Russia. It lasted until the 17th Century when it became the Lithuanian-Polish Commonwealth.

Trakai is the home of a small community of Turkic **Karaites** who only accept the Torah with no rabbinic tradition and who don't consider themselves Jews like the Karaites in Israel. During World War 2, the Germans did not consider the Karaites as Jews so they were not persecuted like the Jews in Lithuania. Even so, several hundred were massacred in **Baby Jar** in Kiev.

The small community of Karaites residing in Trakai live in wooden houses with three windows. The legend goes: one for God, one for fortune, and one for themselves.

Karaite wooden houses in Trakai, Lithuania

We visited the century **Trakai Castle** of the Grand Duke **Gediminas,** the medieval Lithuanian hero. It is the most visited tourist attraction in Lithuania.

Trakai Castle, Trakai, Lithuania

After a couple of hours touring the castle, we stopped at a local restaurant to taste some of their national dishes, like *kibinai,* a tasty meat pie and chilled borscht.

Kibinai, a Lithuanian meat pie

On another occasion at the end of June 2014, I had an invited talk to the 12th Acousto-Optics School in **Druskininkai,** Lithuania. Druskininkai is a beautiful spa resort where the Czars used to spend their vacations. We stayed in the Europa Royal Hotel and visited many of their beautiful spas.

Hotel and Spa in Druskininkai, Lithuania, 2014

The Conference was rather small but very good and for the first time in all our trips, my presentation was attended by Vera who was accompanied by Georges and Françoise also who came along to Lithuania with us. Vera was very happy with my lecture.

63. LATVIA

From Vilnius, we took a short bus ride to **Riga** Latvia. During our scenic ride, our knowledgeable tour guide briefed us on the history of Latvia. After centuries of Swedish, Russian, and Polish rule, Latvia became an independent country, the Republic of Latvia in 1918. Later, at the beginning of World War2, the Soviet Union forcibly annexed Latvia and the other two Baltic countries, Lithuania and Estonia. When the German Army attacked the Soviet Union in 1941, Latvia was occupied by the Germans until 1944. Some of the Latvian population collaborated with the Germans because of their anti-Soviet feelings. Almost all of the Jewish population of 94,000 was murdered during this period.

For the next 45 years, Latvia was again part of the Soviet Union until the end of the Soviet regime when in 1989 it recovered its independence. Today, its population is less than 2 million, one-third of which lives in Riga, the capital city. Riga was one of the cities on the Baltic that made up the Hanseatic League in the 13th century.

Our first visit was to the Grand Central Market which was one of the largest and most colorful we had ever visited, where we had a wonderful lunch of the dark rye bread that one can find everywhere in the Baltic countries.

Grand Central Market, Riga, Latvia

441

Riga is a very beautiful city with probably more Art Nouveau buildings than anywhere else in Europe. At the turn of the century, Mihail Eisenstein an architect of German Jewish paternal roots (and Swedish maternal roots) initiated the design of these magnificent buildings in Riga.

Mihail Eisenstein, chief architect of Art Nouveau buildings in Riga

Art Nouveau buildings in Riga, Latvia

In one of the Eisenstein buildings, they established an Art Nouveau museum with interesting exhibits of turn of the century interiors and many art pieces of the movement.

Art Nouveau Museum in Riga

Eisenstein's son Sergei became a well-known Bolshevik film director in Russia. He produced the classic film *Battleship Potemkin* about the start of the Bolshevik Revolution.

Film by Sergei Eisenstein

His father Mihail Eisenstein hated the Bolsheviks and after the Bolshevik Revolution moved to Berlin in 1917. The father and son broke off their relationship and never saw each other again until Sergei went to his father's funeral in Berlin in 1921.

With Margarita (left) and Ibi, in Riga, Latvia 2011

Walking through the streets of Riga we discovered the Hungarian Embassy, also in an Art Nouveau building similar to the many other interesting examples of Art Nouveau design in Budapest.

Art Nouveau building in Riga

In the center of Riga, we walked around the big beautiful park with a canal connected to the Daugava River where we took a boat ride.

Park in Riga.

In the evening we went to listen to a Russian Chorus singing both religious and Russian folk songs in the beautiful St. John Lutheran Church. We knew many of the folk songs.

St. John Church in Riga, Latvia

The following day we visited the Jewish Community Center of Riga. There is a sizable Jewish population of 4800 in Riga which is only twenty percent of the pre Holocaust population but there is a revival of Jewish life with a Jewish Museum and lots of cultural activities.

Jewish Community Center and Museum of "Jewish Latvia", in Riga

We had a nice lunch at the Flying Frog restaurant. The frog legs were at least as good as the *grenouilles* at our favorite restaurant "Le Petit Lutetia" in Paris.

Lidojosa Varde (Flying Frog) restaurant, Riga

Frogs' Legs in Garlic Sauce

Serves 2

Ingredients:

1 lb. of fresh frog legs (or frozen)

4 tbsp. flour

8 oz. butter

2 cloves garlic

4 tbsp. Muscadet

A handful of parsley, finely chopped

Juice of one lemon

Salt

Freshly ground pepper

Directions:

1. Quickly rinse frog legs in cold water, dry them thoroughly cover them with the flour.

2. Melt in a large nonstick skillet 6 oz. butter over high heat.

3. Once the butter is melted and hot, brown the frog legs for 5 minutes on each side. Remove and drain the frog legs.

4. Deglaze the pan by adding the Muscadet.

5. Add salt and pepper, then stir well and keep warm over low heat.

6. Combine the finely chopped parsley with the mashed garlic

7. Add the parsley, garlic, lemon juice, and remaining butter to the pan and stir well.

8. Add the frog legs. Adjust the seasoning, adding salt and pepper as needed.

9. Simmer a few minutes stirring and serve.

Riga has a very beautiful opera house, the Latvian National Opera House, and many talented singers, conductors, and composers have triumphed all around the world from their beginnings there. Unfortunately, we did not have the opportunity to watch a performance.

Latvian National Opera House, Riga

It has been more than nine years since we visited Riga, this old historical city with many of its beautiful attractions. In 2020 as we sit home for the last few months locked in because of the Covid 19 pandemic, every evening we revived pleasant memories of the city by watching operas transmitted by the Metropolitan Opera of New York. We have watched more than hundred and thirty Operas in the last several months. We remarked that a large number of the singers were from Riga, Latvia. It is puzzling that such a small country with a population of only two million could produce so many musical talents.

To name just a few of the big stars who perform at the Met: the mezzo-soprano Elina Garanca; the sopranos Kristine Opolais, Marina Rebeka, and Maija Kovalevska; the tenor Aleksandrs Antonenko, and the list goes on for many more. Even among the Metropolitan conductors, many like Andris Nelson are from Riga. One night we watched one of the best performances we have ever seen of the Rossini Opera, *Cinderella with* Elina Garanca who is not only a fantastic singer but beautiful as well.

64. ESTONIA

The third Baltic Country we visited on our 2011 tour was Estonia. It is the smallest of the three, with a population of 1.3 million. Estonia's history is very similar to that of Latvia. After hundreds of years under Swedish, Polish, and Russian rule, it became an independent country after World War 1. But the Soviet Union took Estonia over to be part of the Union at the beginning of World War 2. When the German Army occupied it in 1941, the majority of the population welcomed them hoping that their situation would be better than under the Soviets.

It was not the case, many people were murdered by the Nazis, including not only the Jews but the Roma and Estonian progressives were eliminated as well. After World War 2, it became part of the Soviet Union again. After 45 years with the disintegration of the Soviet Union, the Estonian Republik was established.

As opposed to the other two Baltic States where Russian speaking people are very few, more than one-third of the Estonian population is of Russian origin. Some came on their own for better economic conditions while others were forcibly relocated under the Soviet regime. When we talked with some ethnic Russians they told us that they felt mistreated by the majority and gave the example that the Russian language spoken by a large minority is not an official language.

Speaking about languages, although the Lithuanian and Latvian languages are Indo-European, Estonian is Finno-Ugric, like Hungarian. Even so, we could not communicate with our Estonian hosts in a common Finno-Ugric language, so we used American English!

On our way to Tallinn, we stopped at the beautiful sea resort town Pärnu.

With Joe and Margarita on the Main street of Pärnu Estonia, 2011

Enjoying a snack with friends in Pärnu 2011

After a couple of hours spent in Pärnu, we went to **Tallinn**, the capital of Estonia which is an hour away by bus. It is one of the oldest capital cities in Northern Europe. The Alexander Nevsky Orthodox Cathedral is the tallest building in Tallinn.

451

Tallinn, Estonia

Tallinn was once Europe's greatest fortified city and still houses a vast range of magnificent defense towers and historic gates. These unique constructions are a precious treasure of medieval architecture and have witnessed important moments of Baltic history.

Defensive Towers built in the 14th Century, Tallinn

Tallinn has a very colorful old town with unique downspouts (gutters).

Old Town Tallinn

Aerial view of Tallinn

Our going away party in the Peppersack, Tallinn 2011

Our two-week Baltic tour concluded in Tallinn's traditional restaurant, the Peppersack. At the restaurant, I noticed on the menu a Hungarian word for a roasted meat dish *Sült*. When I ordered it, I was surprised. It was not roast pork but it was headcheese which was quite good. Even though both Estonian and Hungarian are from Finn-Ugric roots they are not easily translated from one to another. From Tallinn, our group took a flight to Berlin for another short tour.

Hungarian Sült, roasted pig

Estonian Sült, headcheese

65. BAHAMAS

The year 2012 started with a Disney cruise to the **Bahamas** for the six of us: Richard, Suzika, Hannah, Talia, Vera, and me. We drove to Cape Canaveral to take a 4-day cruise on this beautiful Disney ship.

Taking the Disney Cruise to the Bahamas, 2012

Happy Family on our way to the Bahamas 2012

Both Hannah and Talia were exuberant. All the cartoon figures that they only knew from TV or from books became "reality" and they could hold hands and dance with Mickey and Minnie, Pluto, and with other cartoon characters. They were occupied all day in the children's section of the boat with games and fun activities under close supervision. The rest of us could go our own way to enjoy this comfortably organized cruise and all its offerings. There were several gourmet restaurants on the boat in addition to the delicious meals in the dining halls. Not only Hannah and Talia, we all had a ball!

Enjoying Snow White

and Pluto, on our Disney Cruise 2012

Entertainment on the Disney Cruise 2012

After a long cruise of over 500 miles, we landed in Nassau, the capital of the Bahamas with a population of more than a quarter of a million. First, we went sight-seeing in this unique city, neither colonial nor British.

Bahamian Parliament

Later, we just wandered around the shopping area before we boarded again to head for the Disney Island, "Castaway Cay".

Shopping street in Nassau, Bahamas

Castaway Cay is a private island purchased by the Disney Company from the Bahamian government where the Disney ships can board directly. The island is developed to look like the site of a castaway community with buildings made to look as if they had been improvised after a shipwreck. The main attraction however for Hannah and Talia was to continue in their dream world of Disney figures, but we adults also enjoyed the theme.

Having fun on Castaway Cay, 2012

On our way back to Cape Canaveral we stopped at Key West Florida for a one-day tour. We all have lifetime memories of this family trip.

66. CUBA

Travel to Cuba was restricted in 2012 but through a suggestion of our friends Janie and Marty, we learned that it was possible to sign up for a humanitarian tour to **Havana, Cuba.** The tour requirement was to take a 50 lb. gift package with medication, clothing, toys, etc. to some Cuban organization. We signed up for a weeklong tour with a Jewish group organized by a Temple from Flint Michigan. Vera and I drove to Miami in February 2012 and we stayed overnight at an airport hotel. The next morning about 25 of us took a flight to Havana. Our guide and organizer of the Cuba mission, Marla from Flint lead the group.

Vera is happy as we land in Havana, 2012

It was a short flight from Miami to Havana and we all were anxious to begin our adventure.

Welcome to Cuba

After collecting our suitcases including the 50 lb. gift packages per person, we had to go through a rather elaborate passport control handled by very efficient and polite officials. We met our Cuban guide Carlos, a knowledgeable young man who together with Marla informed us about all the important official details. We could not use credit cards or any currency other than the **CUC** (pronounced kook) a convertible peso equivalent to the US dollar. We had our breakfast in the hotel and twice a day for lunch and dinner we dined in local restaurants.

Our guides in Cuba, Marla, American and Carlos Cuban 2012

We stayed in the beautiful 5-star hotel, Hotel **Melia Cohiba** next to the Malecón, an eight-mile stretch of walkway and wall along the ocean.

Hotel Melia Cohiba, Havana

Our Cuban tour group 2012

Even though it was February, we had very nice sunny weather so after settling in at the hotel we started to explore the colorful city of Havana. The first impression we had of Cuba was that as opposed to the Communist countries of Eastern Europe where people are visibly unhappy and many are depressed, the Cuban people were dancing and singing anywhere we went. People are poor but we did not hear too many complaints. Perhaps the Latin mentality and the fact that the Cubans selected their way of living without any external power forcing it on them, makes the difference.

Enjoying the street entertainment, Havana 2012.

Unfortunately, due to the shortage of supplies, many of the beautiful old buildings are crumbling.

462

Street scene in Havana, 2012

Havana 2012

With Margarita in Havana, 2012

After running for more than 40 years and finishing 5 Marathons, Vera started to have some back problems (she is fine now) and could not keep up with our strenuous walking in Havana so she shared transportation with Walter Loebenberg, one of our tour companions. Walter was a refugee from Germany who came to Cuba at the age of 15 before he was admitted to the United States. In 1939, when the SS St. Louis carrying 900 Jewish refugees was turned away from Cuba, he saw a man jump off the boat and die rather than go back to Germany.

Disgracefully, when the boat sailed to Florida, the American authorities also refused the landing of the refugees and they were sent back to Germany to be murdered. Walter was the founder of the Florida Holocaust Museum in St. Petersburg. Unfortunately, he passed away in 2019 and we miss him.

Vera with Walter Loebenberg taking "public transportation" Havana 2012

Part of our mission to Cuba was to bring badly needed medicine and clothing to the local Jewish population so we visited the Jewish Community Center, where we met members and were briefed by a woman who was a university professor of history.

464

Jewish Community Center Havana.

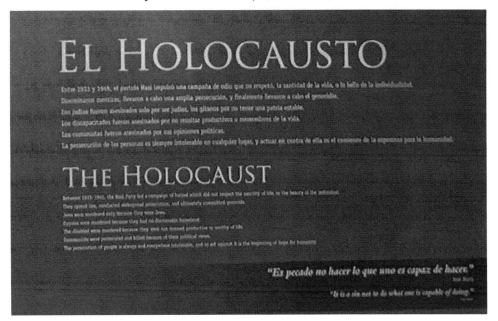

Holocaust Memorial in Havana

Cuba has a small Jewish community of about 1500 people most of whom live in Havana. There are three functioning Synagogues. Before the Revolution, over 24,000 Jews were living in Cuba but most of them came to the US or emigrated to Israel. There were some Jews who supported the Revolution headed by Fidel Castro and among them, there were several ministers and high officials in the Revolutionary government.

When we visited the Jewish cemetery in Havana, the professor told us an interesting story. A man named Alex Friedman, who was the pilot of Batista's private plane, deserted and joined the anti-Batista group and became Fidel Castro's pilot. They had no idea of Friedman's background, where was he born, or where he came from. After his plane was shot down and he was buried, a single word *Viszontlatasra* was carved next to his name on his grave. When we read it, we knew where he came from. Viszontlatasra means "until next time", in Hungarian!

Fidel Castro was very friendly with the Jewish community. Once when he visited the Jewish Community Center he asked about Hanukkah, and when he was told that it was a kind of revolution of the Israelites, he had a satisfied smile on his face. We were told that Cubans have never been Anti-Semitic and they still are not. Interestingly, even though there was a meat shortage in Cuba, a Kosher butcher shop was still functioning.

The breakfasts in the Melia Cohiba were the best one could hope for. Lots of fresh fruit, pastries, omelets, or eggs prepared to order. However, the luncheons and dinners were something else. We went to different restaurants for each meal but the food was always very plain: rice, beans and either a piece of chicken or a piece of fish. The ambiance, however, was always great. Every restaurant we went to had a band, and we often participated in the great Cuban music.

Joining the band in a restaurant. Havana 2012

For years all businesses and establishments including restaurants were state-owned and there were no private businesses but by 2012 there were some small privately-owned shops and restaurants. Some Cuban Americans sent money to their relatives to invest, which was allowed by the Cuban Government. So we went to some restaurants where the food was much better.

Happy times in Havana, 2012

Several evenings we went to a Jazz Club near our hotel, called *La Zorra y El Cuervo*, (the Vixen and the Raven) where the world-famous jazz pianist and composer **Roberto Fonseca** played. One of his memorable compositions was about his wife who died in an airplane accident. Fonseca was one of the biggest hits in Paris when he performed. Even the heavy cigar smoke, did not dampen our enthusiasm and we returned to listen to Fonseca several evenings.

Our favorite Jazz Club and world-famous Jazz pianist and composer Robert Fonseca in Havana, 2012

One afternoon we visited the famous **Floridita**, the favorite place of **Hemingway**. We had some good drinks, Cuban sandwiches, and more fun.

Ernest Hemingway's favorite bar, El Floridita, Havana

Enjoying a great band in El Floridita, Havana, 2012

We visited the former home of Ernest Hemingway, the **Finca Vigia** in the San Francisco de Paula district of Havana.

The former home of Hemingway now is the Finca Vigia museum

The building was originally a farmhouse built in 1886 on 14 acres. Hemingway lived there with his third wife from 1939 -1960. It was here that he wrote the book "For Whom the Bell Tolls" about the Spanish Civil War as well as the "Old Man on the Sea".

Another marvel of this fantastic city is **Fusterlandia**, a Cuban variation of the famous Park Güell, the Gaudi park in Barcelona. The creator, Jose Rodriguez Fuster, graduated from Havana's Art Instructor's School in 1965 and continued his education in Europe. He was very impressed by Antoni Gaudi in Barcelona and decided to develop Fusterlandia in **Jamainatas,** a neighborhood of Havana which had been a rundown fishing village. It is still under development and five years later in 2017, when we returned to Havana, Fusterlandia had increased its size at least 5-fold.

Scenes in Fusterlandia in Jamainatas, a suburb of Havana

Jose Rodriguez Fuster

One afternoon we went to the beautiful Bacuranao beach, about 25 km from Havana, where besides a good swim, we enjoyed some fresh seafood at a small bistro on the beach.

Bacuranao Beach, Cuba

Vera likes Cuba,2012

One of the couples originally from Colombia of our group had an accident. As they stepped out of a taxi, a car hit them and both were taken to the hospital. Because of the shortage of medicine due to the United States embargo, the doctors had to suture the man's head injury without any anesthesia. The injured man is a physician practicing in Chicago and he was very complimentary about the skill and educational level of the Cuban doctors, one of the highest in Latin America. All in all, the educational system in Cuba has a very high standard and has one of the highest percentages of literacy in the world. The island's educational conditions improved significantly after the Batista regime was overthrown by the revolution in 1959.

I went jogging along the Malecón every morning but I had to be very careful because it was very slippery because of the waves that crashed over the wall onto the walkway.

Giant waves along the Malecón, Havana

We also went to an afternoon performance of **La Traviata** at the *Gran Teatro de La Habana*, the opera house in Havana which has a beautiful exterior built in 1914 by immigrants from Galicia. The interior was somewhat neglected. Just like everywhere else in Havana, there was a shortage of materials for its restoration and repair.

On the other hand, it was a good performance, although we had to pay 25 CUC for a ticket, the equivalent of $25, the locals only paid the equivalent of 25 cents. Cultural offerings are accessible to everyone in Cuba. Their ballet performances are outstanding and we were impressed by the very talented young dancers.

El Gran Teatro de La Habana, the Havana Opera House

Waving adios at the Havana airport with Janie and Marty (2012)

A very nice album of our 2012 Cuban tour was given to us by Janie and Marty Borell. We used many of the photos from their album.

In 2017 we returned to Havana just for a day celebrate Sanyi's 80th birthday with a 3-day cruise from Tampa Seaport. The boat stopped at Key West and landed in Havana where we spent a day sightseeing. In addition to Mari, Agi from Knoxville together with Harvey joined Vera and me. It was nice to see Havana and Cuba's good-looking young people again. The time was rather short but we made an effort to see as much as we could. As I mentioned earlier, Fusterlandia had expanded considerably since 2012 and we spent several hours there. It is getting to be as big as Gaudi's Park Güell in Barcelona.

67. THE CAYMAN ISLANDS

In January 2013 together with Françoise and Georges, we took another Caribbean Cruise from Tampa Seaport. After stopping at Key West and Cozumel, we spent a day on Cayman Island. The beaches are beautiful but the shopping is not much different from other seaport towns. All in all, it was a nice day but the best part was to be with friends.

Cayman Island

68. UKRAINE

My first visit to what is Ukraine today was in 1941. I visited a cousin of my father in **Uzhgorod,** a city in the Carpathian mountain area in western Ukraine. At that time, it was part of Hungary and was called **Ungvar**. Just like most of the towns in the Carpathians, Ungvar had a large Jewish population, about 35%. Many of the Jews came from Galicia in the late 19th and early 20th Century and their primary language was Yiddish. In March 1944 when the German Army occupied Hungary, the city's Jewish population including my relatives were deported to Auschwitz and murdered. After World War 2, in 1945 the area became part of Ukraine and today it is called Uzhgorod.

Uzhgorod, Ukraine

Following the suggestions of Françoise and Georges, we signed up for a five-day tour to **Odessa** which left from Paris in April 2019. The tour was organized by the Valiske Association, a husband and wife owned travel agency located in Strasbourg. For some time, we had considered taking a trip to this fascinating city on the Black sea with its very significant Jewish history.

At the end of the 19th and the beginning of the 20th Century, Odessa was a leading center of Zionist political and literary movements in Europe. Many well-known Zionist leaders like Borochov, Achad Ham, and Jabotinsky lived here, as well as literary figures like Bialik, Babel, and others. In the 1930s, the Jewish population of Odessa totaled close to two hundred thousand people, the largest ethnic group in the city followed by the Ukrainians and then by the Russians.

Terribly, during the Holocaust, a large percentage of the Jewish population was brutally murdered by the German and Romanian occupying forces who were aided by the local Ukrainian population. On October 22, 1941, an explosion wrecked a part of the general headquarters of the Romanian army causing the death of a General, the city's military commander, and many Romanian and German officers and soldiers. In the first reprisals carried out the following day, 5,000 persons, most of them Jews, were killed. Many of them were hanged at crossings and in the public squares.

Antonescu, the head of the Romanian Government, ordered the execution of 200 persons for every officer who had been killed, and 100 for every soldier, and ordered that one member of every Jewish family be taken hostage. Nineteen thousand Jews were arrested and brought to the square at the harbor, doused with gasoline, and burned. Another 16,000 were taken the following day to the outskirts, where all of them were massacred.

Northern Transylvania, which had been taken away from Hungary by the Trianon Treaty and given to Romania in 1920, was given back to Hungary by the 2nd Viennese Award in 1941. To compensate Romania, (both Hungary and Romania were allies of Nazi Germany), the territories of Bessarabia, Bukovina and Transnistria with its capital Odessa that was occupied by the Germans, was given to Romania.

On our visit in the spring of 2019 during Passover, there was a much smaller but sizable Jewish population of around 15-20 thousand souls. There are several functioning Synagogues, Jewish elementary and middle schools, and a Jewish University. Odessa which was called the cradle of Israeli culture, is enjoying a Jewish Renaissance.

Downtown Odessa

Israeli Café, "Tel Aviv on the Black Sea"

We stayed in a beautiful historical hotel, the Hotel Londonskaja (London) facing the Black sea. We had a beautiful two-level suite and excellent breakfast with both English and Continental offerings.

Hotel Londonskaja in Odessa

We visited many of the museums and attended Shabbat morning service at the Grand Synagogue, which was crowded with many young people. We dined in nice restaurants, but because it was Passover the choices were somewhat limited but still very good.

It was interesting to see the statue of Mishka (Moshe) Yaponchik in the middle of Odessa. Yaponchik was an Odessa gangster, a Jewish revolutionary, and even a Soviet military leader. He was a hero to the oppressed Jews, a Jewish Robin Hood robbing the rich and helping the poor. He and his gang were very well armed and he organized Jewish defense groups to prevent pogroms against the Jews. He was executed by the Soviets despite his having helped them to defeat the anti-Soviet forces in 1919. A book written by Isaak Babel about Yaponchik and Jewish life in Odessa in the early twentieth century, was recently made into" Once upon the time in Odessa", a TV series with 12 episodes. We watched and enjoyed it all.

The city of Odessa erected statues for both the famous Jewish writer Isaak Babel and for Mishka (Moshe) Yaponchik

Mishka (Moshe) Yaponchik

Isaak Babel Jewish writer

The Opera House in Odessa

We had the pleasure of seeing an excellent performance of the opera "Tosca" at the beautiful Odessa Opera House. Coincidentally, just a few weeks earlier we saw Tosca at the Opera House in Tel Aviv. The contrast

478

between the new modern Opera House in Tel Aviv and the classic historic Opera House in Odessa was striking. We liked both.

The Opera House in Tel Aviv

After a very memorable and educationally enriching visit to Odessa, we spent a day in Kiev, the capital of the Ukraine. We toured the city and were impressed by the wide boulevards and imposing buildings.

Kiev, Ukraine

Golda Meier, the former prime minister of Israel was born in Kiev and we visited her home. She as well as many of her compatriots turned toward Zionism believing that the pogroms in Ukraine and the murder of Jews could only be stopped if they established their own country. She was honored by the Ukrainian government on the 120th anniversary of her birth in Kiev.

Memorial of Golda Meier at the house of her birth in Kiev

While we were in Ukraine, there was a presidential election and a Jew by the name of Zelensky was elected with a large majority of well over 75%. This was the first time in the history of the Ukraine that such a thing happened. As a matter of fact, Ukraine, historically one of the most anti-Semitic countries, is the only country outside Israel, whose president and the prime minister are both Jewish. There is hope for humanity.

S11. FLORIDA

After having described our travels to more than sixty-five countries and many states in the USA, it is appropriate to highlight our life in **Florida**, our home state for the last twenty-five years.

Our first trip to the Sunshine State was in 1969 from Knoxville Tennessee. In those years, almost all our travel was limited to Toronto in Canada to visit Vera's parents or to the Smokey Mountains only 35 miles away. We had limited resources because my low paying faculty position at the University of Tennessee and Vera's studies did not leave us much money for extended vacations elsewhere.

We were surprised and pleased to get an unexpected letter of invitation from an unknown organization that offered us a 4-day vacation in Miami Beach with all hotel and meal expenses covered. It was hard to resist so we took off for a week's vacation to Florida. Leaving Knoxville in the early morning and after driving straight through for close to 600 miles, we arrived at our first stop in Florida, **St Augustine**. Suzika who was only two years was fast asleep but I took Michael who was a big boy of five for an exploratory walk. St Augustine was founded in 1565 and is the oldest European settlement in the United States. Its founder, a Spanish admiral, Pedro Menendez de Aviles, was the first governor of Florida. Menendez named the place San Augustin, because he first sighted it on August 28, the feast of Saint Augustine. For 200 years the city was the capital of Spanish Florida.

Recent studies indicate that a group of Marranos, converted Jews, arrived to St Augustin with Menendez. This would be 100 years earlier than the officially accepted date of 1656 when the Jews first settled in the Dutch colony of New Amsterdam which later became New York. Furthermore, Menendez's wife's maiden name was Solis, a common Sephardic Jewish name.

Anyway, we had a wonderful time spending the following day in this historic city and even though we planned on returning there, we never found time in the last 50 years to go back. But it's never too late.

Aviles Street in St Augustine, Florida, the oldest street in the USA.

We still had our VW square back which we brought back from Germany four years earlier. It took us about five hours to drive from St Augustine to Miami Beach. The "free hotel accomondation" which was part of the package was quite satisfactory for us as we were not demanding. Both Michael and Suzika enjoyed the ocean and the nice swimming pool. It was the first time that Suzika at 2 years old swam in a pool without any aids. Both kids are good swimmers and later on, they raced with the University of Tennessee swimming team.

Having fun in Miami Beach, Florida, 1969

During the four days of our stay, we had our meals in the hotel's dining room which was ok. The second evening after we just finished our meal, the four connecting doors to the dining room suddenly opened and about 10 well-dressed men entered, smiling as each of them sat down at one of the guests' tables. We had no experience with this approach and did not know what to expect. But we learned quickly. After introducing himself, the man at our table took out some brochures with nice photos of prospective condominium buildings, that would be built somewhere in the middle of Florida.

We were told that we were fortunate to be able to purchase one by signing a contract and putting down a *mere* $ 5000 to secure it. He said reassuringly that in a year or two when the project is completed, the price of the condos will quadruple at least. We did not even have $500 in the bank at that time, but I asked anyway if we could see the project before we purchase anything? He said no, but that we shouldn't worry since it was a great location.

When I told him that we were not interested, he got really angry and started to insult me pointing at Michael and Suzika saying, "how could you be so cruel as to not think of the future of these two beautiful children?". Then I got up and told him, "Don't lecture me on how to take care of my children", and we walked out of the dining room. I am sure some of the guests were less skeptical because we saw some people signing papers. That was the first and last time that we took advantage of a *free vacation*.

Since we had just saved $5000 by not buying anything in the swamps of Florida, we felt we deserved a reward. We wanted to have some hard shell crabs at the famous *Joe's Stone Crab* restaurant. I knew that many Hungarians who came to America had impacted significantly this country, like von Neuman, Wigner, Szilard and Teller, the four scientists, who initiated the Manhattan project or the numerous musicians and conductors like Dorati who conducted the Minneapolis and Detroit Symphony, Ormandy (born Blau) who conducted the Philadelphia Orchestra for 40 years, and Sir Solti (born Stern), the conductor of the Chicago orchestra, but I was surprised to find out that Joe Weiss, the owner of Joe's restaurant was born in Hungary also.

In 1913, Joe Weiss arrived in Miami Beach from New York hoping to relieve his asthma. Five years later, he opened up the original Joe's Restaurant in the front room of the bungalow that he shared with his wife Jennie on Biscayne Street and although he most likely was raised on gefilte fish and chopped chicken liver he made the most successful stone crab restaurant in Florida. We came back many times. It is superb!

Joe's Stone Crab Restaurant in Miami Beach, Florida

By 1972 when we returned to Miami Beach, we were in much better financial conditions than three years earlier, so we could spend a week enjoying the ocean and Joe's for more stone crab. On our way back we stopped at the newly opened Disney World in Orlando. The kids loved the Magic Kingdom. We returned many times together with friends, and of course with Rachel, Hannah, and Talia.

Magic Kingdom, Disney World Orlando, Florida

Vera with Rachel in Disney World, 1997

In 1985 our exposure to Florida took a significant leap beyond just fun and vacation. My childhood friend Steve Szasz with whom I was a partner in his construction business in Toronto along with several of our other friends suggested we all meet in **Dunedin** a small town in Florida on the Gulf of Mexico, to discuss some business opportunities, such as a half-finished townhouse project that was up for sale by a Canadian group at a low price. After visiting Suzika who was a freshman at Tufts, I flew from Boston to Sarasota, and then drove to Dunedin to meet Steve. With the involvement of all the friends, we purchased the project in Dunedin, a small historic town. That was the beginning of a lucrative construction business in Florida for the next 20 years. We bought one unit for ourself in the Dunedin project when it was completed.

Downtown Dunedin, Florida

Steve with his son Robi built approximately 600 units in the Clearwater-St Petersburg-Tampa area. Vera and I visited Steve and Marika often after they moved from Toronto to Belleair Beach.

We went to Florida in 1993 to participate in a surprise 60th birthday party for Steve. He had just moved into his new house which he built in **Belleair Beach** right on the inter-coastal bay of the Gulf of Mexico. It was a beautiful 6-bedroom 6-bathroom house that Steve designed. Both Vera and I thought that one day we might want to move to Florida and that Belleair Beach would be a perfect place. Luckily, two houses away from Steve's place, a small bungalow had a for-sale sign. Within a few days, after some offers and counteroffers, we bought 301 Harbor Drive for $209,000. It was a tiny 2-bedroom 2-bathroom house with a tiny swimming pool but with a long waterfront lot. Soon after the closing, we rented the house to a doctor. So that time we had two properties in the area: a townhouse in Dunedin which was also rented and a house in Belleair Beach. Steve was happy that we showed up for his surprise birthday party and we were too.

We were all back in Miami in 1994 to participate in the wedding of Robi, Steve's and Marika's son. In the wedding, I had the honor of giving the blessing for the challah and also that of quoting an old Hebrew expression to wish for the wellbeing of the new couple. The highlight of the wedding was the Hora danced by the seven friends all in our sixties just like we used to dance when we were sixteen. Suzika also gave a very emotional speech, emphasizing the deep and long friendship of the seven of us, which made most of us cry.

Suzika speaking at Robi's and Bonnie's wedding in Florida, 1994

Friends and their families at Robi's and Bonnie's wedding in Florida, 1994

After the wedding, we rented a minivan and about 10 of us drove to **Key West**, the picturesque southern-most part of the USA. We went sailing, fishing, and enjoyed the dynamic life of the city. Through the years as we took cruises on the Caribbean, we spent a lot more time in Key West.

We went to see Hemingway's house. It always fascinates me that wherever I go, Hemingway had already put his fingerprints around the area. However, his home in Key West had more cats than my allergy could have had handled, so I stayed outside.

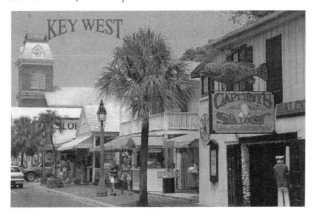

Downtown   *Hemingway's Home Key West, Florida*

We decided to take early retirement and move to Belleair Beach in 1995. Steve kindly offered to design and build a house on the lot after tearing down the little bungalow that we had just purchased. He built us the most beautiful palace one could hope for. I had always heard about the headaches involved in getting a new house built. Not for us! Steve took care of everything. Of course, he discussed our needs with us, rather mostly with Vera who likes detail more than me, and all we had to do was just move in. When we arrived to Belleair Beach on July 15 1995 and saw our gorgeous house, we felt that we were moving into Paradise.

301 Harbor Drive, Belleair Beach, Florida. Our house. 1995

Despite our over 150 trips from Florida for over 25 years, we still enjoy our life in Florida. We furnished our new home with comfortable furniture and built-in appliances so we were ready for visitors. On the second floor, we had four bedrooms and three bathrooms which could accommodate quite a few people. Everybody loves to come to Florida, especially when the weather is cold elsewhere. We had a beautiful pool with a heated Jacuzzi, a nice terrace facing the inter-coastal bay, and a 60-foot dock and although we had no boat, we did buy a kayak.

From day one we started to have visitors: our kids, our relatives from abroad, our friends, and my colleagues from the US and abroad. Often, our house was full, especially during the last few weeks in December when George Bozoki and Poncike with their wives, George Burger with his wife, and Janos from California would be our guests. Some mornings when we woke up, Vera would ask me, "Can you tell me who's staying with us today? I can't remember."

With George Sarkadi, Vera, Myra, Gabi Nadai, Eva Nadai, 1995

With Mari Pollak, 1995

Year after year we celebrated New Year's Eve in our home with our local friends and visitors. Often, we were more than twenty-five altogether. It was always a feast with Vera's gourmet cooking and our singing and dancing until early morning. The celebration was followed by dinner the next day in Steve and Marika's home or back in ours. It was convenient that we were neighbors.

New Year's Eve party with friends, 1995

Having fun, 1995

Food was always important, with Steve and with George Bozoki

```
******************************************************************
                        MENU
                     CHEZ ADLER
                        *****
                     SZILVESZTER
                     DEC 31, 2003
```

Crudités avec pâté de foie, sauce Hongrois.
Spectacular Japanese delights : sushis and sashimis

Salad gourmande

Filet de veau a la Vera de Bellair Beach (Freedom from BSE is
guaranteed, certificate on request) avec pommes de terre lyonaise, haricot vert

Fromages exclusives de campagne

Strudels with mouthwatering fillings

Sherbet, fagy, palna es seh deli gyumolcs (Toldi Miklos by Arany Janos)

Assorted fine French wines and champagne despite admonitions from Dubya.

To boost the festive spirits you may treat yourselves to terrific spirits all night
long.

New Year's Eve Menu

This memorable menu was written up by Poncike, who utilized three languages; French, English, and Hungarian,

We were very happy (and still are) that we made our move to Florida. The triangle of Tampa-Clearwater-Saint Petersburg referred to as Tampa Bay, has a population of over two million people (not counting the millions of visitors) and everything is accessible. There are several concert halls, theaters, and many good restaurants to make life enjoyable, not counting the endless beaches along the Gulf of Mexico. Our house was built on a narrow island having the Gulf of Mexico on one side and the inter-coastal bay on the other, so the cross breeze keeps the weather pleasant all year round.

We continued our daily run of 5-6 miles and on Saturdays, we usually would do 10-11 miles. It was much easier to run here than in Columbus in the winter when it snows. Once on a real snowy day in Columbus when I was out of town, Vera was the only one outside. One of the TV station reporters spotted her and she was broadcast as the "lone runner". Here in Florida, we participated in a 15K Gasparilla race in Tampa which was a major event with lots of top runners from many countries. We did not win any races until 2013 when I got first place in the age group of over 80! If you wait long enough, your time will come!

Winning first place for over 80 at the Gasparilla 15 K race, Tampa Florida, 2013

We also participated in the 10K Turkey Trot runs on Thanksgiving Day and some 5Ks along the Beach. One day Vera was running alone along Gulf Boulevard when a minivan full of people pulled up in front of her. She got scared for a moment until a big husky guy came out saying, "Hi Vera I am Tamas Magyar, from Hungary. We met in La Jolla some years ago and I recognized your jogging style." What he spotted was that Vera runs with very short steps. Vera invited all the people who were in the van for lunch later on. There were over 10 of them and we met the Wahls, a very nice family of Feri and Vali and their daughter Vicky. We became close friends. Vicky who is married now to Eric is a talented graphic artist who designed the cover page for our last book, *Honor the Past and Build the Future,*

Within a few weeks after Richard proposed to Suzika in Bermuda, the wedding was set for the Ritz Carlton **Sarasota** on February 4th, 2006. We had only a few months to prepare but everything went according to schedule. Living close to Sarasota we were able to make all the arrangements with Clara, the very capable wedding planner at the Ritz. Initially, an outdoor wedding was planned but due to bad weather, it had to be inside. Even so, a number of people said that it was the "Wedding of the Millennium". We all had a great time, dancing, enjoying excellent food and sharing our happiness with our friends and family from all around the world.

Susan and Richard with the bridesmaids and the groomsmen, 2006

Susan and Richard with their happy parents, 2006

Table at the wedding, 2006

Seven friends reunited at "The Wedding of the Millennium", 2006

Sarasota, became one of our favorite cities in Florida, it is a cultural center with many good restaurants, foreign film festivals, and even an Opera House, so we took our visitors there many times. We always tried to stay in the Ritz Carlton and usually, we got a very good deal. The ceviche at the Peruvian restaurant Selva is as good as anything we found in Peru.

Ritz Carlton | *Our favorite Peruvian restaurant* | *The Opera House, Sarasota, Florida*

For Thanksgiving in 2007, we went to Baltimore where Richard's sister arranged a dinner. When we arrived at the Baltimore airport, we met Richard and Suzika. Next, we saw the 17-month-old Hannah running away from everybody and looking back toward us, smiling and showing how well she could walk already. She was and still is a performer!

We had a nice time with Richard's family and when we said goodbye to Judy and Howard, I said to them, "I hope we'll see you soon". Actually, in less than a week they showed up in Florida to participate in my surprise **75th birthday party**.

George Burger came to see me a couple of weeks before my birthday and gave me a realistic statue of me running.

Statue of "The Runner"

Suzika arranged the whole surprise event, inviting many of our friends, and arranging for the catering and music, etc. The most important thing she did was the DVD which she put together with the music and photographs of my 75 years. It was a Hollywood type performance! It was admirable that she was almost eight months pregnant when she accomplished this. There were over 40 people in the party held in the party room in Ultimar 3. The Szasz family (10), the Sarkadis, the Nadais, Csetris and Rokhlins from Columbus, my friends George Bozoki and George Gomory, Margarita from Boston, Vera's childhood friend's children, Michele and Andy, the locals, the Koenigs, the Wahls, and the Imredis... all came to celebrate my big event. Of course, our family, Judy and Howard, Michael and Rachel, Richard, Suzika and Hannah were there. Several people gave speeches before the DVD was shown which was narrated by Suzika. It was one of the best days of my life!

Our family at my 75th birthday celebration, 2007

75 Years of Friendship, Family, Fortune and Fulfillment

Laszlo Adler's Wonderful World

Suzika's DVD production

A few weeks later, in the beginning of January 2008, we moved out of our beautiful home in Belleair Beach. I had some hesitation about moving into a condo in ***Ultimar 3, Sand Key***, after having lived in a house for more than 45 years, but Vera had enough of walking up and down stairs and taking care of the big house and yard. So, we were ready for the move and I have never regretted it! There are three buildings built in the 1990s called Ultimar 1,2 and 3.

The Ultimar complex in Sand Key, Ultimar 3 in on the right.

Before our move, Vera ran a garage sale where she sold lots of junk and made quite a bit of money. We sold half of our furniture to the new owners of 301 Harbor Drive. We bought a few more new pieces for our new home: 1560 Gulf Blvd. #1002. It was a definite downsizing but we love it.

Dining room in the old house   *Dining room in the condo*

But even with our downsizing, we had enough space in our 3-bedroom, 3-bathroom condo to continue welcoming our friends and our growing family. Our happiness grew as we welcomed our third granddaughter Talia on February 11, 2008.

Ever since she was a few months old, she would sit on my lap in front of the computer where I would play music for her like the "Banana Boat" by Harry Belafonte, as performed by the "Jewish Monkeys". One of her first words was "dayo", implying that she wanted the song, and then she would climb up on my lap to listen to it. Both Hannah and Talia loved to listen to the music I played for them. They danced with the Georgian Dancers and even learned the Japanese words for breakfast", "asa gohan" performed with Beethoven's fifth symphony.

Talia in Florida and in the refrigerator, 2009

The Sisters: Talia and Hannah, 2008

Hannah and Talia, 2020

In2009 Michael moved to Bradenton which is next to Sarasota and came here often with Rachel and our family of eight enjoyed spending quality time together.

Our family after dinner at Hyatt Regency, Clearwater, 2013

With our three beautiful granddaughters Clearwater, 2013

A couple days after New Year's in 2013, Vera and I got a nice present, a coupon to a spa in the Hyatt Regency for our special 50th anniversary. The plan was that after the spa, we would go out to the Salt Rock Grill to celebrate with the family. Richard picked us up at the hotel and told us that the girls were practicing piano in the party room and that we had to go get them to take them along with us. As we entered the party room in Ultimar 3, we were greeted by about thirty of our local friends with a surprise party arranged by our daughter Suzika. It was an unbelievable arrangement, with catered food and music, all the speeches, especially Hannah's, and with the presence of our loved ones, although Michael and Rachel could not come. We felt very fortunate to celebrate our anniversary. It is always a joyful occasion to be with our family and friends and we feel very fortunate to be able to do it this time and many others.

At our 50th wedding anniversary surprise party, 2013

At our 50th anniversary in the Ultimar party room, 2013

New Year celebration in Florida, 2014

Celebrating Hanukkah in our home, 2015

Thanksgiving, 2019

After receiving her Master's Degree in Social Work at Ohio State University, Rachel moved near us to St Petersburg. We feel very fortunate that both Rachel and Michael, who lives only three miles from us, are located nearby. Rachel who worked for three years as a therapist for a Florida company recently opened her own practice as a Clinical Social Worker Therapist.

Rachel's Website

and her proud father

Michael and Rachel make up the part of our family live nearby but we also see Suzika, Richard and the girls several times a year either in Boston, Florida, or traveling abroad together

While the rest of us are dining, Hannah is flying at Clearwater Beach, February 2020

In 2020, Rosh Hashana, the Jewish New Year, fell on September 18, and because of the COVID 19, we stayed at home and only Michael joined us for the festive dinner.

Since the COVID 19 virus broke out, we are all at a standstill and can only enjoy the connection with our family on Skype or ZOOM. However, we are confident that it will be over soon and we will continue our travels all around the world. We are scheduled for Morocco in February 2021, Prague in July 2021, and South Korea in 2022, but more importantly, we look forward to getting together with family and friends again.

We are ready

Contents

35025777R00285